Thai

An Essential Grammar

2nd edition

This second edition of *Thai: An Essential Grammar* provides an up-to-date and concise reference guide to Thai grammar.

Using clear, jargon-free explanations, it sets out the complexities of Thai in short, readable sections and presents an accessible description of the language. Focus is kept on the real patterns of use today and grammar forms are demonstrated through a wide range of relevant examples. No prior knowledge is assumed on the part of the reader.

Features include:

- coverage of crucial topics, such as sentence particles, negation, questions and quantification
- examples given in both Thai script and romanised transliteration
- pronunciation section
- guidance on speech conventions and the Thai writing system
- glossary of grammatical terms
- two appendices covering romanisation systems and three key verbs
- bibliography

This unique reference work will prove invaluable to all learners looking to master the grammar of Thai. It is ideal for both independent study and for students in schools, colleges, universities and adult classes of all types.

David Smyth is Senior Lecturer in Thai at the School of Oriental and African Studies, University of London.

Routledge Essential Grammars

Essential Grammars are available for the following languages:

Arabic
Chinese
Czech
Danish
Dutch
English
Finnish
Modern Hebrew
German
Greek
Hindi
Hungarian
Korean
Latvian
Norwegian
Polish
Portuguese
Romanian
Serbian
Spanish
Swedish
Thai
Turkish
Urdu

Thai

An Essential Grammar

2nd edition

 **David Smyth**

 Routledge
Taylor & Francis Group

LONDON AND NEW YORK

Second edition published 2014
by Routledge
2 Park Square, Milton Park, Abingdon, Oxon OX14 4RN

and by Routledge
711 Third Avenue, New York, NY 10017

Routledge is an imprint of the Taylor & Francis Group, an informa business

First edition published by Routledge 2002

British Library Cataloguing in Publication Data
A catalogue record for this book is available from the British Library

Library of Congress Cataloging in Publication Data
Smyth, David, 1954– author.
 Thai : an essential grammar / David Smyth. – Second edition.
  pages cm. – (Routledge essential grammars)
 Includes bibliographical references and index.
 1. Thai language–Grammar. I. Title.
 PL4163.S64 2013
 495.9′182421–dc23

                                        2013019254

ISBN: 978-0-415-51033-2 (hbk)
ISBN: 978-0-415-51034-9 (pbk)
ISBN: 978-1-315-87105-9 (ebk)

Typeset in Sabon and Gill Sans
by Graphicraft Limited, Hong Kong

Printed and bound in the United States of America by Publishers Graphics,
LLC on sustainably sourced paper.

Contents

Preface   x

Introduction   1

    Thai and its speakers   1
    Romanisation   2
    Learning Thai   2
    Dictionaries   3
    Linguistic literature on Thai   4

Chapter 1   Pronunciation   5

1.1   Consonants   5
1.2   Vowels   7
1.3   Tones   8
1.4   Stress   10

Chapter 2   The writing system   11

2.1   Consonants   11
2.2   Consonants by class   14
2.3   Vowels   15
2.4   Live syllables and dead syllables   17
2.5   Tone rules   17
2.6   Miscellaneous   21

Chapter 3   Nouns, classifiers and noun phrases   25

3.1   Proper nouns   25
3.2   Common nouns   26

3.3   Making new nouns   27
3.4   Noun phrases and classifiers   34
3.5   Word order in noun phrases   36

Chapter 4   Pronouns   **42**

4.1   Personal pronouns: basics   42
4.2   Reflexive pronouns   50
4.3   Emphatic pronoun   52
4.4   Reciprocal: 'each other'   54
4.5   Possessive pronouns   54
4.6   Demonstrative pronouns   54
4.7   Interrogative pronouns   55
4.8   Indefinite pronouns   55
4.9   Relative pronouns   59

Chapter 5   Verbs   **61**

5.1   The verb 'to be'   61
5.2   Stative verbs   64
5.3   Verb compounds   65
5.4   Resultative verbs   66
5.5   Directional verbs   67
5.6   Modal verbs   69
5.7   Time and aspect   74
5.8   Passives   83
5.9   Verbs of utterance, mental activity and perception
      with **wâh**   85
5.10 Verbs of emotion with **têe**   86
5.11 Causatives   87
5.12 'To give': direct and indirect objects   91
5.13 Verb serialisation   92

**Chapter 6   Adjectives (stative verbs) and
              adjectival constructions**   **94**

6.1   Compound adjectives   95
6.2   Modification of adjectives   96
6.3   Special intensifiers   98
6.4   Reduplication   101
6.5   Comparison of adjectives   103

Chapter 7 Adverbs and adverbial constructions   109

7.1	Adverbs of manner	109
7.2	Modification of adverbs	114
7.3	Comparison of adverbs	115
7.4	Adverbs of time	117
7.5	Adverbs of frequency	119
7.6	Adverbs of degree	120

Chapter 8 Location markers and other prepositions   123

8.1	Location: têe and yòo	123
8.2	'To'	127
8.3	'For'	127
8.4	'By'	129
8.5	'With'	131
8.6	'From'	132

Chapter 9 Clauses and sentences   133

9.1	Word order and topicalisation	133
9.2	Subordinate clauses	136
9.3	Direct and indirect speech	143
9.4	Imperatives	143
9.5	Exemplification	144
9.6	Exclamatory particles	144

Chapter 10 Sentence particles   145

10.1	Question particles	145
10.2	Polite particles	145
10.3	Mood particles	149

Chapter 11 Negation   158

11.1	Negating main verbs	158
11.2	Negating resultative verbs	159
11.3	Negating auxiliary verbs	160
11.4	mâi dâi + VERB (PHRASE)	162
11.5	mâi châi + NOUN	164
11.6	mâi mee	164

11.7   Modifying negatives: intensifying and softening   165
11.8   Negative imperatives   166
11.9   Negative causatives   167
11.10   Negative questions   170
11.11   Negative conditional clauses   171
11.12   Saying 'no'   172
11.13   Useful negative expressions   173
11.14   Two further negatives: **mí** and **hăh . . . mâi**   173

Chapter 12   Questions   **174**

12.1   Yes/no questions   174
12.2   Wh- questions   180
12.3   Alternative questions   192
12.4   Indirect questions   193

**Chapter 13   Numbers, measurement and
                quantification**   **194**

13.1   Cardinal numbers   195
13.2   Cardinal numbers with **sùk** and **dtûng**   198
13.3   Ordinal numbers   199
13.4   Sanskrit numbers   200
13.5   Once, twice . . .   201
13.6   Fractions, decimals, percentages, multiples and averages   202
13.7   Collective numbers   204
13.8   Some idiomatic expressions involving numbers   205
13.9   Measurements   206
13.10   Distances   207
13.11   Distribution: 'per'   207
13.12   Quantifiers   208
13.13   Negative quantification   210
13.14   Approximation: 'about'   210
13.15   Restriction: 'only'   211
13.16   'More than'   212
13.17   'Less than'   214
13.18   'As many as'   215

Chapter 14 Time   **216**

14.1 Days   216
14.2 Parts of the day   217
14.3 Months   217
14.4 Years   218
14.5 Dates   219
14.6 Seasons   220
14.7 Useful expressions of time   220
14.8 Telling the time   225

Chapter 15 Thai speech conventions   **230**

15.1 Politeness   230
15.2 Thanks   230
15.3 Apologies   231
15.4 Polite requests   232
15.5 Misunderstandings   237
15.6 Socialising   239

Appendix 1   Romanisation systems   **246**
Appendix 2   The verbs hâi, dâi/dâi: **and** bpen:
               a summary   **251**

Glossary   **256**
Bibliography and further reading   **259**
Index   **262**

Preface

The aim of the first edition of this book was to provide a description of the main features of Thai grammar which would be accessible to the ordinary learner with little or no knowledge of linguistic terminology.

This second edition differs only slightly in content from the first edition. The major difference is cosmetic: examples are given in Thai script first, while the Mary Haas-based phonemic system of romanising Thai has been abandoned in favour of a less-technical system. In addition, some new examples have been included, some explanations simplified and some errors eliminated.

I am grateful to those people who have written messages of appreciation for the first edition and offered suggestions and advice on how it might be improved. I am indebted to Routledge's anonymous reviewers of the first edition for their valuable suggestions and encouraging comments. I am especially grateful to Sujinda Khantayalongkoch and Vantana Cornwell for sharing their insights on the language, often at great length, and for checking the Thai entries. Errors, omissions and other shortcomings that may remain are, however, entirely my own responsibility.

Introduction

Thai and its speakers

Thai (formerly called 'Siamese') is a member of the *Tai* family of languages, which are spoken by an estimated 70 million people dispersed over a wide area of Asia, from northern Vietnam to northern India. Thai, with over 50 million first-language speakers, is the most important language in the Tai family, which also includes Lao, Shan (spoken in northern Burma) and some 15 million speakers in south-western China. Despite common structural features, even closely-related Tai languages are often mutually unintelligible because of phonological and lexical differences. Tai speakers were once thought to have originated from China and migrated southwards, but today, the border area between northern Vietnam and China's Guangxi province is regarded as a more likely origin. From the eighth century AD Tai speakers began to migrate westwards and south-westwards into what is present-day Thailand.

Thai is the national language of Thailand. Distinct regional dialects of Thai are spoken in the north, north-east and south of the country, but the language of the Central Region is regarded as the standard and is used both in schools and for official purposes throughout the country.

Thai is a tonal language, with the meaning of each syllable determined by the pitch at which it is pronounced. Standard Thai has five tones – mid, low, high, rising and falling. Thai has no noun or verb inflections: a noun has a single form, with no distinction between singular and plural, while past, present and future time can be conveyed by a single verb form. Like many other South-East Asian languages, Thai has a complex pronoun system, which reflects gender, age, social status, the formality of the situation and the degree of intimacy between speakers. Much of the original Thai lexicon is monosyllabic; a high percentage of polysyllabic words are foreign borrowings, particularly from the classical Indian languages, Sanskrit and Pali.

 ## Romanisation

There are many ways of romanising Thai but no universally recognised system. Academic linguists use one system, librarians another, the Royal Thai Institute yet another, while writers of textbooks, phrasebooks and dictionaries often adapt or devise their own personal systems. Thais can neither systematically write their language in the Western alphabet nor easily read Westerners' romanisations of Thai; the average Thai, when called upon to romanise Thai words, will almost certainly do so in a quite unsystematic way.

Some romanisation systems use special phonetic symbols to represent the sounds of Thai more precisely and accents to represent tones and vowel length, while other less-precise systems use a near equivalent in the author's own language – which may confuse learners who do not share the author's mother tongue or even just his regional dialect. The complexities and ambiguities of romanised Thai can be bypassed by learning to read the Thai script.

The romanisation system used in this book is similar to that used in *Complete Thai* (2010). The system appears in full in Appendix 1, alongside the Mary Haas/AUA type system favoured by academic linguists, and the Library of Congress system used by librarians.

 ## Learning Thai

A number of readily available Thai courses can be used in conjunction with this grammar. *Complete Thai* (2010), for example, equips the learner with the necessary language to deal with a range of everyday situations, provides a structured introduction to the script and has accompanying CDs; the *Linguaphone Thai Course* (1984) and *Colloquial Thai* (2005) cover similar ground. The two-volume *Thai Language and Culture for Beginners* (2007) by Yuphaphann Hoonchamlong is an excellent and attractively produced course with accompanying DVDs.

Of earlier materials, *Spoken Thai* (1945–9) by Mary Haas, although dated in places, is an extremely solid work, which offers many valuable insights into the language. *Foundations of Thai* (1968) by Edward Anthony et al., and *Thai Basic Course* (1970) by Warren G. Yates and Absorn Tryon likewise provide very thorough introductions to the language with comprehensive grammar notes. The *AUA Language Center Thai Course* (1967), prepared by J. Marvin Brown, was designed for classroom use with a native speaker, rather than self-tuition, but other works produced by AUA, including Brown's *AUA Language Center Thai Course: Reading and Writing* (1979), and Adrian Palmer's imaginative dialogue books, *Small Talk* (1974) and *Getting Help with your Thai* (1977) are well worth consulting. Reprints of *Fundamentals of the Thai Language* (1957) by Stuart Campbell and Chuan Shaweewongse continue to appear periodically, and the book has long provided the Bangkok expatriate with a sound introduction to the language, despite its traditional grammar-translation approach.

For many years the only available grammar of Thai was *Thai Reference Grammar* (1964) by Richard Noss, which was based on his doctoral thesis. Although it is outstandingly comprehensive and insightful, it is addressed to those with a background in linguistics, and is at times bewildering or even intimidating for the average beginner. *Teaching Thai Grammar* (1992) by William Kuo does not go into anywhere near as much depth, but it serves as a very useful workbook for practising key structures, using Thai script. In addition to the first edition of this volume (2002), two other notable grammars have appeared in recent years: *Thai Reference Grammar: the structure of spoken Thai* (2001) by James Higbie and Snea Thinsan, which is aimed at the layman, and *A Reference Grammar of Thai* (2005) by Shoichi Iwasaki and Preeya Ingkaphirom, which is written with an audience of more advanced learners and linguists in mind.

 Dictionaries

The last twenty years have seen the appearance of a number of excellent dictionaries reflecting up-to-date usage. These include Domnern and Sathienpong's *Thai-English Dictionary* (1994), Thianchai Iamwaramet's *A New Thai Dictionary with Bilingual Explanation* (1993) and Wong Watthanaphichet's *New Age Thai-English Dictionary* (2010), the latter providing a romanised pronunciation guide for each entry.

Of earlier dictionaries, *Thai-English Student's Dictionary* (1964) compiled by the American linguist, Mary Haas, remains a valuable tool for the learner. Each Thai script entry is followed by a phonemic transcription and English gloss. A particularly useful feature for the learner is that for every noun the appropriate classifier is indicated; many of the entries also include well-chosen examples of everyday usage. George B. McFarland's *Thai-English Dictionary* (1944), although dated, also remains a valuable reference work for the more advanced student of Thai, for it contains many words of Sanskrit origin and extensive listings of flora and fauna not found in the Haas volume. Robertson's pocket-sized *Practical English-Thai Dictionary*, first published in 1969, is useful for the beginner, with Thai equivalents of about 2,500 common English words in both romanised transcription and Thai script.

 ## Linguistic literature on Thai

There is a rich English-language literature on many aspects of Thai linguistics, most of which is catalogued in Franklin E. Huffman's *Bibliography and Index of Mainland Southeast Asian Languages and Linguistics* (1986). Much of this literature is in the form of unpublished doctoral theses written in American university linguistics departments during the 1970s and 1980s and therefore not readily available. A number of collections of essays produced to honour leading scholars of Thai, most notably William J. Gedney (1975), Fang-Kuei Li (1976) and Vichin Panupong (1997), include contributions which the serious learner can benefit from. Anthony Diller's essays on levels of language use (1985) and the role of Central Thai as a national language (1991) and William A. Smalley's *Linguistic Diversity and National Unity: Language Ecology in Thailand* (1994), a masterful study of the relationship between the national language, regional dialects and minority languages, are accessible to the layman and offer invaluable insights into the language and language situation in Thailand.

Chapter 1

Pronunciation

Thai differs radically from English and other European languages in being a *tone language*. In tone languages the meaning of a syllable is determined by the pitch at which it is pronounced. The Thai sound system also includes a small number of consonant and vowel sounds which have no close equivalent in English. The lists of consonant and vowel sounds in this section include, where possible, a close equivalent sound in standard British English; speakers of American English need to be aware that the final 'r' in words like **jer** ('to meet') is not sounded. An example of each sound in a word is given for confirmation with a Thai native speaker. For a more technical description of the sounds of Thai, see Noss (1964) or Iwasaki and Preeya (2005).

1.1 Consonants

1.1.1 Initial consonants

The consonants **d, b, f, l, m, n, r, y, w, s, h** are similar to English; the following consonants, however, need further clarification:

g similar to *g* in *get* e.g. **gài** (ไก่) 'chicken'

k similar to *k* in *kick* e.g. **kài** (ไข่) 'egg'

ng similar to *ng* in *singer* e.g. **ngahn** (งาน) 'work'

j similar to *j* in *jar* e.g. **jahn** (จาน) 'plate'

ch similar to *ch* in *chart* e.g. **chai:** (ชาย) 'male'

dt similar to *t* in *stop* e.g. **dtahm** (ตาม) 'to follow'

t similar to *t* in *too* e.g. **tai** (ไทย) 'Thai'

bp similar to *p* in *spin* e.g. **bpai** (ไป) 'to go'

p similar to *p* in *part* e.g. **pah-săh** (ภาษา) 'language'

Many Thais find it difficult to produce an **r** at the beginning of a word or syllable and will substitute **l**. Thus **róo** ('to know') is often pronounced **lóo**, and **a-rai** ('what?') as **a-lai**.

1.1.2 | Final consonants

A Thai syllable can end in two types of consonant sounds:

(a) **-p**, **-t**, **-k** sounds

These final consonants are *unreleased*. Technically, the airstream is closed to make the sound, but not re-opened, so that no air is released. Examples in English include the 'p' in the casual pronunciation of 'yep!' and the 't' in 'rat', when 'rat trap' is said quickly. Beginners sometimes find it difficult to hear the difference between words like **rúk** ('to love'), **rút** ('to bind') and **rúp** ('to receive'), while in attempting to reproduce these sounds, they may inadvertently 'release' the final consonant.

(b) **-m**, **-n**, **-ng** sounds

These sounds are familiar from English and present no problem.

1.1.3 | Consonant clusters

The following consonant clusters (combinations of two or more consonant sounds) exist in Thai; they occur only at the beginning of a word.

gr- as in **grOOng** (กรุง) 'city'

gl- as in **glai** (ไกล) 'far'

gw- as in **gwâhng** (กว้าง) 'wide'

kr- as in **krai** (ใคร) 'who?'

kl- as in **klái:** (คล้าย) 'to resemble'

kw- as in **kwǎh** (ขวา) 'right'

bpr- as in **bpra-dtoo** (ประตู) 'door'

bpl- as in **bplah** (ปลา) 'fish'

pr- as in **prá** (พระ) 'monk'

pl- as in **plâht** (พลาด) 'to miss, fail'

dtr- as in **dtrong** (ตรง) 'straight'

In everyday speech many Thais from Bangkok will omit the second consonant in a cluster:

bplah (ปลา) 'fish' becomes **bpah**

krai (ใคร) 'who?' becomes **kai**

bpra-dtoo (ประตู) 'door' becomes **bpa-dtoo**

A more radical transformation, associated with Bangkok working-class speech, is the change of initial **kw-** to **f-**:

kwăh (ขวา) 'right' becomes **făh**

kwahm sÒOk (ความสุข) 'happiness' becomes **fahm sÒOk**

1.2   Vowels

The distinction between short and long vowels is important in Thai. Learners are likely to experience some difficulty at first in hearing and producing differences between the short and long vowel sounds **-ao/-ao:** and **-ai/-ai:**:

rao (เรา) 'we'	**rao:** (ราว) 'about'
kâo (เข้า) 'to enter'	**kâo:** (ข้าว) 'rice'
dtai (ไต) 'liver'	**dtai:** (ตาย) 'to die'
săi (ใส) 'clear'	**săi:** (สาย) 'late morning'

When reading Thai script it is essential to be able to distinguish between long and short vowel symbols, as vowel length influences tone (see Chapter 2):

-u short vowel, similar to *u* in *run* e.g. **yung** (ยัง) 'still'

-ah long vowel, similar to *a* in *father* e.g. **mah** (มา) 'to come'

-e short vowel, similar to *e* in *let* e.g. **dèk** (เด็ก) 'child'

-ay long vowel, similar to *ay* in *may* e.g. **tay** (เท) 'to pour'

-er as a short vowel, similar to *er* in *number* e.g. **ngern** (เงิน) 'money';
as a long vowel, similar to *er* in *her* e.g. **jer** (เจอ) 'to meet'

-air a short or long vowel, similar to *air* in *hair* e.g. (short vowel)
kăirng (แข็ง) 'hard'; (long vowel) **mâir** (แม่) 'mother'

-i similar to *i* in *bin* e.g. **bin** (บิน) 'to fly'

-ee similar to *ee* in *fee* e.g. **mee** (มี) 'to have'

-or a short or long vowel, similar to *or* in *corn* e.g. (short vowel)
dtôrng (ต้อง) 'must'; (long vowel) **bòrk** (บอก) 'to say'

-o similar to *o* in *Ron* e.g. **jon** (จน) 'poor'

-oh similar to *o* in *go* e.g. **dtoh** (โต) 'big'

-OO similar to *oo* in *book* e.g. **yÓOk** (ยุค) 'era'

-oo similar to *oo* in *coo* e.g. **róo** (รู้) 'to know'

-eu short vowel, with no equivalent in English, e.g. **nèung** (หนึ่ง) 'one'

-eu: long vowel, with no equivalent in English, e.g. **meu:** (มือ) 'hand'

-ee-a similar to *ear* in *hear* e.g. **sěe-a** (เสีย) 'to lose'

-oo-a similar to *oer* in *doer* e.g. **róo-a** (รั้ว) 'fence'

-eu-a long vowel with no equivalent in English, e.g. **bèu-a** (เบื่อ) 'bored'

-ee-o similar to *io* in *Rio* e.g. **dee-o** (เดียว) 'single'

-oo-ay similar to *oué* in *roué* e.g. **roo-ay** (รวย) 'rich'

-eu-ay long vowel with no equivalent in English, e.g. **nèu-ay** (เหนื่อย) 'tired'

-oo-ee similar to *ewy* in *chewy* e.g. **koo-ee** (คุย) 'to chat'

-oy-ee long vowel with no equivalent in English, e.g. **doy-ee** (โดย) 'by'

-er-ee long vowel with no equivalent in English, e.g. **ner-ee** (เนย) 'butter'

-oy short or long vowel, similar to *oy* in *boy*, e.g. (short vowel) **bòy** (บ่อย) 'often'; (long vowel) **róy** (ร้อย) 'hundred'

-ai short vowel, similar to *ai* in *Thai* e.g. **tai** (ไทย) 'Thai'

-ai: long vowel, similar to *ai* in *Thai* e.g. **dtai:** (ตาย) 'dead'

-ew short vowel, similar to *ew* in *few* e.g. **hěw** (หิว) 'hungry'

-ay-o short or long vowel, similar to *ayo* in *Mayo* e.g. (short vowel) **ray-o** (เร็ว) 'fast'; (long vowel) **lay-o** (เลว) 'bad'

-air-o long or short vowel, with no equivalent in English, e.g. (short vowel)

  tǎir-o (แถว) 'row, line'; (long vowel) **láir-o** (แล้ว) 'already'

-ao short vowel, similar to *ao* in *Lao* e.g. **rao** (เรา) 'we'

-ao: long vowel, similar to *ao* in *Lao* e.g. **rao:** (ราว) 'about'

1.3 Tones

Each syllable in Thai is pronounced with a specific tone. Standard Thai has five different tones, which are represented in the transcription system by an accent over the first vowel in the syllable. They are mid tone (no accent), high tone (´), low tone (`), rising tone (ˇ) and falling tone (ˆ).

(a) Mid tone (**sĕe-ung săh-mun**): normal voice pitch:

> **bpai** (ไป) 'to go' **mah** (มา) 'to come' **pairng** (แพง) 'expensive'

(b) High tone (**sĕe-ung dtree**): higher than normal voice pitch:

> **rót** (รถ) 'car' **séu:** (ซื้อ) 'to buy' **lék** (เล็ก) 'small'

(c) Low tone (**sĕe-ung àyk**): lower than normal voice pitch:

> **sìp** (สิบ) 'ten' **jàhk** (จาก) 'from' **yài** (ใหญ่) 'big'

(d) Rising tone (**sĕe-ung jùt-dta-wah**): starting from a lower than normal voice pitch with a distinctive rising contour:

> **kŏrng** (ของ) 'of' **sŏo-ay** (สวย) 'pretty' **pŏrm** (ผอม) 'thin'

(e) Falling tone (**sĕe-ung toh**): starting from a higher than normal voice pitch with a distinctive falling contour:

> **têe** (ที่) 'at' **chôrp** (ชอบ) 'to like' **pôot** (พูด) 'to speak'

1.3.1 *Tone change*

There are a few common words which have a different tone in normal conversation to when pronounced slowly and deliberately in isolation. For example, **káo** (เขา) 'he, she, they', **chún** (ฉัน) 'I' and **mái?** (ไหม) (question particle) are all pronounced with a high tone in normal conversation but a rising tone when pronounced in isolation.

In one form of adjectival reduplication (see 6.4), the first element is pronounced with a high tone for the purpose of emphasis or intensification:

sŏo-ay	สวย	'beautiful'
sóo-ay sŏo-ay	ส๊วยสวย	'so beautiful!'

In certain situations tones may also change; the unstressed first syllable in a two-syllable word is usually pronounced with a mid tone (see 1.4), while when two syllables with rising tones follow one another, the first is often pronounced as a high tone:

núng-sĕu:	หนังสือ	'book'
sórng săhm kon	สองสามคน	'two or three people'

1.4 Stress

In words of two syllables, it is the second syllable (in italics) which is stressed. When the vowel in the first syllable is -a, it is normally reduced to a 'neutral' vowel (an 'er' sound like the 'o' in 'tonight') and in normal speech the tone is mid:

bpra-*dtoo*	ประตู	'door'
sa-*dòo-uk*	สะดวก	'convenient'

When the vowel -ah occurs in both the first and second syllable, it is commonly shortened in the first syllable:

ah-*hăhn* or **a-*hăhn***	อาหาร	'food'
pah-*săh* or **pa-*săh***	ภาษา	'language'

Chapter 2

The writing system

Thai is written in a unique script. This has evolved from a script which originated in South India and was introduced into mainland South-East Asia during the fourth or fifth century AD. The neighbouring Lao and Cambodian scripts bear some close similarities to Thai. The first recorded example of Thai writing is widely believed to be a stone inscription found by the future King Mongkut (Rama IV, 1851–68) at Sukhothai in 1833, and dated 1292 AD. In this inscription, the author, King Ramkhamhaeng, records that he actually devised the script. There has been lively debate in academic circles about the authenticity of the inscription, much of which can be found in Chamberlain (1991).

The Thai writing system is alphabetic. It is written across the page from left to right with no spaces between words; when spaces are used, they serve as punctuation markers, instead of commas or full stops. There is generally a close match between spelling and pronunciation. The following sections provide a broad outline of the key features of the Thai writing system; for practical, structured lessons in reading Thai, see Brown (1979) and Smyth (2010).

2.1 Consonants

The Thai alphabet is conventionally described as having 44 consonants, although two of these, **kǒr kòo-ut** and **kor kon**, fell out of use more than a century ago. The letters **réu** and **reu**, and **léu** and **leu** are not regarded as consonants, but follow the letters **ror reu-a** and **lor ling** respectively in dictionary arrangements.

Consonants are arranged according to the order of letters in the traditional Indian alphabet. All consonants are pronounced with an inherent -**or** vowel sound. Each consonant has a name, rather like 'a-for-apple, b-for-bat', which children learn in school. For the foreign learner, knowing these names can be useful when asking how to spell a word, but it is not necessary for learning to read.

Many consonant symbols change their pronunciation at the end of a word. Because of the very limited number of final consonant sounds that exist in Thai (1.1.2), the *letters* representing initial **g, j, ch, d, dt, b, bp, s** and **f** sounds (as well as initial **k, p, t** sounds) are each channelled into one of just three possible final consonant *sounds* – **k, p, t** – when they occur at the end of a word. The following chart lists the consonants in dictionary order with their names and pronunciations, both as initial and as final consonants:

Name			Initial	Final
ก	**gor gài**	(chicken)	**g**	**k**
ข	**kŏr kài**	(egg)	**k**	**k**
ฃ	**kŏr kòo-ut**	(bottle)	**k**	**k**
ค	**kor kwai:**	(buffalo)	**k**	**k**
ฅ	**kor kon**	(person)	**k**	**k**
ฆ	**kor ra-kung**	(bell)	**k**	**k**
ง	**ngor ngoo**	(snake)	**ng**	**ng**
จ	**jor jahn**	(plate)	**j**	**t**
ฉ	**chŏr chìng**	(small cymbals)	**ch**	**t**
ช	**chor cháhng**	(elephant)	**ch**	**t**
ซ	**sor sôh**	(chain)	**s**	**t**
ฌ	**chor (ga)cher**	(tree)	**ch**	**t**
ญ	**yor yǐng**	(girl)	**y**	**n**
ฎ	**dor chá-dah**	(theatrical crown)	**d**	**t**
ฏ	**dtor bpa-dtùk**	(goad)	**dt**	**t**
ฐ	**tŏr tǎhn**	(base)	**t**	**t**
ฑ	**tor mon-toh**	(Montho, wife of the god Indra)	**t**	**t**
ฒ	**tor tâo**	(old man)	**t**	**t**
ณ	**nor nayn**	(novice)	**n**	**n**
ด	**dor dèk**	(child)	**d**	**t**

Name			Initial	Final
ต	dtor dtào	(turtle)	dt	t
ถ	tŏr tǒOng	(bag)	t	t
ท	tor ta-hăhn	(soldier)	t	t
ธ	tor tong	(flag)	t	t
น	nor nŏo	(mouse)	n	n
บ	bor bai mái:	(leaf)	b	p
ป	bpor bplah	(fish)	bp	p
ผ	pŏr pêung	(bee)	p	p
ฝ	fŏr făh	(lid)	f	p
พ	por pahn	(tray)	p	p
ฟ	for fun	(tooth)	f	p
ภ	por sŭm-pao	(sailing ship)	p	p
ม	mor máh	(horse)	m	m
ย	yor yúk	(giant)	y	depends on preceding vowel
ร	ror reu-a	(boat)	r	n
ฤ	réu	–	réu/rí/rer	–
ฤๅ	reu:	–	reu:	–
ล	lor ling	(monkey)	l	n
ฦ	léu	–	léu	–
ฦๅ	leu:	–	leu:	–
ว	wor wăirn	(ring)	w	depends on preceding vowel
ศ	sŏr săh-lah	(pavilion)	s	t
ษ	sŏr reu-sĕe	(ascetic)	s	t
ส	sŏr sĕu-a	(tiger)	s	t
ห	hŏr hèep	(box)	h	–
ฬ	lor jOO-lah	(kite)	l	n
อ	or àhng	(bowl)	–	–
ฮ	hor nók hôok	(owl)	h	–

The chart below summarises the representation of final consonant sounds. Although there are theoretically 15 ways of writing a final -t sound, less than half of these are likely to be encountered in normal usage.

Final consonant sound	Thai consonant symbol
-p	บ ป พ ภ ฟ
-t	ด ต ฎ ฏ จ ถ ฐ ท ธ ฑ ช ซ ศ ษ ส
-k	ก ข ค ฆ
-m	ม ำ
-n	น ณ ญ ร ล ฬ
-ng	ง

2.2 Consonants by class

Thai consonants are divided into three classes – *high*, *mid* and *low*. The class of the initial consonant is one factor in determining the tone of a word or syllable. In order to be able to read, the learner has to memorise the class of each consonant; the easiest way to do this is to memorise the shorter lists of mid-class and high-class consonants so that everything not on those lists can be assumed to be low-class.

Low class:	น	ม	ง	ร	ล	ย	ว		
	n	m	ng	r	l	y	w		
	ค	ช	ซ	ท	พ	ฟ			
	k	ch	s	t	p	f			
	ฅ	ธ	ภ	ญ	ณ				
	k	t	p	y	n				
	ฌ	ฑ	ฒ	ฬ	ฮ				
	ch	t	t	l	h				
Mid class:	ก	จ	ด	ต	บ	ป	อ	ฎ	ฏ
	g	j	d	dt	b	bp	zero	d	dt
High class:	ข	ฉ	ถ	ผ	ฝ	ศ ษ ส		ห	ฐ
	k	ch	t	p	f	s		h	t

2.3 Vowels

Vowel symbols can only be written in combination with a preceding consonant; they can appear after, before, above, or below a consonant, and even surrounding the consonant on three sides; in the following table, a dash is used to indicate the position of the consonant in relation to the vowel symbol. A few vowels change their form, depending on whether or not they are followed by a consonant. Thus, เ-อ and เิ- represent the same -er sound; in a word like **ter** ('you', 'she') where no consonant sound follows -er, then the first form is used; but in **dern** ('to walk'), with a consonant following -er, the second form is used.

When a word begins with a vowel sound, the 'zero' or 'glottal' consonant symbol is used. (Note that the Thai letter representing 'zero' consonant and the **-or** vowel are identical.)

Vowel length is important in Thai because it plays a part in determining the tone of a syllable. Some long vowels use the symbols -ะ and -ั as vowel shorteners.

The following chart lists the vowel symbols in dictionary order, indicating whether the vowel is long or short:

-ร	**-orn**	long	พร	**porn**	(blessing)
-รร	**-un**	short	สรร	**sŭn**	(to choose)
-รร-	**-um**	short	กรรม	**gum**	(karma, fate)
-ว-	**-oo-u-**	long	ด่วน	**dòo-un**	(urgent)
-อ	**-or**	long	หมอ	**mŏr**	(doctor)
-ะ	**-a**	short	ค่ะ	**kâ**	(female polite particle)
-ั	**-u-**	short	ตัด	**dtùt**	(to cut)
-ัว	**-oo-a**	long	รั้ว	**róo-a**	(fence)
-า	**-ah**	long	มา	**mah**	(to come)
-าย	**-ai:**	long	ยาย	**yai:**	(grandmother)
-าว	**-ao:**	long	ลาว	**lao:**	(Lao/Laos)
-ํา	**-um**	short + m	จำ	**jum**	(to remember)

◌ิ	**-i**	short	กิน	**gin**	(to eat)
◌ิว	**-ew**	short + w	ผิว	**pěw**	(skin)
◌ี	**-ee**	long	ดี	**dee**	(good)
◌ึ	**-eu**	short	หนึ่ง	**nèung**	(one)
◌ื	**-eu:**	long	ซื้อ	**séu:**	(to buy)
◌ุ	**-OO**	short	คุณ	**kOOn**	(you)
◌ุย	**-oo-ee**	short + y	คุย	**koo-ee**	(to chat)
◌ู	**-oo**	long	ดู	**doo**	(to look at)
เ-	**-ay**	long	เลข	**lâyk**	(number)
เ็-	**-e**	short	เป็น	**bpen**	(to be)
เ-ย	**-er-ee**	long	เคย	**ker-ee**	(used to, ever)
เ-อ	**-er**	long	เธอ	**ter**	(you, she)
เ-อะ	**-er**	short	เยอะ	**yér**	(a lot)
เ-ะ	**-e**	short	เตะ	**dtè**	(to kick)
เ-า	**-ao**	short	เรา	**rao**	(we)
เ-าะ	**-o'**	short	เกาะ	**gò'**	(island)
เ-ิ-	**-er**	long	เดิน	**dern**	(to walk)
เ-ีย	**-ee-a**	long	เรียน	**ree-un**	(to study)
เ-ือ	**-eu-a**	long	เบื่อ	**bèu-a**	(to be bored)
แ-	**-air**	long	แม่	**mâir**	(mother)
แ็-	**-air**	short	แข็ง	**kǎirng**	(hard)
แ-ะ	**-air**	short	และ	**láir**	(and)
โ-	**-oh**	long	โลก	**lôhk**	(world)
โ-ะ	**-o**	short	โต๊ะ	**dtó**	(table)
ใ-	**-ai**	short	ใน	**nai**	(in)
ไ-	**-ai**	short	ไทย	**Thai**	(Thai)

2.4 Live syllables and dead syllables

Thai syllables are described in Thai as being either *live* or *dead*. A live syllable (**kum bpen**) ends with a long vowel, an **m, n, ng** sound, or the Thai letters -ย, -ว, เ-า, ไ- , ใ-; a dead syllable (**kum dtai:**) ends with either a short vowel, or a **p, t,** or **k** sound.

Live syllables:	**mah**	**doo**	**bin**	**rum**	**yung**	**ao**	**kăi:**
	มา	ดู	บิน	รำ	ยัง	เอา	ขาย

Dead syllables:	**dtó**	**gà**	**dÒO**	**rúp**	**jòrt**	**mâhk**
	โต๊ะ	กะ	ดุ	รับ	จอด	มาก

2.5 Tone rules

The tone of a syllable is determined by a combination of three different factors: (i) the type of syllable (live or dead), (ii) the class of the initial consonant (high, medium or low) and (iii) the length of the vowel (long or short).

2.5.1 Dead syllables

The following chart summarises tone rules for dead syllables with examples:

Initial consonant	Short vowel	Long vowel
Low class	**HIGH TONE**	**FALLING TONE**
	รัก **rúk**	มาก **mâhk**
	to love	much, very
Mid class	**LOW TONE**	**LOW TONE**
	ติด **dtìt**	บาท **bàht**
	to stick	baht
High class	**LOW TONE**	**LOW TONE**
	ขับ **kùp**	สอบ **sòrp**
	to drive	to take an exam

| 2.5.2 | *Live syllables and tone marks* |

Live syllables with no tone mark are pronounced with a mid tone if the initial consonant is either low class or mid class, but a rising tone if it is a high-class consonant.

To represent live syllables with high, falling and low tones, (such as the words **máh** 'horse', **dtôrng** 'must' and **kài** 'egg') tone marks are used. These tone marks are written above the initial consonant. The two most common tone marks are **mái àyk** (˙) and **mái toh** (˝). Unfortunately for the learner, because of a radical change in the tone system that occurred centuries ago, these tone marks no longer represent a specific tone. Words written with **mái àyk** can have either a falling tone or a low tone; words written with **mái toh** can have either a high tone or a falling tone. It is the class of the initial consonant which determines how the tone mark will be interpreted.

The following chart summarises rules for live syllables with examples:

Initial consonant	(no tone mark)	**mái àyk**	**mái toh**
Low class	**MID TONE**	**FALLING TONE**	**HIGH TONE**
	มา **mah**	ไม่ **mâi**	ม้า **máh**
	to come	not	horse
Mid class	**MID TONE**	**LOW TONE**	**FALLING TONE**
	ตาม **dtahm**	ต่อ **dtòr**	ต้อง **dtôrng**
	to follow	to continue	must
High class	**RISING TONE**	**LOW TONE**	**FALLING TONE**
	ขอ **kŏr**	ไข่ **kài**	ข้าง **kâhng**
	to ask for	egg	side

There are two further tone marks, **mái dtree** (˜) and **mái jùt-dta-wah** (˖), although they are much less common. The former always produces a high tone, the latter, always a rising tone.

โต๊ะ	เป๊ปซี่	เก๊
dtó	**bpép-sêe**	**gáy**
table	Pepsi	false, counterfeit

เดี๋ยว	จ๋า	ก๋วยเตี๋ยว
dĕe-o	**jăh**	**gŏo-ay dtĕe-o**
moment	*polite particle*	noodles

2.5.3 | Silent initial consonants: ห and อ

When the high-class consonant ห occurs before the low-class consonants, ง, น, ม, ร, ย, ญ, ว, ล, it is silent but has the effect of transforming the low-class consonants into high-class consonants; such words then follow the tone rules for words with initial high-class consonants (2.5.1; 2.5.2).

หยุด	หลอด	หนี	หญิง	หนึ่ง
yòOt	**lòrt**	**nĕe**	**yĭng**	**nèung**
to stop	tube	to flee	female	one

The mid-class consonant อ occurs silently before the low-class consonant ย and has the effect of transforming the low-class consonant into a mid-class consonant. There are only four words in this category, all of which are pronounced with a low tone:

อยาก	อย่า	อย่าง	อยู่
yàhk	**yàh**	**yàhng**	**yòo**
to want to	don't	like, kind	to live

2.5.4 | Consonant clusters

Consonant clusters occur only at the beginning of a syllable in Thai. In syllables beginning with a consonant cluster, the class of the first consonant in the cluster is used for determining the tone of the syllable. The following chart summarises possible consonant clusters with examples:

กร-	คร-	ขร-	ตร-	ปร-	พร-
กรอก	ใคร	ขรึม	ตรวจ	ปราบ	พระ
gròrk	**krai**	**krĕum**	**dtròo-ut**	**bpràhp**	**prá**
to fill in	who?	solemn	to examine	to suppress	monk

กล-	คล-	ขล-		ปล-	พล-
ใกล้	คล้าย	ขลุ่ย		ปลุก	พลาด
glâi	**klái:**	**klòo-ee**		**bplÒOk**	**plâht**
near	similar	Thai flute		to arouse	to make a mistake

กว-	คว-	ขว-
กว้าง	ควาย	ขวา
gwâhng	**kwai:**	**kwăh**
wide	buffalo	right

2.5.5 Unwritten vowels

2.5.5.1 Monosyllables

Syllables consisting of two consonants with no written vowel symbol are pronounced with an inherent **o** vowel sound:

คน	ยก	จบ	หก	หมด
kon	**yók**	**jòp**	**hòk**	**mòt**
person	to lift	to finish	six	to be finished, used up

2.5.5.2 Two-syllable words

Many two-syllable words in Thai have an unwritten **a** vowel in the first syllable. The first syllable is unstressed and pronounced with a mid tone in normal speech; the tone of the second syllable is determined by the second consonant in the word (i.e. the initial consonant of the second syllable), unless that consonant is ง, น, ม, ร, ย, ญ, ว, or ล, in which case the first consonant 'over-rules' it and determines the tone:

สบาย	สถาน	สภาพ	สนุก	ตลาด
sa-bai:	**sa-tăhn**	**sa-pâhp**	**sa-nÒOk**	**dta-làht**
well, happy	place	condition	fun	market

A small number of two-syllable words consist of three consonant symbols but no written vowel symbols. In words like this, the first unwritten vowel is -**a** and the second -**o**:

ถนน	สงบ	ตลก	ขนม
ta-nǒn	**sa-ngòp**	**dta-lòk**	**ka-nǒm**
road	peaceful	to be funny	sweet, dessert

There are a small number of words beginning with the letters บริ-, in which the unwritten vowel sound is **or**:

บริษัท	บริเวณ	บริการ	บริหาร	บริโภค
bor-ri-sùt	**bor-ri-wayn**	**bor-ri-gahn**	**bor-ri-hăhn**	**bor-ri-pôhk**
company	vicinity, area	service	to administer	to consume

2.6 Miscellaneous

2.6.1 Mismatch between spelling and pronunciation

Overall, the match between spelling and pronunciation in Thai is remarkably close; if you know the rules, you can almost guarantee that you will be able to read a word correctly. However, three common types of mismatch between spelling and normal conversational pronunciation, are:

1 Tone suggested by the spelling is not reflected in pronunciation

Words written with rising tones but pronounced with high tones in normal speech:

เขา ('he, she, they') written **kǎo** but pronounced **káo**

ฉัน ('I') written **chǔn** but pronounced **chún**

ไหม (question particle) written **mǎi** but pronounced **mái**

Words written with falling or high tones but pronounced with low tones:

ประโยชน์ ('advantage') written **bpra-yôht** but pronounced **bpra-yòht**

ประโยค ('sentence') written **bpra-yôhk** but pronounced **bpra-yòhk**

ประวัติ ('history') written **bpra-wút** but pronounced **bpra-wùt**

2 Vowel length in the written form is not reflected in the pronunciation

Words written with long vowels but pronounced with short vowels:

ต้อง ('must') **dtôrng** pronounced with a short vowel

เงิน ('money') **ngern** pronounced with a short vowel

ท่าน ('you') written **tâhn** but pronounced **tûn**

Words written with short vowels but pronounced with long vowels:

น้ำ ('water') written **núm** but pronounced **náhm**

เก้า ('nine') written **gâo** but pronounced **gâo:**

ไม้ ('wood') written **mái** but pronounced **mái:**

2.6.2 | Linker syllables and double-functioning consonants

A number of words that appear to consist of two syllables are joined by
a linker syllable consisting of the final consonant of the first syllable with
an unwritten a vowel between them:

สกปรก	ผลไม้	คุณภาพ	ราชการ
sòk-ga-bpròk	**pǒn-la-mái:**	**kOOn-na-pâhp**	**râht-cha-gahn**
dirty	fruit	quality	government service

2.6.3 | Silenced consonants

Thai words that have been borrowed from Sanskrit, Pali and English usually
try to reflect as much of the original spelling as possible; as this will often
produce pronunciations that are impossible or misleading, a 'killer' symbol is
placed above the redundant consonant to indicate that it should be ignored:

เบียร์	เบอร์	จอห์น	เสาร์	อาทิตย์
bee-a	**ber**	**jorn**	**sǎo**	**ah-tít**
beer	number	John	Saturday	Sunday, week

Sometimes the 'killer' sign, called **gah-run** in Thai, cancels out not only the
consonant above which it appears, but also the one immediately preceding it:

จันทร์	ศาสตร์
jun	**sàht**
Monday, moon	science

Sometimes, even though there is no **gah-run** sign, the final consonant is
not pronounced:

บัตร	สมัคร
bùt	**sa-mùk**
card	to join

2.6.4 | Silent final vowels

A number of words of Indic origin are spelt with a final short vowel which
is not pronounced:

ชาติ	ญาติ	เหตุ
châht	**yâht**	**hàyt**
nation	relative	reason

2.6.5 | Irregular ร

The letter ร, normally pronounced **r** at the beginning of a word and **n** at the end of word, occurs in a number of irregular combinations:

2.6.5.1 | ทร-

These two letters together at the beginning of a word behave like low-class **s**:

ทราบ	ทราย	ทรง
sâhp	**sai:**	**song**
to know	sand	shape, form

2.6.5.2 | สร-

The letter ร is not pronounced in words that begin with these two letters:

สร้าง	สร้อยคอ	สระน้ำ
sâhng	**sôy kor**	**sà náhm**
to build	necklace	pond

2.6.5.3 | Final ร

As a final consonant the letter ร is normally pronounced **n**; but in words where there is no immediately preceding written vowel, it is pronounced **orn**:

การ	ทหาร	พร	นคร	ละคร
gahn	**ta-hăhn**	**porn**	**na-korn**	**la-korn**
business, affair	soldier	blessing	city	play, theatrical performance

2.6.5.4 | -รร

When the letters รร occur at the end of a syllable, they are pronounced **un**; if they are followed by a final consonant they are pronounced **u**:

สรร	รถบรรทุก	กรรม	พรรค
sŭn	**rót bun-tÓOk**	**gum**	**púk**
to choose	lorry	karma, fate	party (political)

23

2.6.5.5 จริง

The letter ร is ignored in the pronunciation of the word จริง (**jing** 'true').

2.6.6 **The symbols ฯ and ๆ**

The symbol ฯ indicates that a word has been abbreviated. It occurs most commonly in the Thai name for Bangkok, **grOOng-tâyp**. The symbol ๆ indicates the reduplication of the preceding word:

กรุงเทพฯ	เพื่อน ๆ	เล็ก ๆ
grOOng-tâyp	**pêu-un pêu-un**	**lék lék**
Bangkok	friends	small(ish)

2.6.7 **Consonants . . . or what?**

The letters **réu** and **reu:**, and **léu** and **leu:** are not counted among the 44 Thai consonants, but follow the letters **ror reu-a** and **lor ling** respectively in dictionary arrangements.

ฤ	ฤๅ	ฦ	ฦๅ
réu	**reu:**	**léu**	**leu:**

The first symbol occurs in only a very small number of words (but including 'English', where it has the value **ri**), while the latter three are very unlikely to be encountered.

อังกฤษ	**ung-grìt**	English
ฤดู	**réu-doo**	season

Chapter 3

Nouns, classifiers and noun phrases

Nouns can be divided into two broad categories: proper nouns and common nouns.

3.1 Proper nouns

Proper nouns refer to unique things, such as personal names, place names, and names of institutions.

3.1.1 Personal names

Names of individuals follow the same order as in English, with the personal name preceding the family name. People are addressed, referred to and known by their personal name rather than their family name; family names are used primarily for administrative purposes. Most Thais will also have a nickname, by which they will be known within the family and among friends.

The polite title **kOOn,** usually written as **Khun,** is used before the personal name, and sometimes the nickname, to address both males and females of similar or higher status. Thus, Mr Suchart Boonsoong and Mrs Yupa Saibua will be known as **Khun Suchart** and **Khun Yupa** respectively. Thais will sometimes use **Khun** followed by the surname when addressing Westerners in formal situations.

3.1.2 Place names

Individual place names, names of rivers, mountains and other geographical features, institutions, organisations, buildings and so on, follow the noun identifying the type of place; an exception is Thailand's oldest university, Chulalongkorn University, which deliberately reverses the order:

จังหวัดนครพนม
jung-wùt na-korn pa-nom
Nakhorn Phanom Province

ภาคอีสาน
pâhk ee-sǎhn
North Eastern Region

แม่น้ำเจ้าพระยา
mâir náhm jâo pra-yah
Chao Phraya River

เมืองไทย
meu-ung tai
Thailand

ถนนสุขุมวิท
ta-nǒn sǒǒ-kǒǒm-wít
Sukhumwit Road

สนามบินสุวรรณภูมิ
sa-nǎhm bin sǒǒ-wun-na-poom
Suvarnabhumi Airport

มหาวิทยาลัยธรรมศาสตร์
ma-hǎh-wít-ta-yah-lai tum-ma-sàht
Thammasat University

จุฬาลงกรณ์มหาวิทยาลัย
jǒǒ-lah-long-gorn ma-hǎh-wít-ta-yah-lai
Chulalongkorn University

3.2 Common nouns

Common nouns are traditionally divided into 'concrete nouns', which are observable, such as 'house', and 'abstract nouns', which are not, such as 'love'.

Common nouns in Thai have a single fixed form. Unlike many European languages, no suffix is added to indicate plural or to show whether the noun is the grammatical subject or object in a sentence; nor are nouns classified by gender. The word **pêu-un** thus means either 'friend' or 'friends', depending on the context. Usually the context provides sufficient information for there to be no confusion. When it is necessary to be more specific, numbers or indefinite quantifier words, such as *many*, *every*, *a few*, can be used; a very small number of nouns may be reduplicated as a means of indicating plurality:

ผมไปกับเพื่อน
pŏm bpai gùp pêu-un
I went with a friend/friends.

ผมไปกับเพื่อนสองคน
pŏm bpai gùp pêu-un sŏrng kon
I went with two friends.

ผมไปกับเพื่อนหลายคน
pŏm bpai gùp pêu-un lăi kon
I went with several friends.

ผมไปกับเพื่อน ๆ
pŏm bpai gùp pêu-un pêu-un
I went with friends.

3.3 Making new nouns

Common nouns make up the largest part of the language's vocabulary and are an ever-growing category. New nouns have, and continue to, come into the language through borrowing from other languages and from the Thai language's own means of generating new words, chiefly the process of compounding.

3.3.1 Borrowings

The Thai lexicon includes a considerable number of loan words, borrowed over the centuries from Khmer (Cambodian), the classical Indian languages, Sanskrit and Pali and, more recently, English. In some instances a word

27

of Indic (Sankrit or Pali) origin is used in preference to a 'pure' Thai word to convey a sense of politeness, refinement or formality:

Informal (Thai origin)		Formal (Indic origin)		
ผัว	**pǒo-a**	สามี	**sǎh-mee**	'husband'
เมีย	**mee-a**	ภรรยา	**pun-ra-yah**	'wife'
หัว	**hǒo-a**	ศีรษะ	**sěe-sà**	'head'
เมือง	**meu-ung**	ประเทศ	**bpra-tâyt**	'country'
หมา	**mǎh**	สุนัข	**sOO-núk**	'dog'

There has been a huge influx of English borrowings over the last 50 years, including scientific, technical and business terms and words associated with food, dress, arts, sports and other leisure activities. Thais' pronunciation of English loanwords will depend very much on their level of education and exposure to English; some English borrowings (e.g. **pút-tìk**, the 'uneducated' pronunciation of *plastic*, or **born**, the abbreviated pronunciation of *football*) may become scarcely recognisable to an English native speaker when adapted to the Thai sound system and assigned tones. Here is just a tiny sample of English words in everyday use in Thai:

กอล์ฟ	**górp**	golf
พลาสติก	**pláh-stìk, pút-tìk**	plastic
ฟีล์ม	**feem**	film
แสตมป์	**sa-dtáirm**	stamp
คอมพิวเตอร์	**korm-pew-dtêr**	computer
ฟุตบอล	**fÓOt-born, born**	football
อีเมล์	**ee-may**	email
มอเตอร์ไซค์	**mor-dter-sai**	motorcycle
คูปอง	**koo-bporng**	coupon
แฟน	**fairn**	fan; boyfriend/girlfriend; husband/wife; partner

3.3.2 | Compounds

Compounding involves joining two or more words together to make a new word. The first word or 'head noun' may be followed by either a 'noun attribute' or a 'verb attribute', which qualifies or restricts the meaning of the head noun; in some compounds, a verb attribute is followed by a grammatical object:

3.3.2.1 | HEAD NOUN + NOUN ATTRIBUTE

รถไฟ	**rót fai**	train	(vehicle + fire)
ร้านอาหาร	**ráhn ah-hăhn**	restaurant	(shop + food)
เงินเดือน	**ngern deu-un**	salary	(money + month)
ช่างไฟฟ้า	**chûng fai fáh**	electrician	(mechanic + electricity)

3.3.2.2 | HEAD NOUN + VERB (+ OBJECT) ATTRIBUTE

น้ำแข็ง	**núm kăirng**	ice	(water + to be hard)
บทเรียน	**bòt ree-un**	lesson	(text + to study)
คำแนะนำ	**kum náir-num**	introduction	(word + introduce)
คนขับรถ	**kon kùp rót**	driver	(person + to drive + car)
เครื่องซักผ้า	**krêu-ung súk pâh**	washing machine	(machine + to wash + clothes)

3.3.3 | Some common head nouns

A number of head nouns occur either normally or exclusively in compounds; some common examples include the following:

3.3.3.1 **núk** ('one skilled in ...') + VERB or NOUN

นักศึกษา	**núk sèuk-săh** student	(**sèuk-săh** to study)
นักเขียน	**núk kĕe-un** writer	(**kĕe-un** to write)
นักกีฬา	**núk gee-lah** sportsman, athlete	(**gee-lah** sport)
นักธุรกิจ	**núk tÓO-rá-gìt** businessman	(**tÓO-rá-gìt** business)
นักโทษ	**núk tôht** prisoner	(**tôht** punishment)
นักหนังสือพิมพ์	**núk núng-sĕu pim** journalist	(**núng-sĕu pim** newspaper)

3.3.3.2 **pôo** ('one who ...') + VERB (*but* note last two examples with noun)

ผู้ใหญ่	**pôo yài**	adult	(**yài** to be big)
ผู้เชี่ยวชาญ	**pôo chêe-o chahn**	expert	(**chêe-o chahn** to be skilled)
ผู้ร้าย	**pôo rái:**	criminal	(**rái:** to be bad)
ผู้ชาย	**pôo chai:**	man	(**chai:** male)
ผู้หญิง	**pôo yĭng**	woman	(**yĭng** female)

3.3.3.3 **bai** ('a sheet of paper') + VERB

ใบรับรอง	**bai rúp rorng** guarantee	(**rúp rorng** to guarantee)
ใบสัญญา	**bai sŭn-yah** contract	(**sŭn-yah** to promise)
ใบอนุญาต	**bai a-nÓO-yâht** permit	(**a-nÓO-yâht** to permit)
ใบขับขี่	**bai kùp-kèe** driving licence	(**kùp-kèe** to drive)
ใบเสร็จรับเงิน	**bai sèt rúp ngern** receipt	(**sèt rúp ngern** finish – receive – money)

3.3.3.4 rohng ('a large building') + NOUN or VERB

โรงรถ	rohng rót	garage	(rót car)
โรงงาน	rohng ngahn	factory	(ngahn work)
โรงหนัง	rohng nǔng	cinema	(nǔng film, movie)
โรงแรม	rohng rairm	hotel	(rairm to stay overnight)
โรงเรียน	rohng ree-un	school	(ree-un to study)

3.3.3.5 gahn ('matters of . . .') + NOUN; gahn ('act of . . .') + VERB

การบ้าน	gahn bâhn homework	(bâhn house, home)
การไฟฟ้า	gahn fai fáh Electricity Authority	(fai fáh electricity)
การเงิน	gahn ngern finance	(ngern money)
การเมือง	gahn meu-ung politics	(meu-ung city, country)
การรักษา	gahn rák-sǎh care, preservation	(rák-sǎh to care for)
การศึกษา	gahn sèuk-sǎh education	(sèuk-sǎh to study)
การช่วยเหลือ	gahn chôo-ay lěu-a assistance	(chôo-ay lěu-a to assist)
การเดินทาง	gahn dern tahng travel	(dern tahng to travel)

The pattern **gahn** + VERB in many instances corresponds to the English gerund, or verbal noun, and it occurs commonly in written Thai:

การกิน	gahn gin	eating	(gin to eat)
การรบ	gahn róp	fighting	(róp to fight)
การเรียน	gahn ree-un	studying	(ree-un to study)
การพูด	gahn pôot	speaking	(pôot to speak)

In normal spoken Thai, however, the English gerund construction is more naturally conveyed simply by the verb without **gahn**:

กินตามร้านอาหารแพง
gin dtahm ráhn ah-hăhn pairng
Eating in restaurants is expensive.

เรียนหนังสือไม่สนุก
ree-un núng-sěu mâi sa-nÒOk
Studying is not fun.

พูดภาษาไทยยาก
pôot pah-săh tai yâhk
Speaking Thai is difficult.

3.3.3.6 **kwahm** (used to form abstract nouns) + VERB

ความรัก	**kwahm rúk**	love	(**rúk** to love)
ความรู้	**kwahm róo**	knowledge	(**róo** to know)
ความคิด	**kwahm kít**	idea	(**kít** to think)
ความสำเร็จ	**kwahm sŭm-rèt**	success	(**sŭm-rèt** to complete)
ความสุข	**kwahm sÒOk**	happiness	(**sÒOk** to be happy)

3.3.3.7 **têe** ('person whom one ..., place where ..., thing which ...')
+ VERB

ที่ปรึกษา	**têe bprèuk-săh** adviser	(**bprèuk-săh** to consult)
ที่พึ่ง	**têe pêung** benefactor	(**pêung** to depend, rely on)
ที่รัก	**têe rúk** darling	(**rúk** to love)
ที่อยู่	**têe yòo** address	(**yòo** to live)

ที่ทำงาน	**têe tum ngahn** place of work	(**tum ngahn** to work)
ที่นั่ง	**têe nûng** seat	(**nûng** to sit)
ที่ระลึก	**têe ra-léuk** souvenir	(**ra-léuk** to think of)
ที่จอดรถ	**têe jòrt rót** car park	(**jòrt rót** to park – car)
ที่เจาะกระดาษ	**têe jò' gra-dàht** paper punch	(**jò' gra-dàht** to punch holes – paper)
ที่เปิดขวด	**têe bpèrt kòo-ut´** bottle opener	(**bpèrt kòo-ut** to open – bottle)

3.3.4 | Co-ordinate compounds

Two or more nouns can occur together to make a new noun in a 'co-ordinate compound' where the second noun does not modify the first:

พ่อแม่	**pôr mâir**	parents (father – mother)
พี่น้อง	**pêe nórng**	brothers and sisters (older sibling – younger sibling)
เสื้อผ้า	**sêu-a pâh**	clothes (upper garment – lower garment)

Often such compounds involve a four-syllable pattern, which may involve one or more of the following features: duplication of the first and third elements, internal rhyme, alliteration or the insertion of a meaningless syllable to preserve the rhythm.

ปู่ย่าตายาย	**bpòo yâh dtah yai:** grandparents (paternal grandfather – paternal grandmother – maternal grandfather – maternal grandmother)
ชาวไร่ชาวนา	**chao: râi chao: nah** farmers (people – dry rice field – people – wet rice field)
ชาวเขาชาวดอย	**chao: kăo chao: doy** mountain people (people – hill – people – mountain)
น้ำพักน้ำแรง	**núm púk núm rairng** one's own effort/labour (water – rest – water – energy)

33

ครูบาอาจารย์   **kroo bah ah-jahn**   teachers
(teacher – rhyming nonsense syllable – teacher)

วัดวาอาราม   **wút wah ah-rahm**   wats/temples
(temple – alliterative/rhyming nonsense syllable –
temple buildings)

3.4   Noun phrases and classifiers

When a noun is accompanied by one or more modifying words, such as
'*three* cars', '*that* car' or '*the red* car' it is called a noun phrase. Noun phrases
in Thai frequently involve the use of a class of words called *classifiers*.

Classifiers are an obligatory component of noun phrases containing numerals.
In both English and Thai, uncountable nouns, such as rice, beer and silk
may be counted by the kilo, the bottle or the metre; in Thai these measure
words are regarded as classifiers. Thai differs from English in that it uses
classifiers for countable nouns such as 'friends', 'dogs' and 'books', where
English simply places the number before the noun. (A rare exception in
English is 'cattle', which are counted by the 'head'; 'head' functions like
a Thai classifier.) Every noun in Thai is counted by a specific classifier;
thus **kon** is used for counting people, **dtoo-a** for animals and **lêm** for books:

เพื่อนสองคน
pêu-un sŏrng kon
two friends (friends – two – classifier)

หมาห้าตัว
măh hâh dtoo-a
five dogs (dogs – five – classifier)

หนังสือสิบเล่ม
núng-sĕu sìp lêm
ten books (books – ten – classifier)

Some common classifiers and the nouns they are used with are:

บาน	**bahn**	doors, windows, mirrors
ใบ	**bai**	fruit, eggs, leaves, cups, bowls, slips of paper documents, hats, pillows
ฉบับ	**cha-bùp**	letters, newspapers, documents

ชนิด	**cha-nít**	types, kinds, sorts (of things)
ชิ้น	**chín**	pieces (of cake, meat, cloth, work)
ชุด	**chÓÓt**	sets of things
เชือก	**chêu-uk**	elephants
ดวง	**doo-ung**	stamps, stars
ดอก	**dòrk**	flowers; keys
ต้น	**dtôn**	trees, plants
ตัว	**dtoo-a**	animals, chairs, tables, items of clothing including trousers, guitars
ฟอง	**forng**	eggs
แห่ง	**hàirng**	places
ห่อ	**hòr**	packages, bundles
ห้อง	**hôrng**	rooms
ขบวน	**ka-boo-un**	trains, processions
คน	**kon**	people (except monks and royalty)
คู่	**kôo**	pairs (e.g. shoes, socks, married couples but not trousers)
ข้อ	**kôr**	items, clauses, points (e.g. in a contract or formal statement)
เครื่อง	**krêu-ung**	radios, tvs, computers, mechanical and technical devices
คัน	**kun**	forks, spoons, umbrellas, objects with long handles; vehicles
เล่ม	**lêm**	books, knives
ลูก	**lôok**	fruit, balls, locks and padlocks
หลอด	**lòrt**	light bulbs, tubes (e.g. toothpaste)
ลำ	**lum**	boats, aeroplanes

หลัง	**lŭng**	houses
เม็ด	**mét**	seeds, pills, buttons
มวน	**moo-un**	cigarettes, cigars
ม้วน	**móo-un**	rolls of toilet paper
องค์	**ong**	members of royalty, Buddha images
แผ่น	**pàirn**	flat objects, sheets of paper
เรื่อง	**rêu-ung**	stories, issues
รูป	**rôop**	pictures, monks
สาย	**săi:**	bus routes, railway lines, roads
ซี่	**sêe**	teeth
เส้น	**sên**	long, thin items; strands of hair, necklaces, noodles
อัน	**un**	small objects
อย่าง	**yàhng**	types, kinds, sorts (of things)

In addition, measure words such as 'kilo', 'inch' and 'month', and containers, such as 'bottle', 'bowl' and 'bag', also function as classifiers.

Classifiers occur not only with cardinal numbers, but also with other quantifiers (ordinal numbers, indefinite quantifiers and 'how many?'), demonstratives ('this', 'that', 'these', 'those' and 'which?') and adjectives.

3.5 Word order in noun phrases

The following list is not exhaustive but covers the most common patterns of noun phrase:

3.5.1 NOUN + CARDINAL NUMBER + CLASSIFIER

ลูกสามคน
lôok săhm kon
three children

บ้านสี่หลัง

bâhn sèe lǔng

four houses

หนังสือหกเล่ม

núng-sěu hòk lêm

six books

The word **nèung** ('one', 'a') can occur either before the classifier or after it. When it occurs before the classifier it functions as the numeral 'one', and when it occurs after the classifier it can be treated as the indefinite article 'a', describing the noun:

ลูกหนึ่งคน

lôok nèung kon

one child

ลูกคนหนึ่ง

lôok kon nèung

a child

3.5.2 **NOUN + QUANTIFIER + CLASSIFIER**

For quantifiers, see 13.12; note that some quantifiers do not occur with classifiers.

ฝรั่งบางคน

fa-rùng bahng kon

some 'farangs' (Westerners)

ปลาทุกชนิด

bplah tÓOk cha-nít

every kind of fish

จดหมายไม่กี่ฉบับ

jòt-mǎi: mâi gèe cha-bùp

not many letters

3.5.3 | NOUN + CLASSIFIER + ORDINAL NUMBER

For ordinal numbers, see 13.3.

ลูกคนที่สาม
lôok kon têe săhm
the third child

บ้านหลังที่สอง
bâhn lǔng têe sŏrng
the second house

หนังสือเล่มแรก
núng-sĕu lêm râirk
the first book

3.5.4 | NOUN + CLASSIFIER + DEMONSTRATIVE

Demonstratives are words like **née** ('this/these'), **nún** ('that/those'), **nóhn** ('that/those over there') and the question word **năi?** ('which?').

หนังสือเล่มนี้
núng-sĕu lêm née
this book

เสื้อตัวนั้น
sêu-a dtoo-a nún
that shirt

บ้านหลังโน้น
bâhn lǔng nóhn
that house over there

ลูกคนไหน
lôok kon năi?
which child?

The noun is often dropped in spoken Thai when the context is unambiguous, as in the response below:

เอาเสื้อตัวไหน

ao sêu-a dtoo-a nǎi?

Which shirt do you want?

– ตัวนั้น

– dtoo-a nún

– That one.

The classifier, too, is also often dropped in spoken Thai:

เสื้อนั้นไม่สวย

sêu-a nún mâi sǒo-ay

That top isn't pretty.

3.5.5 | **NOUN + CARDINAL NUMBER + CLASSIFIER + DEMONSTRATIVE**

ลูกสามคนนี้

lôok sǎhm kon née

these three children

เสื้อสองตัวนั้น

sêu-a sǒrng dtoo-a nún

those two shirts

3.5.6 | **NOUN + ADJECTIVE**

อาหารเผ็ด

ah-hǎhn pèt

spicy food

หนังสือเก่า

núng-sěu gào

an old book

บ้านใหญ่

bâhn yài

a big house

39

3.5.7 | NOUN + ADJECTIVE + CLASSIFIER + DEMONSTRATIVE

หนังสือเก่าเล่มนั้น
núng-sěu gào lêm nún
that old book

บ้านใหญ่หลังนั้น
bâhn yài lǔng nún
that big house

3.5.8 | NOUN + ADJECTIVE + CARDINAL NUMBER + CLASSIFIER (+ DEMONSTRATIVE)

หนังสือเก่าสองเล่ม(นี้)
núng-sěu gào sǒrng lêm (née)
(these) two old books

บ้านใหญ่ห้าหลัง(นั้น)
bâhn yài hâh lǔng (nún)
(those) five big houses

3.5.9 | NOUN + ADJECTIVE + CLASSIFIER + ORDINAL NUMBER

หนังไทยเรื่องที่สอง
nǔng tai rêu-ung têe sǒrng
the second Thai movie

บ้านใหญ่หลังที่สาม
bâhn yài lǔng têe sǎhm
the third big house

3.5.10 | NOUN + CLASSIFIER + ADJECTIVE

This pattern is used to distinguish the noun referred to from other members of the same class:

เสื้อตัวใหม่
sêu-a dtoo-a mài
the new shirt

หนังสือเล่มเก่า
núng-sěu lêm gào
the old book

3.5.11 NOUN + NOUN

Some nouns can be used adjectivally to modify the preceding noun:

ตำรวจผู้สอบสวน
dtum-ròo-ut pôo sòrp sǒo-un
the investigating police officer (policeman – one who – investigate)

ข้าราชการชั้นผู้ใหญ่
kâh-râht-cha-gahn chún pôo yài
a high-ranking civil servant (civil servant – rank – senior person)

3.5.12 NOUN + (kǒrng) + POSSESSOR

In possessive phrases, **kǒrng** ('of') is optional and very frequently omitted:

บ้าน(ของ)ฉัน
bâhn (kǒrng) chún
my house

ลูก(ของ)เขา
lôok (kǒrng) káo
his child

Chapter 4

Pronouns

4.1   Personal pronouns: basics

Thai has many more personal pronouns than English; age, social status, gender, the relationship between the speakers, the formality of the situation and individual personality all play a part in helping a Thai to decide the most appropriate way to refer to him/herself and address and refer to others in any one situation.

Kin terms (aunt, older brother), status/occupation terms (teacher, doctor) and personal names or nicknames are also commonly used as personal pronouns.

As a starting point for learners, the personal pronoun system can be simplified to the following:

ผม	**pŏm**	I/me (male)
ฉัน	**chún**	I/me (female; informal)
ดิฉัน	**di-chún**	I/me (female; formal)
เรา	**rao**	we/us
คุณ	**kOOn**	you (sing. and plur.)
ท่าน	**tûn**	you (sing. and plur.); he/him, she/her, they/them. To address or refer to people of significantly higher social status
เขา	**káo**	he/him; she/her; they/them
เธอ	**ter**	she/her; they/them (female)
มัน	**mun**	it

Note that male and female speakers use a different word for 'I/me', while a single third person pronoun in Thai covers 'he/him', 'she/her', 'they/them'. Usage of these and other pronouns are discussed in more detail in the next section.

Pronouns have a single form for subject and object:

ผมชอบเขา
pǒm chôrp káo
I like him.

เขาชอบผม
káo chôrp pǒm
He likes me.

The plural reference of a pronoun can be clarified or made explicit by (a) a number or other quantifier expression or (b) the pluraliser word **pôo-uk** ('group'):

เราสามคน
raw sǎhm kon
the three of us

คุณทั้งสอง(คน)
kOOn túng sǒrng (kon)
the two/both of you

เขาทั้งหลาย
káo túng lǎi
all of them

พวกเรา
pôo-uk rao
we, us, 'us lot'

Pronouns are frequently omitted when it is clear from the context who is speaking, being addressed or being referred to:

ไปพรุ่งนี้
bpai prÔOng née
I'm/we're/he's/she's/they're going tomorrow. (lit. go tomorrow)

ชอบไหม
chôrp mái?
Do you/do they/does he/does she like it? (lit. like + question word)

In these and many of the other examples in this book, an arbitrary choice of pronoun is supplied in the English translation. Since pronouns reflect relative status and intimacy, a speaker can, by omission, avoid the possibility of using an inappropriate pronoun. But the omission of pronouns is not simply a strategy for the cautious to avoid linguistic faux-pas; it is also a means of denying or avoiding the behavioural or attitudinal expectations of intimacy or deference implicit in the use of any pronoun.

4.1.1 | More personal pronouns

Thais will use a much wider range of pronouns than those given in the previous section. Some of these are given below with an indication of whether they are specifically male (M) or female (F) pronouns and the context in which they are used; certain first person pronouns are normally 'paired' with a specific second person pronoun. Note that some pronouns (e.g. **tûn** and **ter**) function as both second and third person pronouns.

ผม	**pŏm**	M	1st person; general pronoun that can be used in most situations, ranging from polite to intimate; not used with young children.
กระผม	**gra-pŏm**	M	1st person; highly deferential.
ดิฉัน	**di-chún**	F	1st person; very formal, often avoided because it creates distance between speaker and addressee.
ฉัน	**chún**	M/F	1st person; commonly used by female speakers as a less formal, more friendly variant of **di-chún**; also used by males as an expression of intimacy, when it is paired with **ter** (เธอ), and when speaking to children.
ข้าพเจ้า	**kâh-pa-jâo**	M/F	1st person pronoun used formally in public statements, and official documents.
เรา	**rao**	M/F	1st person plural; also used as 1st person singular pronoun in informal speech by both males and females.

หนู	nŏo	M/F	1st/2nd person pronoun used by children talking to adults; literally means 'rat'; used by girls and young women to superiors, for example female students to teachers, secretaries to bosses, etc.
กู	goo	M/F	1st person pronoun used mainly by males as a male-bonding pronoun in informal situations, such as drinking, and brothel visits; also used to show anger; paired with **meung** (มึง) 'you'.
อั๊ว	óo-a	M	1st person pronoun, from Teochiu dialect of Chinese; used mainly by males with close friends as an informal pronoun; paired with **léu:** (ลื้อ) 'you'.
ข้า	kâh	M	1st person pronoun; from English 'I'; used mainly by males with close friends as an informal pronoun; paired with **eng** (เอ็ง) 'you'.
ไอ	ay	M/F	1st person pronoun; from English 'I'; informal, paired with **yuu** (ยู) 'you'.
กัน	gun	M	1st person pronoun; used among close male friends; paired with **gair** (แก) 'you'.
คุณ	kOOn	M/F	2nd person, sing. and plur.; polite, formal use among equals; also used as a polite title before names, kin terms and certain occupations.
ท่าน	tûn	M/F	2nd/3rd person, sing. and plur.; to address or refer to people of significantly higher social status; also used as a deferential title with certain high status positions (see 4.1.4).
เธอ	ter	M/F	2nd/3rd person, sing. and plur.; as a 2nd person pronoun it is paired with **chún** (ฉัน) 'I' and signals a relationship of closeness; as a 3rd person pronoun it usually refers to a female.

45

เขา	**káo**	M/F	3rd person, sing. and plur.; also a 1st person pronoun, used among girls and between husband and wife, when it is paired with **dtoo-a** (ตัว) 'you'.
แก	**gair**	M/F	3rd person, sing. and plur.; also as a 2nd person intimate pronoun among members of the same sex, when it is paired with **chún** (ฉัน) (F) or **gun** (กัน) (M), 'I'.
มัน	**mun**	–	'it'; regarded as unrefined and often avoided in polite, formal speech and writing; used widely in informal situations – including to refer to people, either derogatively or familiarly.

4.1.2 | Kin terms as personal pronouns

Kin terms are commonly used as pronouns. A father, for example, will refer to himself as **pôr** ('father') rather than **pŏm** ('I') when talking to his son and address his son as **lôok** ('child') rather than **kOOn** ('you'):

พ่อไม่ชอบ
pôr mâi chôrp
I (father speaking) don't like it.

ลูกไปไหน
lôok bpai năi?
Where are you (parent addressing child) going?

Kin terms can be used as first, second or third person pronouns; thus depending on the context, the sentence **pôr mao láir-o** could mean (a) I (father speaking) am drunk, (b) You (addressing father) are drunk, or (c) He (referring to father) is drunk.

The use of kin terms extends to include those who are not blood relations; by addressing an elderly man as **lOOng** ('uncle') or a friend or colleague as **pêe** ('older brother/sister') the speaker immediately creates an atmosphere of congeniality. **pêe** has a particularly wide range of use, which includes wives addressing their husbands, service-industry workers addressing customers and complete strangers striking up a conversation with someone older.

Kin terms are often followed by personal names or nicknames (see 4.1.3).
They can also be preceded by the polite title **kOOn** as a sign of further
respect; thus children may address and refer to their parents as **kOOn pôr**
and **kOOn mâir** (or collectively, as **kOOn pôr kOOn mâir**) and address
a younger friend of their father as **kOOn ah** ('uncle/aunt').

The kin terms most commonly used as personal pronouns are:

พ่อ	**pôr**	father
แม่	**mâir**	mother
พี่	**pêe**	older brother/sister
น้อง	**nórng**	younger brother/sister
ลูก	**lôok**	child
หลาน	**lăhn**	grandchild; niece/nephew
ป้า	**bpâh**	aunt (older sister of parents)
ลุง	**lOOng**	uncle (older brother of parents)
น้า	**náh**	aunt/uncle (younger brother/sister of mother)
อา	**ah**	aunt/uncle (younger brother/sister of father)
ปู่	**bpòo**	grandfather (father's father)
ย่า	**yâh**	grandmother (father's mother)
ตา	**dtah**	grandfather (mother's father)
ยาย	**yai:**	grandmother (mother's mother)

4.1.3 | Personal names as personal pronouns

Personal names or nicknames are also commonly used as personal
pronouns. Using one's name or more commonly, nickname, instead of
the 'I' word is characteristic of female speech but much less common
among men. When used as second or third person pronouns names
and nicknames can be preceded by **kOOn** or a kin term, such as **pêe** as
a sign of deference:

ต้อยไม่ทราบค่ะ

dtôy mâi sâhp kâ

I (Toi speaking) don't know.

คุณสุวรรณีว่างไหม

kOOn sÒO-wun-nee wâhng mái?

Are you (addressing Suwannee) free?

คุณอ้วนกลับบ้านแล้ว

kOOn ôo-un glùp bâhn láir-o

Khun Uan has gone home.

พี่สุจะไปด้วยไหม

pêe sÒO ja bpai dôo-ay mái?

Is (older sister) Su going too?

| **4.1.4** | *Occupation and status terms as personal pronouns* |

A number of occupation terms are commonly used instead of pronouns. In the medical and education worlds the following occupation terms are used not only as second or third person pronouns, when addressing or referring to individuals, but also as first person pronouns to mean 'I':

อาจารย์	**ah-jahn**	teacher, university lecturer
ครู	**kroo**	teacher
หมอ	**mǒr**	doctor
พยาบาล	**pa-yah-bahn**	nurse

Note that when addressing teachers, doctors, or nurses the polite title kOOn commonly precedes the occupation term (e.g. **kOOn kroo, kOOn mǒr**); but kOOn does not occur with **ah-jahn**.

เมื่อเช้าวันนี้ คุณพ่อเธอโทรศัพท์มาถึงครู

**mêu-a cháo: wun née kOOn pôr ter toh-ra-sùp mah
tĕung kroo**

Earlier this morning your father telephoned me. (teacher speaking)

ขอหมอดูหน่อย . . . หมอว่าไม่เป็นอะไรมาก
kǒr mǒr doo nòy . . . mǒr wâh mâi bpen a-rai mâhk
Let me have a look . . . I don't think it's anything very much/serious.
(doctor speaking)

คุณหมออยู่ไหมคะ
kOOn mǒr yòo mái ká?
Is the doctor in?

Taxi drivers, however, do not refer to themselves as **táirk-sêe**; the following occupation terms are used only as second and third person pronouns:

กระเป๋า	**gra-bpǎo**	bus conductor
สามล้อ	**sǎhm-lór**	pedicab driver
แท็กซี่	**táirk-sêe**	taxi driver
ตุ๊กตุ๊ก	**dtÓOk dtÓOk**	motorised pedicab driver

The occupants of certain high-ranking positions, such as ambassadors, director generals, rectors, ministers and prime ministers are often addressed and referred to using the deferential title **tûn** before their position, or an abbreviated form of it:

ท่านทูต	**tûn tôot**	Ambassador
ท่านอธิบดี	**tûn à-tí-bor-dee**	Director General
ท่านอธิการฯ	**tûn à-tí-gahn**	(University) Rector
ท่านรัฐมนตรี	**tûn rút-ta-mon-dtree**	Minister
ท่านนายกฯ	**tûn nah-yók**	Prime Minister

4.1.5 | *Monks and monarchs: sacred pronouns*

When speaking to monks or royalty, further complicated sets of pronouns are used, which vary according the ecclesiastical or royal rank of the individual. The learner needs to be aware that an ordinary monk will address a non-monk as **yohm** and will refer to himself as **àht-dta-mah**. The

49

non-monk should use the polite formal first person pronouns **pŏm** (males) or **di-chún** (females) and address or refer to the monk as **lŏo-ung pôr** or **lŏo-ung dtah** (for older monks), **lŏo-ung pêe** or **lŏo-ung náh** (for younger monks), or simply by the deferential second person pronoun, **tûn**.

อาตมา	àht-dta-mah	I (monk speaking)
โยม	yohm	you (monk speaking)
หลวงพ่อ/ หลวงตา	lŏo-ung pôr/ lŏo-ung dtah	you/he (layman addressing/ referring to a monk)
หลวงพี่/ หลวงน้า	lŏo-ung pêe/ lŏo-ung náh	you/he (layman addressing/ referring to a monk)

Using the complex system of royal pronouns correctly is a daunting prospect even for the vast majority of educated Thais. At the simplest level, one should refer to oneself as **kâh pra-pÓOt-ta-jâo** ('Your Majesty's servant') when addressing the King or other high-ranking members of royalty, and use **dtâi fáh la-orng tÓO-lee pra-bàht** as a second person pronoun to the King and **dtâi fáh la-orng pra-bàht** to other high-ranking members of royalty; both terms can be translated as 'dust under sole of royal foot'. Members of royalty, unlike monks, do not use special pronouns when talking to ordinary people.

ข้าพระพุทธเจ้า
kâh pra-pÓOt-ta-jâo
I (to King)

ใต้ฝ่าละอองธุลีพระบาท
dtâi fàh la-orng tÓO-lee pra-bàht
you (to King)

ใต้ฝ่าละอองพระบาท
dtâi fàh la-orng pra-bàht
you (to high-ranking royalty)

4.2 Reflexive pronouns

The reflexive pronoun, **dtoo-a** ('body') is used with first, second and third persons. It occurs in such verbs as:

เจียมตัว	jee-um dtoo-a	to be self-effacing
ขายตัว	kăi: dtoo-a	to sell oneself
ขยายตัว	ka-yăi: dtoo-a	to expand
ขอตัว	kŏr dtoo-a	to excuse oneself
เล่นตัว	lên dtoo-a	to play hard to get
ลืมตัว	leu:m dtoo-a	to forget oneself
ปรับตัว	bprùp dtoo-a	to adapt oneself
รู้ตัว	róo dtoo-a	to be aware
เสนอตัว	sa-něr dtoo-a	to put oneself forward
เสียตัว	sěe-a dtoo-a	to lose one's virginity
เสียสละตัว	sěe-a sa-là dtoo-a	to sacrifice oneself
ซ่อนตัว	sôrn dtoo-a	to hide oneself
แต่งตัว	dtàirng dtoo-a	to get dressed
เตรียมตัว	dtree-um dtoo-a	to prepare oneself
ถ่อมตัว	tòrm dtoo-a	to be self-effacing
ถือตัว	těu dtoo-a	to be aloof

The verb 'to kill oneself/commit suicide' is irregular, translating literally as 'kill-body/self-dead':

ฆ่าตัวตาย	kâh dtoo-a dtai:	to commit suicide

For a smaller category of verbs, the reflexive pronoun must be followed by the emphatic pronoun **ayng** (self):

ช่วยตัวเอง	chôo-ay dtoo-a ayng	to help oneself
ดูแลตัวเอง	doo lair dtoo-a ayng	to look after oneself
มั่นใจตัวเอง	mûn jai dtoo-a ayng	to be self-confident
มองตัวเอง	morng dtoo-a ayng	to look at oneself

ภูมิใจตัวเอง	**poom jai dtoo-a ayng**	to be proud of oneself
พึ่งตัวเอง	**pêung dtoo-a ayng**	to rely on oneself
ถามตัวเอง	**tăhm dtoo-a ayng**	to ask oneself
วาดรูปตัวเอง	**wâht rôop dtoo-a ayng**	to draw a picture of oneself

The idea of doing something 'by oneself' uses either **dôo-ay** ('by') **dtoo-a ayng** or **dôo-ay dton ayng**; the latter is less common in speech and carries a slightly formal or literary flavour:

ผมซ่อมรถด้วยตัวเอง
pǒm sôrm rót dôo-ay dtoo-a ayng
I mended the car by myself.

เราทำด้วยตัวเอง
rao tum dôo-ay dtoo-a ayng
We did it by ourselves.

เขาเรียนด้วยตนเอง
káo ree-un dôo-ay dton ayng
He studied by himself.

4.3 Emphatic pronoun

The emphatic pronoun **ayng** ('self') is used with first, second and third persons; it occurs in the following patterns, each conveying a slightly different shade of emphasis:

4.3.1 | PERSONAL PRONOUN + ayng + VERB

ผมเองทำ
pǒm ayng tum
I myself did it.

4.3.2 | *PERSONAL PRONOUN* + *VERB* + ayng

ผมทำเอง
pŏm tum ayng
I did it myself.

4.3.3 | *PERSONAL PRONOUN* + ayng + bpen kon + *VERB*

ผมเองเป็นคนทำ
pŏm ayng bpen kon tum
I myself was the one who did it.

4.3.4 | dtoo-a + *PERSONAL PRONOUN* + ayng + *VERB*

ตัวผมเองทำ
dtoo-a pŏm ayng tum
I myself did it.

ayng also occurs after demonstratives to convey the sense of 'the very same (one)', 'precisely':

วันนี้เอง
wun née ayng
this very day

เดี๋ยวนี้เอง
dĕe-o née ayng
this very moment, right now

รถคันนั้นเอง
rót kun nún ayng
that very car

สามร้อยบาทเท่านั้นเอง
săhm róy bàht tâo-nún ayng
precisely three hundred baht

4.4 Reciprocal: 'each other'

The reciprocal pronoun *each other/one another* is expressed by the pattern,
SUBJECT + VERB + **gun** (together):

เขารักกัน
káo rúk gun
They love each other.

เราต้องช่วยกัน
rao dtôrng chôo-ay gun
We must help one another.

4.5 Possessive pronouns

The possessive pronouns 'mine', 'yours', 'his', etc. are formed using **kǒrng**
('of') + PERSONAL PRONOUN:

ของฉัน
kǒrng chún
Mine.

ของคุณสวย
kǒrng kOOn sǒo-ay
Yours is pretty.

รถนั้นของเขา
rót nún kǒrng káo
That car is his.

4.6 Demonstrative pronouns

There are three demonstrative pronouns, **nêe** ('this one'), **nûn** ('that one')
and **nôhn** – sometimes pronounced **nôon** – ('that one over there'):

นี่ไม่สวย
nêe mâi sǒo-ay
This one isn't pretty.

โน่นของใคร

nôhn kŏrng krai?

Whose is that one over there?

Demonstrative pronouns also occur in these common idiomatic expressions:

นี่ยังไง

nêe yung-ngai

Here you are (when giving someone something).

นั่นนะสิ

nûn ná sì

Exactly! That's right!

แต่นั่นแหละ

dtàir nûn làir

even so; nevertheless

4.7 Interrogative pronouns

For the use of interrogative pronouns (listed below) in questions, see 12.2:

ใคร	**krai**	who?
อะไร	**a-rai**	what?
เมื่อไร	**mêu-rài**	when?
ที่ไหน	**têe-năi**	where?
ไหน	**năi**	which?
อย่างไร	**yung-ngai**	how?

4.8 Indefinite pronouns

Interrogative pronouns also act as the indefinite pronouns, 'somebody', 'something', 'somewhere', etc.:

'Somebody', 'anybody', 'nobody'

krai as an indefinite pronoun means 'somebody', 'anybody', 'whoever';
mâi mee krai ('there is not anyone') means 'nobody':

ผมคุยกับใครคนหนึ่ง
pŏm koo-ee gùp krai kon nèung
I chatted to somebody.

ฉันไม่ได้พบใคร
chún mâi dâi póp krai
I didn't meet anybody.

มีใครจะกินไหม
mee krai ja gin mái?
Is anybody going to eat?

ใครเสร็จไปได้
krai sèt bpai dâi:
Whoever is finished can go.

ไม่มีใครรู้
mâi mee krai róo
Nobody knows.

'Something', 'anything', 'nothing'

a-rai as an indefinite pronoun means 'something', 'anything', 'whatever';
mâi mee a-rai ('there is not anything') means 'nothing':

เขาอยากซื้ออะไรบางอย่าง
káo yàhk séu a-rai bahng yàhng
She wants to buy something.

คุณอยากกินอะไรไหม
kOOn yàhk gin a-rai mái?
Do you want to eat anything?

ผมไม่ได้พูดอะไร

pǒm mâi dâi pôot a-rai

I didn't say anything.

ไม่มีอะไรน่าสนใจ

mâi mee a-rai nâh sǒn jai

There is nothing interesting.

4.8.3 'Whenever'

mêu-rài as an indefinite pronoun means 'whenever'; it can occur either before or after the verb in the first clause:

กินเมื่อไรก็ท้องเสีย

gin mêu-rài gôr tórng sěe-a

Whenever I eat it, I get diarrhoea.

เมื่อไรว่างก็โทรมาหา

mêu-rài wâhng gôr toh mah hǎh

Whenever you are free, phone me.

4.8.4 'Somewhere', 'anywhere'

têe nǎi as an indefinite pronoun means 'somewhere', 'anywhere', 'wherever'; note that when it immediately follows the verb **bpai** ('to go') the word **têe** is frequently dropped:

ฉันอยากไปอยู่ที่ไหนที่เงียบ ๆ

chún yàhk bpai yòo têe nǎi têe ngêe-up ngêe-up

I want to go and live somewhere quietish.

วางไว้ที่ไหนที่สะดวก

wahng wái têe nǎi têe sa-dòo-uk

Put it down somewhere convenient.

อยากไปไหนไหม

yàhk bpai nǎi mái?

Do you want to go anywhere?

ไม่อยากไปไหน

mâi yàhk bpai nǎi

I don't want to go anywhere.

| **4.8.5** | **'Whichever'** |

nǎi as an indefinite pronoun means 'whichever one'; it always follows a classifier and normally occurs with **gôr dâi:** (see 4.8.7).

ผมจะซื้ออันไหนก็ได้ที่ไม่แพง

pǒm ja séu un nǎi gôr dâi: têe mâi pairng

I'll buy whichever one is not expensive.

| **4.8.6** | **'However'** |

yung-ngai as an indefinite pronoun means 'however', 'whatever way'; it always follows a verb:

ทำอย่างไรก็พลาดทุกที

tum yung-ngai gôr plâht tÓOk tee

However I do it, I always get it wrong.

| **4.8.7** | **Indefinite pronouns with gôr dâi:** |

Indefinite pronouns occur before **gôr dâi:** to show amenability or indifference, as in expressions such as 'whoever/whenever/whatever you like'. Note that the vowel in **dâi:** is pronounced as a long vowel, although written in Thai script with a short vowel symbol:

สั่งอะไรก็ได้

sùng a-rai gôr dâi:

Order whatever you like.

บอกใครก็ได้

bòrk krai gôr dâi:

Tell whoever you like.

เราพบกันเมื่อไรก็ได้
rao póp gun mêu-rài gôr dâi:
We'll meet whenever you like.

เราไปไหนก็ได้
rao bpai năi gôr dâi:
We can go anywhere you like.

ซื้ออันไหนก็ได้
séu: un năi gôr dâi:
Buy whichever one you like.

กินอย่างไรก็ได้
gin yung-ngai gôr dâi:
You can eat it however you like.

ให้เท่าไหร่ก็ได้
hâi tâo-rài gôr dâi:
You can give however much you like.

4.9 Relative pronouns

A single relative pronoun **têe** is used to refer to people, places and things:

เขาเป็นคนที่ไว้ใจไม่ได้
káo bpen kon têe wái jai mâi dâi:
He is a person who you can't trust.

บ้านที่เขาอยู่เล็ก
bâhn têe káo yòo lék
The house where they live is small.

กล้วยที่เขาซื้อแพง
glôo-ay têe káo séu pairng
The bananas which she bought are expensive.

sêung can be used interchangeably with **têe** but it is a rather formal-sounding word and much less common in spoken Thai:

ช้างซึ่งมีสองประเภท . . .

cháng sêung mee sǒrng bpra-pâyt . . .

Elephants, of which there are two kinds, . . .

ไม่เหมือนภาษาของท่าน ซึ่งท่านใช้มาตั้งแต่เกิด

mâi měu-un pah-sǎh kǒrng tûn sêung tûn chái mah dtûng-dtàir gèrt

It's not like your language, which you have been using since birth.

un also functions rather like a relative pronoun, in a formal, stylised linking of noun and adjective (or stative verb); it cannot link a noun and an action verb:

โชคดีที่ได้มีงานทำอันมั่นคง

káo chôhk dee têe dâi mee ngahn tum un mûn kong

He was lucky to have a secure job.

วันรุ่งขึ้นจะเป็นวันที่ ๑ อันเป็นกำหนด

wun rÔOng kêun ja bpen wun têe nèung un bpen gum-nòt

The next day was the first scheduled day.

ผู้ดีเมื่อยืน นั่ง ต้องรู้จักตำแหน่งอันสมควร

**pôo dee mêu-a yeu:n nûng dtôrng róo-jùk dtum-nàirng un
    sǒm-koo-un**

People of good breeding must know the appropriate place to stand or sit.

ขอขอบพระคุณอาจารย์เป็นอย่างยิ่งที่สละเวลาอันมีค่า
    ของอาจารย์ในวันนี้

**kǒr kòrp-pra-kOOn ah-jahn bpen yàhng yîng têe sa-là way-lay
    un mee kâh kǒrng ah-jahn nai wun née**

I would like to express my deep gratitude to you for giving up your
    precious time today.

Chapter 5
Verbs

Thai is a verb-oriented language, often using verbs where English uses nouns (3.3.3.5) or prepositions. Verbs have a single form: they are not inflected for number or tense. Thus **bpai** can mean 'go', 'went', 'will go', etc.; ambiguity can be avoided by the addition of time expressions, such as 'yesterday', 'next week', etc., or auxiliary verbs and particles (5.3), but often the context alone is sufficient to clarify the situation. A common feature of Thai is verb serialisation (5.13).

5.1 The verb 'to be'

Thai uses several different verbs to translate English 'is/are', 'was/were', etc; the most important are **bpen, keu:, mee** and **yòo**.

5.1.1 bpen

When **bpen,** means 'to be' it is always followed by a noun or noun phrase; only rarely is it followed by an adjective (see 5.2). Note the use of **bpen kon** + ADJECTIVE to describe a person's character:

เขาเป็นเพื่อน
káo bpen pêu-un
He is a friend.

พี่สาวเป็นครู
pêe săo: bpen kroo
Her sister is a teacher.

น้องชายเป็นคนขี้เกียจ

nórng chai: bpen kon kêe gèe-ut

My younger brother is lazy.

แม่เป็นคนใจดี

mâir bpen kon jai dee

My mother is kind.

When **bpen** means 'to be', unlike other verbs, it cannot be negated by placing the negative word **mâi** immediately before it. Instead, the negative form 'is not' is either **mâi châi** or **mâi dâi bpen**; of these, the former is neutral in tone, while the latter conveys the sense of contradicting a spoken or unspoken assumption:

เขาไม่ใช่คนอเมริกัน

káo mâi châi kon a-may-ri-gun

He isn't American.

ไม่ใช่ผม

mâi châi pŏm

It wasn't me.

เขาไม่ได้เป็นเพื่อน

káo mâi dâi bpen pêu-un

He's not a friend.

For a summary of different usages of **bpen**, see Appendix 2.

5.1.2 | **keu:**

keu: means 'is equal to' or 'namely'; it often occurs when giving explanations, clarifications and definitions; it is also used as a hesitation device. **keu:** does not occur in the negative:

สามบวกสี่คือเจ็ด

săhm bòo-uk sèe keu: jèt

Three plus four is seven.

มีปัญหาสามอย่างคือ . . .

mee bpun-hăh săhm yàhng keu: . . .

There are three problems, namely . . .

คำเมืองคือภาษาที่คนเชียงใหม่พูด
kum meu-ung keu: pah-săh têe kon chee-ung mài pôot
'Kham Muang' is the language people speak in Chiangmai.

คืออย่างนี้นะ ...
keu: yàhng née ná ...
It's like this, right? ...

In some instances, such as introductions and identifying people in photographs, **bpen** and **keu:** are interchangeable:

นี่คือ/เป็นสามีฉัน
nêe keu:/bpen săh-mee chún
This is my husband.

สมชาย คือ/เป็นใคร
sŏm-chai keu/bpen krai?
Who is Somchai?

Note, however, that **bpen**, not **keu:**, is used in the contrastive construction **mâi châi . . . , bpen . . .** ('it's not . . . , it's . . .'):

ไม่ใช่อย่างนั้น เป็นอย่างนี้
mâi châi yàhng nún, bpen yàhng née
It's not like that, it's like this.

ไม่ใช่แฟน เป็นน้องสาว
mâi châi fairn bpen nórng săo
She's not his girlfriend. She's his younger sister.

| 5.1.3 | mee |

mee ('to have') is also used to translate 'there is/there are'; often, especially in written Thai, it occurs after the topic (9.1):

มีนักเรียนสี่ร้อยคน
mee núk ree-un sèe róy kon
There are four hundred pupils.

ไม่มีเวลา

mâi mee way-lah

There isn't time.

คนไทยที่พูดภาษาฝรั่งเศสได้ดีมีน้อย

kon tai têe pôot pah-săh fa-rùng-sàyt dâi: dee mee nóy

There are few Thais who can speak French well.

(people – Thai – who – speak – language – French – can – well –
  there are – few)

5.1.4 | **yòo**

yòo ('to be situated at') is used to describe the location of things:

บ้านคุณอยู่ที่ไหน

bâhn kOOn yòo têe năi?

Where is your house?

อยู่ในตู้เย็น

yòo nai dtôo yen

It's in the fridge.

5.2   **Stative verbs**

Adjectives in Thai also function as stative verbs (verbs which describe
a state rather than an action). Thus lék is both the adjective 'small' and
the verb 'to be small':

บ้านเล็ก

bâhn lék

a small house / The house is small.

เสื้อสวย

sêu-a sǒo-ay

a pretty shirt (top, blouse) / The shirt (top, blouse) is pretty.

อาหารแพง

ah-hăhn pairng

expensive food / The food is expensive.

Adjectives occur only rarely with the verb **bpen** ('to be'); the following idiomatic expressions are exceptional:

เป็นห่วง	**bpen hòo-ung**	to be concerned
เป็นโสด	**bpen sòht**	to be single, unmarried
เป็นใหญ่	**bpen yài**	to have power, authority; be a bigwig

ลูกกลับบ้านดึก พ่ออดรู้สึกเป็นห่วงไม่ได้
lôok glùp bâhn dèuk pôr òt róo-sèuk bpen hòo-ung mâi dâi:
When the children come home late, their father can't help feeling concerned.

5.3   Verb compounds

Many verbs, such as **dtàirng ngahn** ('to get married'), are made up of two words and are called verb compounds. Verb compounds in Thai can consist of (a) VERB + NOUN; (b) NOUN + VERB; or (c) VERB + VERB:

5.3.1   VERB + NOUN

เข้าใจ	**kâo jai**	to understand (to enter + heart)
ดีใจ	**dee jai**	to be happy (good + heart)
แต่งงาน	**dtàirng ngahn**	to marry/be married (to arrange + work/party)
ทำงาน	**tum ngahn**	to work (to do + work)

5.3.2   NOUN + VERB

ใจดี	**jai dee**	to be kind (heart + good)
มือไว	**meu wai**	to be light-fingered, a thief (hand + quick)
ปากร้าย	**bpàhk rái:**	to be malicious (mouth + bad)
หัวแข็ง	**hǒo-a kǎirng**	to be stubborn (head + hard)

5.3.3 | VERB + VERB

เปลี่ยนแปลง	**bplèe-un bplairng**	to change (change + transform)
เปรียบเทียบ	**bprèe-up têe-up**	to compare (compare + compare)
อดอยาก	**òt yàhk**	to be starving (go without + want)
ดูแล	**doo lair**	to look after (see + watch)
ตกลง	**dtòk long**	to agree (fall + descend)
เดินเล่น	**dern lên**	to go for a walk (walk + play)
พูดเล่น	**pôot lên**	to joke (speak + play)

Verb compounds are negated by the pattern **mâi** + VERB COMPOUND (11.1):

ผมไม่เปรียบเทียบ
pǒm mâi bprèe-up têe-up
I'm not making any comparisons.

5.4 Resultative verbs

A number of verbs, such as **norn lùp** 'to sleep' (lie down + sleep) and **morng hěn** 'to see' (look at + see) resemble verb compounds as they consist of two verbs. They differ in that the second verb describes a state that results from the action of the first verb; thus, sleep 'results' from lying down and seeing from looking. Verb compounds and VERB (PHRASE) + RESULTATIVE VERB constructions are negated differently (11.1, 11.2).

lùp and **hěn** occur as resultative verbs only with **norn** and **morng** respectively. Other verbs have a much less restricted role as resultative verbs. These include the completive verbs, **sèt** ('to finish'), **jòp** ('to complete'), **mòt** ('to be all used up/gone'), the directional verbs **kêun** ('to rise'), **long** ('to descend'), **kâo** ('to enter') and **òrk** ('to leave') (see 5.5), and words such as **tun** ('to be in time') and **tòok** ('to be correct, accurate'):

ฉันทำอาหารเสร็จแล้ว
chún tum ah-hǎhn sèt láir-o
I've finished cooking.

เขาอ่านหนังสือจบแล้ว
káo àhn núng-sĕu jòp láir-o
He's finished the book.

ผมใช้เงินหมดแล้ว
pŏm chái ngern mòt láir-o
I've spent all my money.

คุณจะไปทันไหม
kOOn ja bpai tun mái?
Will you get there in time?

Resultative verbs are negated by the pattern VERB (PHRASE) + **mâi** +
RESULTATIVE VERB (11.2):

ฉันมองอะไรไม่เห็น
chún morng a-rai mâi hĕn
I can't see anything.

5.5 Directional verbs

The verbs **bpai** ('to go') and **mah** ('to come') are used after a number of
verbs or verb phrases as 'direction markers' to indicate whether the action
of the verb is directed towards or away from the speaker. They commonly
follow such verbs as **dern** ('to walk'), **glùp** ('to return'), **yái:** ('to move
home'), **toh(ra-sùp)** ('to telephone'), **ao/num/pah** ('to take/bring'), **bplèe-un**
('to change') and **sòng** ('to send'). Some verbs conveying a sense of loss,
such as **hăi:** ('to disappear') and **leu:m** ('to forget') occur only with **bpai**:

เราย้ายมาอยู่กรุงเทพ ฯ ตั้งแต่ฉันยังเด็ก
rao yái: mah yòo grOOng-tâyp dtûng-dtàir chún yung dèk
We moved (here) to Bangkok when I was still a child.

วันเสาร์หน้าเราจะขับรถไปหัวหิน
wun săo nâh rao ja kùp rót bpai hŏo-hĭn
Next Saturday we'll drive to Hua Hin.

พรุ่งนี้เขาจะเอาหนังสือมาให้ดู
prÔOng née káo ja ao núng-sĕu mah hâi doo
Tomorrow he'll bring the book to show me.

คุณจะพาลูกสาวไปด้วยหรือ

kOOn ja pah lôok sǎo: bpai dôo-ay lěr?

You're taking your daughter with you, then?

ฉันลืมไปแล้ว

chún leu:m bpai láir-o

I've forgotten.

เมื่อเช้านี้ฉันโทร(ศัพท์)ไปคุยกับพี่สาว

mêu-a cháo: née chún toh(ra-sùp) bpai koo-ee gùp pêe sǎo:

I phoned your sister this morning.

Note, however, that in the expression, 'I'll ring you back', the directional verb is **mah**:

เย็น ๆ ฉันจะโทร(ศัพท์)มาใหม่

yen yen chún ja toh(ra-sùp) mah mài

I'll ring you back in the evening.

bpai and **mah** sometimes occur in the pattern VERB + **bpai** + VERB + **mah**, where the same verb is repeated, to convey the idea of the action occurring repetitively back and forth:

ผมเดินไปเดินมาสิบนาที

pǒm dern bpai dern mah sìp nah-tee

I walked back and forth for ten minutes.

เราคุยกันไปคุยกันมาทั้งคืน

rao koo-ee gun bpai koo-ee gun mah túng keu:n

We chatted (back and forth) all night.

เขาชอบเปลี่ยนไปเปลี่ยนมา

káo chôrp bplèe-un bpai bplèe-un mah

He likes/is always chopping and changing.

Other common directional verbs are **kêun** ('to rise'), **long** ('to descend'), **kâo** ('to enter') and **òrk** ('to leave'):

เขาปีนขึ้นต้นไม้

káo bpeen kêun dtôn-mái:

He climbed up the tree.

ฉันวิ่งลงบันได
chún wîng long bun-dai
I ran down the stairs.

เราเดินเข้าห้อง
rao dern kâo hôrng
We entered the room.

เขารีบออกไป
káo rêep òrk bpai
He hurried out.

In negative sentences, directional verbs are not negated; note, however, that **kêun, long, kâo** and **òrk** also function as resultative verbs when they are negated by the pattern, VERB (PHRASE) + **mâi** + RESULTATIVE VERB (11.2):

ฉันกินไม่ลง
chún gin mâi long
I can't eat it.

5.6 Modal verbs

Modal verbs are auxiliary verbs which express such ideas as possibility, probability, ability, necessity, volition and obligation. Most Thai modal verbs can be followed by the particle **ja**. They are negated according to one of three different patterns (11.3).

5.6.1 Possibility and probability

The main modal verbs used for expressing possibility and probability are:

อาจ(จะ)	**àht (ja)**	may/might
คง(จะ)	**kong (ja)**	will probably, sure to
ย่อม(จะ)	**yôrm (ja)**	likely to
มัก(จะ)	**múk (ja)**	tends to, usually
เห็น(จะ)	**hĕn (ja)**	seems that

69

They all occur before the main verb and are negated by the pattern,
MODAL VERB (+ **ja**) + **mâi** + VERB (PHRASE):

เราอาจ(จะ)ไปดูหนัง
rao àht (ja) bpai doo nǔng
We may go to see a movie.

เขาคง(จะ)ไม่มา
káo kong (ja) mâi mah
He probably won't come.

5.6.2 │ Ability and permission

The word 'can' can be translated by three Thai modal verbs – **dâi:, bpen**
and **wǎi**. All three verbs occur after the main verb and are negated by the
pattern VERB (PHRASE) + **mâi** + MODAL VERB.

5.6.2.1 │ VERB (PHRASE) + dâi:

dâi: conveys the sense of both ability and permission; although written in
Thai with a short vowel symbol, it is normally pronounced with a long
vowel:

เรากลับมาพรุ่งนี้ได้
rao glùp mah prÔOng née dâi:
We can come back tomorrow.

ผมช่วยเขาไม่ได้
pǒm chôo-ay káo mâi dâi:
I can't help her.

ขอยืมรถคุณได้ไหม
kǒr yeu:m rót kOOn dâi: mái?
Can I borrow your car?

คุณทำอย่างนั้นไม่ได้
kOOn tum yàhng nún mâi dâi:
You can't do that.

The following idiomatic expressions are also commonly used for talking about possibility:

เป็นไปได้	bpen bpai dâi:	It's possible.
เป็นไปได้ไหม	bpen bpai dâi: mái?	Is it possible?
เป็นไปไม่ได้	bpen bpai mâi dâi:	It's impossible.

5.6.2.2 VERB (PHRASE) + **bpen**

bpen conveys the sense of knowing how to do something:

เขาเล่นกีตาร์เป็น
káo lên gee-dtah bpen
He can play the guitar.

ผมทำอาหารไม่เป็น
pŏm tum ah-hăhn mâi bpen
I can't cook.

คุณขับรถเป็นไหม
kOOn kùp rót bpen mái?
Can you drive?

5.6.2.3 VERB (PHRASE) + **wăi**

wăi conveys the sense of being physically able to do something:

ไม่ค่อยไกลเท่าไหร่ คิดว่าคงเดินไหว
mâi kôy glai tâo-rài kít wâh kong dern wăi
It's not very far. I think we can walk.

อิ่มมากแล้ว ฉันกินไม่ไหว
ìm mâhk láir-o chún gin mâi wăi
I'm really full. I can't eat it.

ระวังหนักนะ ยกไหวไหม
ra-wung nùk ná yók wăi mái?
Be careful, it's heavy. Can you lift it?

5.6.3 | *Necessity: 'must' and 'need'*

Necessity can be expressed by the following modal verbs which all occur before the main verb:

(จะ) ต้อง	(ja) dtôrng	must
ต้องการ (จะ)	dtôrng-gahn (ja)	need; want
จำเป็นต้อง	jum-bpen dtôrng	necessary to

คุณต้องช่วยเขาหน่อยนะ
kOOn dtôrng chôo-ay káo nòy ná
You must help him a bit, OK?

คุณต้องการพูดกับใคร
kOOn dtôrng-gahn pôot gùp krai?
Who do you want / need to speak to?

จำเป็นต้องทำให้เสร็จวันนี้หรือเปล่า
jum-bpen dtôrng tum hâi sèt wun née réu bplào:?
Is it necessary to finish it today?

dtôrng-gahn (ja) and **jum-bpen dtôrng** are negated by the pattern **mâi +
MODAL VERB + VERB (PHRASE)**:

ไม่ต้องการพบเขาอีกแล้ว
mâi dtôrng-gahn póp káo èek láir-o
There's no need / I don't want to meet him again.

คุณไม่จำเป็นต้องจ่ายเงิน
kOOn mâi jum-bpen dtôrng jài: ngern
There's no need for you to pay any money.

Note also:

ไม่จำเป็น
mâi jum-bpen
It's not necessary.

(ja) dtôrng can be negated in two ways, but with different meanings:
(a) **(ja) mâi + dtôrng + VERB (PHRASE)** ('there is no need to . . .'); and
(b) **(ja) dtôrng + mâi + VERB (PHRASE)** ('must not . . .'):

ผมไม่ต้องไป

pŏm mâi dtôrng bpai

There's no need for me to go / I don't need to go.

ไม่ต้องเกรงใจ

mâi dtôrng grayng jai

There's no need to be shy/diffident (about something).

ไม่ต้องหรอก

mâi dtôrng lòrk

There's no need. (when declining an offer)

เราต้องไม่ลืม

rao dtôrng mâi leu:m

We must not forget.

5.6.4 *Obligation*

Obligation is expressed by **koo-un (ja)** ('should/ought') or **nâh (ja)** ('should/ought') before the main verb. Both are most commonly negated by the pattern, **mâi** + MODAL VERB (+ **ja**) + VERB (PHRASE):

คุณควรจะบอกผมล่วงหน้า

kOOn koo-un ja bòrk pŏm lôo-ung nâh

You should've told me in advance.

เราไม่น่าจะกลับดึก

rao mâi nâh ja glùp dèuk

We ought not to return late.

5.6.5 *'want to'*

The idea of wanting to do something is expressed by **yàhk (ja)** ('want to, would like to'), which occurs before the verb or verb phrase. Negative sentences follow the pattern, **mâi** + **yàhk (ja)** + VERB (PHRASE):

ฉันอยากจะกลับบ้าน

chún yàhk ja glùp bâhn

I'd like to go home.

อยากไปดูหนังไหม

yàhk bpai doo nŭng mai?

Do you want to go and see a film?

ฉันไม่อยากไปกินตามร้าน

chún mâi yàhk bpai gin dtahm ráhn

I don't want to go and eat in a restaurant.

5.7 Time and aspect

Whether an action occurs in the future or the past (time), and whether it is a completed, continuous, or habitual action (aspect), can, when necessary, be clarified by using auxiliary verbs or particles.

5.7.1 *Future actions:* **ja** + *VERB (PHRASE)*

Actions that occur in the future can be described using the pattern, **ja** + VERB (PHRASE):

พรุ่งนี้ผมจะไม่มาทำงาน

prÔOng née pŏm ja mâi mah tum ngahn

Tomorrow I'm not coming in to work.

สิ้นปีเราจะกลับไปต่างประเทศ

sîn bpee rao ja glùp bpai dtàhng bpra-tâyt

At the end of the year we'll go back overseas.

เขาจะจัดงานเลี้ยงเมื่อไร

káo ja jùt ngahn lée-ung mêu-rài?

When will they organise the party?

5.7.2 *Completed actions:* VERB (PHRASE) + láir-o
Attained states: STATIVE VERB + láir-o

Completed actions can be described by the pattern, VERB (PHRASE) + láir-o ('already'):

เขาไปทำงานแล้ว
káo bpai tum ngahn láir-o
He has gone to work.

เรากินข้าวแล้ว
rao gin kâo: láir-o
We have eaten already.

รถเมล์มาแล้ว
rót may mah láir-o
The bus has arrived / Here comes the bus.

láir-o occurs with stative verbs to indicate that the specified state or condition has been attained:

ถูกแล้ว
tòok láir-o
That's correct.

พอแล้ว
por láir-o
That's enough.

ดีแล้ว
dee láir-o
That's fine.

Note that some non-stative verbs also occur with **láir-o** to convey the sense of a state having been attained:

เข้าใจแล้ว
kâo jai láir-o
(Now) I understand.

ฝนตกแล้ว
fŏn dtòk láir-o
It's (started) raining.

5.7.3 | Continuous actions: gum-lung + VERB (PHRASE) + yòo

Continuous actions, whether in the present or past, can be described by the pattern, **gum-lung** + VERB (PHRASE) + **yòo**:

ฉันกำลังอ่านหนังสืออยู่
chún gum-lung àhn núng-sěu yòo
I am/was reading.

Either **yòo** or **gum-lung** may be dropped:

เรากำลังกินข้าว
rao gum-lung gin kâo:
We are/were eating.

เขาดูทีวีอยู่
káo doo tee-wee yòo
He is/was watching TV.

คุณทำอะไรอยู่
kOOn tum a-rai yòo?
What are you doing?

5.7.4 | Actions about to happen: gum-lung ja + VERB (PHRASE)

Actions about to happen, whether in the immediate future or when narrating events in the past, are described by the pattern, **gum-lung ja** + VERB (PHRASE):

แม่กำลังจะเตรียมอาหาร
mâir gum-lung ja dtree-um ah-hǎhn
Mum is/was about to prepare the food.

เรากำลังจะไปตลาด
rao gum-lung ja bpai dta-làht
We are/were about to go to the market.

ผมกำลังจะหิว
pǒm gum-lung ja hěw
I am/was getting hungry.

5.7.5 | Actions that have just happened: pêrng + VERB (PHRASE)

Actions that have just happened are described by the pattern, **pêrng** +
VERB (PHRASE):

เขาเพิ่งซื้อรถใหม่

káo pêrng séu: rót mài

He has just bought a new car.

ผมเพิ่งเห็นเขาเมื่อกี้นี้เอง

pǒm pêrng hěn káo mêu-a gêe née ayng

I have just seen him, just a moment ago.

คุณเพิ่งรู้หรือ

kOOn pêrng róo lěr?

You've only just found out, right?

5.7.6 | Single and habitual actions in the past: ker-ee + VERB (PHRASE)

The pattern **ker-ee** + VERB (PHRASE) is used to describe an action that
(a) has occurred on at least one occasion in the past, or (b) that has
occurred habitually in the past; it can occur with **láir-o** for added emphasis.
When preceded by the negative word **mâi** it means 'never' and often occurs
in the pattern **mâi ker-ee . . . mah gòrn** ('never . . . before'):

ฉันเคยไปเที่ยวเชียงใหม่

chún ker-ee bpai têe-o chee-ung-mài

I've been to/visited Chiangmai.

ผมเคยดูแล้ว

pǒm ker-ee doo láir-o

I've seen it already.

เราเคยอยู่ที่กรุงเทพ ฯ

rao ker-ee yòo têe grOOng-tâyp

We used to live in Bangkok.

ฉันไม่เคยกินทุเรียน

chún mâi ker-ee gin tOO-ree-un

I've never eaten durian.

ผมไม่เคยเห็นมาก่อน

pǒm mâi ker-ee hěn mah gòrn

I've never seen it before.

When **ker-ee** occurs in questions, it means 'have you ever . . . ?'; a 'yes' answer is **ker-ee**, a 'no' answer, **mâi ker-ee**:

เคยไปเที่ยวภูเก็ตไหม

ker-ee bpai têe-o poo-gèt mái?

Have you ever been to Phuket?

– เคย/ไม่เคย

– **ker-ee / mâi ker-ee**

– Yes/No.

5.7.7	**Negative past tense: mâi dâi + VERB (PHRASE)**

The pattern **mâi dâi** + VERB (PHRASE) is used to describe actions that did not take place in the past; it cannot be used with stative verbs:

เราไม่ได้ไป

rao mâi dâi bpai

We didn't go.

ฉันไม่ได้บอกเขา

chún mâi dâi bòrk káo

I didn't tell him.

Note that it should not be assumed that the positive past tense is formed by **dâi** + VERB (PHRASE); this pattern is relatively uncommon.

For other uses of **mâi dâi** + VERB (PHRASE), see 5.1.1, 11.4.

5.7.8	**Past continuous tense: VERB (PHRASE) + mah + (dâi:) + TIME EXPRESSION + láir-o**

Actions that began in the past and continue through to the present can be described by the pattern, VERB (PHRASE) + **mah** + (**dâi:**) + TIME EXPRESSION + **láir-o**:

เรานั่งรถไฟมา(ได้)สองชั่วโมงแล้ว
rao nûng rót fai mah (dâi:) sǒrng chôo-a mohng láir-o
We have been sitting on the train for two hours.

เขาเรียนภาษาไทยมา(ได้)หลายปีแล้ว
káo ree-un pah-sǎh tai mah (dâi:) lǎi: bpee láir-o
He has been studying Thai for many years.

For use of **dâi:** to express duration of time, see Appendix 2.

5.7.9	*Changed states: STATIVE VERB + kêun/long*

The verbs **kêun** ('to ascend') and **long** ('to descend') are used with pairs of contrasting stative verbs to indicate an increase or decrease in state; they are similar to English 'up' in 'heat up', 'speed up', etc. and 'down' in 'cool down', 'slow down', etc.

อ้วนขึ้น	**ôo-un kêun** to get fatter	ผอมลง	**pǒrm long** to slim down
เร็วขึ้น	**ray-o kêun** to speed up	ช้าลง	**cháh long** to slow down
ดีขึ้น	**dee kêun** to improve	แย่ลง	**yâir long** to worsen
มากขึ้น	**mâhk kêun** to increase	น้อยลง	**nóy long** to decrease

Note that **kêun** and **long** also occur with verbs of motion as direction markers (5.5).

5.7.10	*VERB (PHRASE) + wái*

The verb **wái** occurs after a verb of action or verb phrase to convey the idea that the action is being done for future use or reference:

ฝากของไว้ที่นี่ได้ไหม
fàhk kǒrng wái têe nêe dâi mái?
Can I leave my things here?

เราจองตั๋วไว้แล้ว
rao jorng dtǒo-a wái láir-o
We've booked tickets already.

เราต้องนั่งตามที่ที่เขาจัดไว้ให้
rao dtôrng nûng dtahm têe têe káo jùt wái hâi
We had to sit in the places they'd arranged for us.

อยากจะอนุรักษ์กีฬาไทยๆ ไว้ด้วย
yàhk ja a-nÓO-rúk gee-lah tai tai wái dôo-ay
I want to preserve traditional Thai sports, too.

เอาไว้วันหลังนะ
ao wái wun lǔng ná
Let's put it off to another day.

| 5.7.11 | *VERB (PHRASE) + ao*

The verb **ao** occurs after a verb of action or a verb phrase to convey the idea that the subject is doing something for himself; often **ao** is followed by **wái**. The beginner is best advised to simply memorise examples from the speech of native speakers rather than to attempt to create sentences of their own using this pattern.

ผมเตรียมเอาไว้แล้ว
pǒm dtree-um ao wái láir-o
I've prepared things.

คุณเก็บเอาไว้แล้วใช่ไหม
kOOn gèp ao wái láir-o châi mái?
You've kept it, right?

ฉันคิดเอาเอง
chún kít ao ayng
I thought so myself.

เดาเอาซิคะ
dao ao sí ká
Have a guess!

5.7.12 VERB (PHRASE) + sĕe-a/sá

sĕe-a as a main verb has a range of meanings, including 'to lose', 'to waste', 'to be spoiled', 'to be broken' and 'to die'. But when it occurs after a verb, or verb phrase, it is usually not translated, while its precise function often appears obscure to the foreign learner and impossible to use, other than in pre-memorised expressions. However, a number of distinct usages can be identified.

Often it is used to convey some sense of loss which cannot be remedied, sometimes tinged with regret, sometimes with the sense 'too bad it happened that way'; in such cases it is often pronounced sá:

เขามาสายไปเสียแล้ว

káo mah săi: bpai sá láir-o

He came too late.

ฉันลืมไปเสียแล้ว

chún leu:m bpai sá láir-o

I've forgotten.

ต่อมานายสโมกี้เดินทางมาพบเข้า จึงรู้ว่าแหม่มภริยารับ
นายจำรัสเป็นสามีใหม่ไปเสียแล้ว

**dtòr mah nai: sa-moh-gêe dern tahng mah póp kâo jeung róo
wâh màirm pa-ri-yah rúp nai: jum-rút bpen săh-mee mài bpai
sá láir-o**

After that, Mr Smokey went to meet up with her and thus learned that his English wife had taken Mr Jamrat as her new husband.

วันหนึ่งเธอได้บอกความจริงแก่ผมว่า เธอได้เสียตัวกับ
ชายอื่นเสียแล้ว

**wun nèung ter dâi bòrk kwahm jing gàir pŏm wâh ter dâi sĕe-a
dtoo-a gùp chai: èu:n sá láir-o**

One day she told me the truth that she had lost her virginity with another man.

Another use of sĕe-a is in gentle commands:

กินเสียลูก

gin sĕe-a lôok

Eat up, now. (mother to child)

ลืมเสียเถิด
leu:m sĕe-a tèrt
Let's forget about it.

นิ่งเสียเถิด ไม่ต้องร้อง
nîng sĕe-a tèrt mâi dtôrng rórng
Shhh, now, there's no need to cry.

sĕe-a is also used for emphasising or intensifying the preceding verb:

ไม่ได้พบกันเสียตั้งนาน
mâi dâi póp gun sĕe-a dtûng nahn
We haven't seen each other for a long time.

บางครั้งดื่มมากเสียจนไม่สบาย
bahng krúng dèu:m sĕe-a jon mâi sa-bai:
Sometimes he drank a lot until he was ill.

ลูกๆพากันร้องให้เสียจนตาบวม
lôok lôok pah gun rórng hâi sĕe-a jon dtah boo-um
The children cried until their eyes swelled up.

การบ้านที่ครูให้ก็มักจะลอกกันเสียมาก
gahn bâhn têe kroo hâi gôr múk ja lôrk gun sĕe-a mâhk
(homework – which – teacher – gives – (students) – then – tend to –
    copy – together – a lot)
Students tend to copy among themselves a lot of the homework that the
    teacher gives them.

sĕe-a in its shortened form, sá, occurs in the pattern, mêu-rài ja + VERB
(PHRASE) + sá tee, to show irritation or impatience that something has
not happened:

เมื่อไรจะเสร็จเสียที
mêu-rài ja sèt sá tee
When are you going to be finished?

เมื่อไรฝนจะหยุดตกเสียที
mêu-rài fŏn ja yÒOt dtòk sá tee
When is it going to stop raining?

5.8 Passives

The passive construction is used much less commonly in Thai than in English. It is more usually associated with sentences with a negative connotation, where the subject is a victim of something unpleasant, such as being beaten, fined, robbed, arrested, criticised, gossiped about, cheated, attacked, shot and so on; however, it sometimes occurs in sentences with no negative connotations, such as 'children are taught to . . .'. The passive is formed using the passive-marker **tòok**, in the pattern, SUBJECT + **tòok** + (AGENT) + VERB (PHRASE):

ฉันถูกยุงกัด
chún tòok yOOng gùt
I've been bitten by a mosquito.

มาลีถูกรถชน
mah-lee tòok rót chon
Malee was hit by a car.

เขาถูกตำรวจจับ
káo tòok dtum-ròo-ut jùp
He was arrested by a policeman.

เราถูกขโมย
rao tòok ka-moy-ee
We were robbed.

เพื่อนถูกยิงตาย
pêu-un tòok ying dtai:
My friend was shot dead.

เด็กอเมริกันถูกสอนให้หาเงินไว้ใช้จ่ายเองตั้งแต่เด็ก
dèk a-may-ri-gun tòok sǒrn hâi hǎh ngern wái chái jài: ayng dtûng-dtàir dèk
American children are taught to earn their own spending money from an early age.

Much less common than **tòok**, but used identically is the passive-marker **dohn**:

เขาโดนตี
káo dohn dtee
He was beaten.

English passive sentences that carry a neutral or positive connotation can often be rendered by the pattern SUBJECT + **dâi rúp** ('received') + VERB (PHRASE):

เราได้รับเชิญไป...

rao dâi rúp chern bpai...

We were invited to...

ผมได้รับอนุญาต...

pŏm dâi rúp a-nÓO-yâht...

I was permitted to...

เขาได้รับเลือกเป็น...

káo dâi rúp lêu-uk bpen...

He was chosen to be...

The pattern SUBJECT + **dâi rúp** + NOUN is also commonly translated by the passive in English:

เขาได้รับอิทธิพลจาก...

káo dâi rúp ìt-tí-pon jàhk...

He was influenced by...

เขาได้รับการศึกษาจากอเมริกา

káo dâi rúp gahn sèuk-săh jàhk a-may-ri-gah...

He was educated in America.

ข้อเสนอได้รับความเห็นชอบ

kôr sa-nĕe dâi rúp kwahm hĕn chôrp

The proposal was approved.

English passive expressions like 'it was agreed that...', 'it is well known that...' and so on, are formed using the pattern, **bpen têe** + VERB + **gun** + **wâh...**:

เป็นที่ตกลงกันว่า...

bpen têe dtòk long gun wâh...

It was agreed that...

เป็นที่ทราบกันดีว่า...

bpen têe sâhp gun dee wâh...

It is well known that...

Verbs of
utterance,
mental
activity and
perception
with **wâh**

เป็นที่ยอมรับกันโดยทั่วไปว่า...

bpen têe yorm rúp gun doy-ee tôo-a bpai wâh ...

It is generally accepted that ...

The pattern **mee** + VERB (PHRASE) also occurs where English normally uses a passive verb.

ภาษาแสกมีพูดอยู่ที่จังหวัดนครพนม

pah-sǎk sàirk mee pôot yòo têe jung-wùt na-korn pa-nom

The Saek language is spoken in Nakhorn Phanom Province.

กระเป๋ายี่ห้อนี้มีขายที่ไหน

gra-bpǎo yêe hôr née mee kǎi: têe nǎi?

Where is this brand of bag sold?

วิชานั้นไม่มีสอนปีนี้

wí-chah nún mâi mee sǒrn bpee née

That subject isn't being taught this year.

5.9 Verbs of utterance, mental activity and perception with wâh

Verbs of utterance ('to say/whisper/call', etc.), mental activity ('to think/remember/hope', etc.) and perception ('to see/understand/know', etc.) are followed by **wâh** + SUBORDINATE CLAUSE. **wâh** is similar in function to the English 'that' ('say *that* . . .', 'think *that* . . .', 'know *that* . . .', etc.), but unlike 'that', which is optional in English, **wâh** should, at least in the early stages of learning, be regarded as compulsory.

คิดว่าจะกลับพรุ่งนี้

kít wâh ja glùp prÔOng née

I think (that) I'll return tomorrow.

หวังว่าจะไม่เผ็ดเกินไป

wǔng wâh ja mâi pèt gern bpai

I hope (that) it's not too spicy.

รู้สึกว่า น่าเบื่อไหม

róo-sèuk wâh nâh bèu-a mái?

Did you feel (that) it was boring?

Some of the most common verbs that are followed by **wâh** are:

บอก	**bòrk**	to say, tell
เป็นห่วง	**bpen hòo-ung**	to be concerned, worried
เชื่อ	**chêu-a**	to believe
ได้ยิน	**dâi yin**	to hear
เห็น	**hěn**	to see, think
จำได้	**jum dâi:**	to remember
เข้าใจ	**kâo jai**	to understand
คิด	**kít**	to think
แน่ใจ	**nâir jai**	to be certain
พูด	**pôot**	to speak
รู้	**róo**	to know (facts)
รู้สึก	**róo-sèuk**	to feel
ทราบ	**sâhp**	to know (facts)
สงสัย	**sǒng-sǎi**	to suspect
หวัง	**wǔng**	to hope

For further examples of the use of **wâh**, see 9.3 and 12.4.

5.10 Verbs of emotion with tês

Verbs of emotion ('to be angry/sorry/excited', etc.) are generally followed by **tês** + SUBORDINATE CLAUSE. **tês** is similar in function to the English 'that' ('happy *that* …', 'angry *that* …', 'sorry *that* …', etc.), but unlike 'that', which is optional in English, **tês** is obligatory:

ผมดีใจที่ไม่ได้ไป
pǒm dee jai têe mâi dâi bpai
I'm pleased (that) I didn't go.

เขาโกรธที่ฉันซื้อ

káo gròht têe chún séu:

He was angry (that) I bought it.

เราเสียใจที่หน้าร้อนผ่านไปเสียแล้ว

rao sěe-a jai têe nâh rórn pàhn bpai sá láir-o

We're sorry that the hot season is over.

5.11 Causatives

Causative constructions in Thai are formed using either (a) **tum** + VERB; (b) **hâi** + VERB (PHRASE), or (c) SUBJECT + **tum hâi** + VERB (PHRASE). The nature of the subject (whether it is human or non-human) and object (whether it is animate or inanimate) and the degree of intention, determine the appropriate construction.

5.11.1 SUBJECT (human or non-human) + tum + (inanimate OBJECT) + VERB

เขาทำถ้วยตก

káo tum tôo-ay dtòk

She dropped the cup.

ฉันทำหนังสือหาย

chún tum núng-sěu hǎi:

I've lost the book.

Some common compound verbs in which the causative **tum** is the first element are:

ทำ...เปื้อน	**tum...bpêu-un**	to make something dirty
ทำ...แตก	**tum...dtàirk**	to break something
ทำ...ตก	**tum...dtòk**	to drop something
ทำ...หก	**tum...hòk**	to spill something
ทำ...หัก	**tum...hùk**	to make something break off

87

ทำ...หล่น	**tum...lòn**	to make something fall off
ทำ...หลุด	**tum...lòot**	to let something slip
ทำ...เสีย	**tum...sĕe-a**	to spoil something

5.11.2 SUBJECT (human) + hâi + (animate OBJECT) + VERB (PHRASE)

hâi can convey a range of meanings, from the zero coercion of 'to let someone do something', to the more forceful 'to have someone do something' and 'to make someone do something':

แม่ให้ผมเรียนบัญชี
mâir hâi pŏm ree-un bun-chee
My mother had me study accountancy.

เขาให้ฉันกลับมาเดือนหน้า
káo hâi chún glùp mah deu-un nâh
They got me to come back next month.

พ่อไม่ให้ลูกกลับบ้านดึก
pôr mâi hâi lôok glùp bâhn dèuk
The father doesn't let his children come home late.

hâi occurs as the first element in a number of common compound verbs which convey a sense of causation:

ให้...ดู	**hâi...doo** (let/have + see)	to show
ให้...เกิด	**hâi...gèrt** (let/have + happen)	to cause, create
ให้...เช่า	**hâi...châo** (let/have + rent)	to let
ให้...ยืม	**hâi...yeu:m** (let/have + borrow)	to lend

ให้เขาดูหน่อย
hâi káo doo nòy
Show him/let him see.

มีบ้านให้เช่าไหม

mee bâhn hâi châo mái?

Do you have a house to let?

ผมไม่ให้ใครยืมรถ

pŏm mâi hâi krai yeu:m rót

I don't let anyone borrow my car.

hâi may be preceded by another verb specifying the method of causing someone to do something (e.g. by requesting, telling, ordering, etc.). Verbs which commonly precede **hâi** include **bòrk** ('to tell'), **kŏr** ('to request'), **yorm** ('to allow'), **a-nÓO-yâht** ('to allow'), **sùng** ('to order'), **yàhk** ('to want to'), **dteu-un** ('to warn'). Word order in such constructions is SUBJECT (human) + SPECIFYING VERB + **hâi** + (animate OBJECT) + VERB PHRASE:

ผมบอกให้เขาซื้อ

pŏm bòrk hâi káo séu

I told him to buy it.

เขาขอให้ฉันไปรับ

káo kŏr hâi chún bpai rúp

He asked me to go and collect him.

เราอยากให้คุณกลับมาเร็ว ๆ

rao yàhk hâi kOOn glùp mah ray-o ray-o

We want you to come back soon.

ฉันเตือนให้เขามาก่อนเวลา

chún dteu-un hâi káo mah gòrn way-lah

I warned him to come early.

คุณพ่อคุณแม่ไม่เคยเล่าให้ฟังเลย

kOOn pôr kOOn mâir mâi ker-ee lâo hâi fung ler-ee

My parents never, ever told me.

Note, however, that the order of object and **hâi** can be reversed with the verbs **bòrk** ('to tell'), **kŏr** ('to request'), **yorm** ('to allow'), **a-nÓO-yâht** ('to allow'), **sùng** ('to order'), **yàhk** ('to want to'), **dteu-un** ('to warn'):

ผมบอกเขาให้ซื้อ

pŏm bòrk káo hâi séu

I told him to buy it.

89

เขาขอฉันให้ไปรับ

káo kǒr chún hâi bpai rúp

He asked me to go and collect him.

5.11.3	*SUBJECT (human or non-human) + tum hâi +*
	(animate or inanimate OBJECT) + VERB (PHRASE)

This pattern conveys a sense of clear intention, coercion or non-accidental causation by the subject:

เจ้าหน้าที่ทำให้ผมต้องเสียเวลามาก

jâo nâh-têe tum hâi pǒm dtôrng sěe-a way-lah mâhk

The official made me waste a lot of time.

ผู้ใหญ่ไทยจะไม่นิยมการชมเด็กต่อหน้าเพราะจะทำให้
เด็กลืมตัวนึกว่าเก่งหรือดีแล้ว

**pôo yài tai ja mâi ní-yom gahn chom dèk dtòr nâh pró' ja tum
hâi dèk leu:m dtoo-a néuk wâh gèng réu dee láir-o**

Thai adults don't like to praise children to their face because it will make
the children forget themselves and think they're great or good.

เสียงชื่นชมเหล่านี้ทำให้เธอรู้สึกปลาบปลื้มและมีกำลังใจ

**sěe-ung chêu:n chom lào née tum hâi ter róo-sèuk bplàhp
bplêu:m láir mee gum-lung jai**

These admiring voices made her feel overjoyed and gave her encouragement.

อากาศอุ่น ๆ ทำให้เขารู้สึกว่าสุขภาพค่อยๆ ดีขึ้น

**ah-gàht ÒOn ÒOn tum hâi káo róo-sèuk wâh sÒOk-ka-pâhp kôy
kôy dee kêun**

The warm weather made her feel that her health was gradually improving.

การใช้ชีวิตในกรุงเทพฯ ไม่ทำให้การครองชีพดีขึ้นแต่
อย่างใดเลย

**gahn chái chee-wít nai grOOng-tâyp mâi tum hâi gahn krorng
cheep dee kêun dtàir yàhng dai ler-ee**

Living in Bangkok did not make their livelihoods better in any way
whatsoever.

For negative causatives, see 11.9.

5.12 'To give': direct and indirect objects

The order of objects with the verb **hâi** ('to give') is SUBJECT + **hâi** + DIRECT OBJECT (+ **gàir**) + INDIRECT OBJECT. The preposition **gàir** ('to, for') is frequently omitted, and in some instances, such as, 'Have you fed the dog yet?', it must be omitted:

ฉันให้หนังสือ (แก่) เขา

chún hâi núng-sĕu (gàir) káo

I gave him the book.

พ่อไม่ยอมให้เงิน (แก่) ลูก

pôr mâi yorm hâi ngern (gàir) lôok

The father refuses to give his children any money.

คุณให้อาหารหมาหรือยัง

kOOn hâi ah-hăhn măh réu yung?

Have you fed the dog yet?

If the direct object is quantified, the quantifier follows the indirect object:

ฉันให้หนังสือ (แก่) เขาสามเล่ม

chún hâi núng-sĕu (gàir) káo săhm lêm

I gave him three books.

If the direct object is qualified (e.g. by a relative clause), the qualifier follows the direct object, but the preposition **gàir** becomes obligatory:

ฉันให้หนังสือที่ฉันชอบแก่เขา

chún hâi núng-sĕu têe chún chôrp gàir káo

I gave him books which I like.

พ่อให้เงินห้าพันบาทนั้นแก่ลูก

pôr hâi ngern hâh pun bàht nún gàir lôok

The father gave his children the five thousand baht.

The indirect object (i.e. 'me') in sentences like 'he taught me Thai', 'she sent me a letter' and 'they brought me flowers' follows the pattern, VERB + DIRECT OBJECT + **hâi** + INDIRECT OBJECT:

เขาสอนภาษาไทยให้ผม

káo sŏrn pah-săh tai hâi pŏm

He taught me Thai.

เขาส่งจดหมายมาให้ผม
káo sòng jòt-mǎi mah hâi pǒm
She sent me a letter.

เขาเอาดอกไม้มาให้ฉัน
káo ao dòrk-mái: mah hâi chún
They brought me flowers.

5.13 Verb serialisation

Verb serialisation, in which a number of verbs sharing the same subject follow one after the other, with no intervening conjunctions or prepositions, is extremely common in Thai. A random glance through the examples in this book, or – better still – any sample of written Thai, will immediately show just how prevalent this feature is. For beginners, learning to 'string' together two or three verbs is a key strategy in trying to produce authentic-sounding Thai.

Serial verb constructions can describe a number of simultaneous actions:

เขารีบวิ่งหนีไป
káo rêep wîng něe bpai
(he – hurry – run – flee – go)
He hurriedly ran away.

or, more usually, a sequence of consecutive actions:

เขาออกไปซื้อมาทำกินที่บ้าน
káo òrk bpai séu: mah tum gin têe bâhn
(he – exit – go – buy – come – make – eat – at home)
He went out to buy it to bring back to cook and eat at home.

พอเอ่ยปากอยากได้อะไร คนในครอบครัวจะรีบซื้อหามาให้
por èr-ee bpàhk yàhk dâi a-rai kon nai krôrp-kroo-a ja rêep séu:
   hǎh mah hâi
(when – open – mouth – want to – get – something – someone – in –
   family – would – hurry – buy – seek – come – for/give)
The moment I said I wanted something, someone in the family would rush
   out and buy it for me.

บางคนก็หยิบยืมเงินญาติมาต้องกลับไปทำงานชดใช้ก็มี

**bahng kon gôr yìp yeu:m ngern yâht mah dtôrng glùp bpai tum
ngahn chót chái gôr mee**

(some people – borrow – money – relative – come – must – return –
go – work – repay – there are)

And there are some people who borrow money from their relatives and
have to go back and work to repay it.

Beginners are often intimidated by undiluted sequences of verbs, such
as this:

ต้องรีบกลับไปเรียกให้มาบอก

dtôrng rêep glùp bpai rêe-uk hâi mah bòrk

(must – hurry – return – go – summon – cause – come – tell)

which at first sight appears to be a daunting serial verb construction.

Often, as in this case, the problem is not so much the verbs that appear
as the pronouns that don't. Once the 'missing' pronouns are 'restored' – or
understood from the context – things become rather more manageable:

(คุณ)ต้องรีบกลับไปเรียกให้(เขา)มาบอก(ฉัน)

(kOOn)dtôrng rêep glùp bpai rêe-uk hâi (káo) mah bòrk (chún)

(you) – must – hurry – return – go – summon – cause – (him) –
come – tell – (me)

You must hurry back and summon him to come and tell me.

Chapter 6

Adjectives (stative verbs) and adjectival constructions

As mentioned in the previous chapter, the categories 'verb' and 'adjective' overlap in Thai and many of the words that are considered to be adjectives in English are called stative verbs when describing Thai. For simplicity, however, the term 'adjective' is used throughout this chapter.

Adjectives do not occur with the verb **bpen** ('to be') (5.1.1); they follow the noun they modify and in noun phrases they often occur with a classifier. The most common patterns of noun phrase in which an adjective occurs are listed in 3.5.6–3.5.10.

When a noun is modified by two adjectives (e.g. 'a large, red book') the normal word order in Thai is NOUN + ADJECTIVE + CLASSIFIER + ADJECTIVE:

หนังสือสีแดงเล่มใหญ่
núng-sěu sěe dairng lêm yài
a large, red book (book – red – classifier – big)

สาวสวยคนรวย
sǎo: sǒo-ay kon roo-ay
a beautiful, rich girl (girl – beautiful – classifier – rich)

หมาแก่ตัวน่าสงสาร
mǎh gàir dtoo-a nâh sǒng-sǎhn
a pitiful, old dog (dog – old – classifier – pitiful)

In this pattern, the first adjective identifies the general category (red books, beautiful girls, old dogs) while the classifier + second adjective specifies the individual case.

6.1 Compound adjectives

As with nouns and verbs, compounding is a common way of creating new adjectives. The most productive adjectival prefixes are **jai** ('heart'), **nâh** ('worthy of') and **kêe** (having the characteristic of); of more limited usage are **chûng** (given to/good at) and **hŏo-a** ('head'). **jai** ('heart') also occurs as an adjectival suffix.

ใจดี	**jai dee**	kind (heart – good)
ใจเย็น	**jai yen**	calm (heart – cool)
ใจร้อน	**jai rórn**	impatient, impetuous (heart – hot)
ใจแคบ	**jai kâirp**	narrow-minded (heart – narrow)
น่าสนใจ	**nâh sŏn jai**	interesting (**sŏn jai** – to be interested in)
น่าเบื่อ	**nâh bèu-a**	boring (**bèu-a** – to be bored)
น่าลืม	**nâh leu:m**	forgettable (**leu:m** – to forget)
น่ากลัว	**nâh gloo-a**	frightening (**gloo-a** – to be afraid)
ขี้เกียจ	**kêe gèe-ut**	lazy (**gèe-ut** does not exist in isolation)
ขี้อาย	**kêe ai:**	shy (**ai:** – to be embarrassed)
ขี้ลืม	**kêe leu:m**	forgetful (**leu:m** – to forget)
ขี้เหนียว	**kêe nĕe-o**	mean, stingy (**nĕe-o** – to be sticky)
ช่างพูด	**chûng pôot**	talkative (**pôot** – to speak)
ช่างคิด	**chûng kít**	given to thinking (**kít** – to think)
ช่างสังเกต	**chûng sŭng-gàyt**	observant (**sŭng-gàyt** – to observe)
ช่างเถียง	**chûng tĕe-ung**	argumentative (**tĕe-ung** – to argue)
หัวดี	**hŏo-a dee**	clever (head – good)
หัวแข็ง	**hŏo-a kăirng**	stubborn, headstrong (head – hard)

หัวสูง	hŏo-a sŏong	pretentious (head – high)
หัวนอก	hŏo-a nôrk	educated abroad (head – outside)
หัวเก่า	hŏo-a gào	conservative, old fashioned (head – old)
พอใจ	por jai	satisfied (enough – heart)
กลุ้มใจ	glÔOm jai	depressed (gloomy – heart)
สบายใจ	sa-bai: jai	happy (well/happy – heart)
หนักใจ	nùk jai	worried (heavy – heart)

Another common stylistic feature of Thai is the use of two adjectives of identical or similar meaning. Common examples include:

เก่าแก่	gào gàir	old (old – old)
สวยงาม	sŏo-ay ngahm	beautiful (beautiful – beautiful)
ว่างเปล่า	wâhng bplào	vacant, empty (vacant – empty)
ยากจน	yâhk jon	poor (difficult – poor)
ใหญ่โต	yài dtoh	big (big – big)
เยอะแยะ	yér yáir	many (many – many)

6.2 Modification of adjectives

The meaning of adjectives can be modified by the addition of words such as 'not', 'very', 'rather', 'somewhat' and so on. A few adjectival modifiers occur before the adjective, while the majority occur after the adjective:

6.2.1 | MODIFIER + ADJECTIVE

ค่อนข้าง(จะ)	kôrn kâhng (ja)	rather
ไม่	mâi	not
ไม่ค่อย...เท่าไหร่	mâi kôy ...tâo-rài	not very

เป็นครอบครัวที่มีฐานะค่อนข้าง(จะ)ดี
bpen krôrp-kroo-a têe mee tăh-ná kôrn kâhng (ja) dee
They were a rather well-off family.

บ้านไม่ค่อยใหญ่เท่าไหร่
bâhn mâi kôy yài tâo-rài
The house isn't very big.

6.2.2 | ADJECTIVE + MODIFIER

จะตาย	**ja dtai:**	very (informal) (cf. Eng. '*dead* easy')
จัง	**jung**	really
จริง ๆ	**jing jing**	truly
ดี	**dee**	nice and . . .
เกินไป	**gern bpai**	too
กว่า	**gwàh**	more
ขึ้น	**kêun**	increasingly
ลง	**long**	decreasingly
เหลือเกิน	**lĕu-a gern**	excessively
มาก	**mâhk**	very
เหมือนกัน	**mĕu-un gun**	moderately
นัก	**núk**	very
ไปหน่อย	**bpai nòy**	a little bit too
พอ	**por**	enough
พอใช้	**por chái**	enough
พอ (ๆ) กัน	**por (por) gun**	equally

พอสมควร	por sŏm-koo-un	enough
เท่า (ๆ) กัน	tâo (tâo) gun	equally
ทีเดียว	tee dee-o	indeed, really very
ที่สุด	têe sÒOt	most

Two modifiers can modify the same adjective:

ค่อนข้างจะแพงไปหน่อย
kôrn kâhng ja pairng bpai nòy
a little too much on the expensive side

สนุกมากทีเดียว
sa-nÒOk mâhk tee dee-o
It was really a lot of fun.

กินข้าวมากพอสมควร
gin kâo: mâhk por sŏm-koo-un
We had quite enough to eat.

ห้องนี้อุ่นดีจริง ๆ
hôrng née ÒOn dee jing jing
This room is really nice and warm.

6.3 Special intensifiers

Certain adjectives are followed by specific intensifiers, which in the absence of a suitable equivalent in English (e.g. *brand* new, *pitch* black, *fast* asleep, etc.), can be translated as 'very'. Such intensifiers, used in moderation, can add a more lively flavour to descriptions and are a useful addition to the more advanced learner's vocabulary. Note that some adjectives (e.g. 'cold', 'red') have more than one specific intensifier, while some specific intensifiers can be used with more than one adjective.

หลับปุ๋ย	lùp + bpǒo-ee	asleep
งงเต๊ก	ngong + dték	bewildered
ใหญ่เบ้อเร่อ/มหึมา	yài + bêr rêr/ma-hĕu mah	big
สว่างจ้า	sa-wàhng + jâh	bright
มืดตึ๊ดตื๋อ	mêu:t + dtéut dtĕu:	dark
จืดชืด	jèu:t + chêu:t	dull, insipid
ใสแจ๋ว	săi + jăir-o	clear
เย็นเจี๊ยบ/เฉียบ	yen + jée-up/chèe-up	cold
ถูกเป๋ง/เป๊ะ	tòok + bpĕng/bpé	correct
บ้าชมัด	bâh + cha-mút	crazy
แน่นเอี๊ยด	nâirn + êe-ut	crowded
ต่างกันลิบลับ	dtàhng gun + líp lúp	different
แห้งแต๊ดแต๋	hâirng + dtáirt tăir	dry
เท่ากันเปี๊ยบ/เป๊ะ	tâo gun + bpée-up/bpé	equal
แพงลิบลิ่ว	pairng + líp lîw	expensive
ไกล/ห่างลิบลิ่ว	glai/hàhng + líp lîw	far
อ้วนปี๋	ôo-un + bpĕe	fat
เร็วจี๋/ปรื๋อ/รี่	ray-o + jĕe/bprĕu: /rêe	fast
แบนแต๊ดแต๋/แต๋	bairn + dtáirt dtăir/dtăir	flat
ถี่ยิบ	tèe + yíp	frequent, in close succession

เต็มเอี้ยด/ปรี่/แปร้	dtem + êe-ut/bprèe/bprâir	full
อิ่มตื้อ	ìm + dtêu:	full (food)
แข็งปั๋ง	kǎirng + bpǔng	hard
หนักอึ้ง	nùk + êung	heavy
ร้อนจี๋	rórn + jěe	hot
ชุ่มฉ่ำ	chÔOm + chùm	humid, damp
ตรงกันเปี๊ยบ/เป๊ะ	dtrong gun + bpée-up/bpé	identical
หายต๋อม	hǎi: + dtǒrm	lost
ดังแปร๋/ลั่น	dung + bprǎir/lûn	loud
ทันสมัยเจี๊ยบ	tun sa-mǎi + jée-up	modern
ใหม่เอี่ยม	mài + èe-um	new
เก่างั่ก	gào + ngûk	old
แหลมเปี๊ยบ	lǎirm + bpée-up	pointed
กลมดิก	glom + dìk	round
คมกริบ	kom + grìp	sharp
เงียบกริบ	ngêe-up + grìp	silent
เหมือนเปี๊ยบ/เป๊ะ	měu-un + bpée-up/bpé	similar
เหมือนกันเด๊ะ/ดิ๊ก	měu-un gun + dé/dík	similar
คล่องปรื๋อ	klôrng bprěu:	skilful
เล็กกะจิ๊ดริ๊ด/ กะจิ๋วริ๋ว/กะจ้อยร่อย	lék + ga-jít rít/ ga-jěw rěw/ ga-jôy róy	small
ตรงเผง/เป๋ง/เปะ	dtrong + pěng/bpěng/bpè	straight
โง่ชะมัด	ngôh + cha-mút	stupid

สูงปรี๊ด/ลิบลิ่ว	sǒong + bpréet/líp lîw	tall
หนาปึ้ก/เตอะ	năh + bpèuk/dtèr	thick
คับปั๋ง	kúp + bpěung	tight
ด่วนจี๋	dòo-un + jěe	urgent

6.3.2 *Colours*

ดำปี๋/ขลับ	dum + bpěe/klùp	black
เขียวขจี/แปร๋/อื๋อ	kěe-o + ka-jee/bprǎir/ěu:	green
แดงแจ๊ด/แจ๋/แปร๊ด	dairng + jáirt/jǎir/bpráirt	red
ขาวจั๊วะ/จ๊วก	kǎo: + jóo-a/jóo-uk	white
เหลืองอ๋อย/แปร๊ด/จ๋อย	lěu-ung + ǒy/bpráirt/jǒy	yellow

6.3.3 *Flavours*

ขมปี๋	kǒm + bpěe	bitter
จืดชืด	jèut + chêu:t	bland
เค็มปี๋	kem + bpěe	salty
เปรี้ยวจี๊ด	bprêe-o + jéet	sour
เผ็ดจี๋	pèt + jěe	spicy
หวานเจี๊ยบ/จ๋อย/ฉ่ำ	wǎhn + jée-up/jǒy/	sweet

6.4 Reduplication

Reduplication (the repetition of a word, either in part or full) is another
common means of modifying the meaning of adjectives in Thai. The two
main forms of adjectival reduplication are:

Simple repetition of the adjective

One function of this type of reduplication is to make the meaning less precise, corresponding approximately to the adjectival suffix *-ish* in English:

สีแดง ๆ	**sĕe dairng dairng**	a reddish colour
บ้านเล็ก ๆ	**bâhn lék lék**	a smallish house
อาหารเผ็ด ๆ	**ah-hĕhn pèt pèt**	spicy-ish food

This type of reduplication sometimes indicates that the preceding noun is plural:

| ผู้หญิงสวย ๆ | **pôo- yĭng sŏo-ay sŏo-ay** | pretty girls |
| หนังสือดี ๆ | **núng-sĕu dee dee** | good books |

Repetition of adjective with tonal change

The meaning of an adjective is intensified by reduplication when the first element is pronounced with an exaggerated high tone, regardless of the normal tone of the word; this exaggerated high tone is particularly apparent when reduplicating a word with a high tone like **rórn** ('hot') where the first element is pitched considerably higher and is usually accompanied by an exaggerated lengthening of the vowel. This type of reduplication tends to be a feature of female rather than male speech:

อร๊อย อร่อย	**a-róy a-ròy**	Ever so tasty!
เบื๊อ เบื่อ	**béu-a bèu-a**	So bored!
แพ๊ง แพง	**páirng pairng**	Really expensive!

Sometimes the reduplication adds a third element, with the exaggerated high tone on the middle syllable:

| ดี ดี๊ ดี | **dee dée dee** | So good! |

6.5 Comparison of adjectives

The basic comparative construction employs the pattern, ADJECTIVE +
gwàh ('more than'):

ข้าวหน้าเป็ดที่นี่อร่อยกว่า
kâo: nâh bpèt têe nêe a-ròy gwàh
The duck rice here is tastier.

รถโตโยต้าถูกกว่ารถเบนซ์
rót dtoh-yoh-dtâh tòok gwàh rót bens
Toyotas are cheaper than Mercedes.

ค่าเครื่องบินแพงกว่าปีที่แล้ว
kâh krêu-ung bin pairng gwàh bpee têe láir-o
The air fare is more expensive than last year.

จ้างคนทำดีกว่าทำเอง
jâhng kon tum dee gwàh tum eng
Paying someone to do it is better than doing it yourself.

6.5.1 Degrees of comparison

The basic comparative construction, ADJECTIVE + **gwàh**, can be modified
by the addition of degree adverbs, such as **mâhk** ('much, a lot'), **yér** ('much,
a lot'), **nít-nòy** ('a little'):

สนุกกว่ามาก/เยอะ
sa-nÒOk gwàh mâhk/yér
a lot more fun

ไกลกว่านิดหน่อย
glai gwàh nít-nòy
a little bit further

แพงกว่าสองเท่า
pairng gwàh sǒrng tâo
twice as expensive

103

6.5.2.1 | X + ADJECTIVE + **tâo (tâo) gùp/por por gùp** ('as much as') + Y

This pattern is used both for numerically quantifiable and non-quantifiable comparisons.

นครพนมอยู่ห่างกรุงเทพฯ เท่ากับหนองคาย
na-korn pa-nom yòo hàhng grOOng-tâyp tâo gùp nŏrng-kai:
Nakhorn Phanom is as far away from Bangkok as Nongkhai.

ไปเที่ยวภาคใต้สนุกเท่าๆ กับภาคเหนือ
bpai têe-o pâhk dtâi: sa-nÒOk tâo tâo gùp pâhk nĕu-a
Taking a trip to the South was as much fun as the North.

บ้านหลังใหม่ใหญ่พอๆ กับหลังเก่า
bâhn lŭng mài yài por por gùp lŭng gào
The new house is as big as the old one.

6.5.2.2 | X + **gùp** ('with') + Y + ADJECTIVE + **tâo (tâo) gun/ por (por) gun** ('equally')

This pattern is a variation on 6.5.2.1.

นครพนมกับหนองคาย อยู่ห่างกรุงเทพฯ เท่ากัน
na-korn pa-nom gùp nŏrng-kai: yòo hàhng grOOng-tâyp tâo gun
Nakhorn Phanom and Nongkhai are equally far away from Bangkok.

พี่กับน้องสวยพอๆ กัน
pêe gùp nórng sŏo-ay por por gun
The older sister and the younger sister are equally beautiful.

6.5.2.3 | X + ADJECTIVE + **mĕu-un** ('similar') + Y

Non-quantifiable adjectives can also occur in this pattern.

ลูกชายขยันเหมือนพ่อ
lôok chai: ka-yŭn mĕu-un pôr
The son is hard-working like his father.

เขาชอบพูดซ้ำไปซ้ำมาเหมือนครู

káo chôrp pôot súm bpai súm mah měu-un kroo

He always repeats himself like a teacher.

Note that while the pattern X + **gùp** ('with') + Y + ADJECTIVE + **měu-un gun** is possible, it is ambiguous (since . . . **měu-un gun** can mean 'moderately . . .') and therefore best avoided:

พี่กับน้องสวยเหมือนกัน

pêe gùp nórng sŏo-ay měu-un gun

The older sister and younger sister are as beautiful as each other.

or

The older sister and younger sister are moderately good looking.

6.5.2.4 | X + ADJECTIVE + **mâi páir** ('be just as . . .') + Y

mâi páir literally means 'not lose to', but is used to convey the sense of 'just as . . .':

ภาคอีสานสวยไม่แพ้ภาคเหนือ

pâhk ěe-sǎhn sŏo-ay mâi páir pâhk něu-a

The North East (region) is just as beautiful as the North.

ลูกสาวปากร้ายไม่แพ้แม่

lôok sǎo: bpàhk rái: mâi páir mâir

The daughter is just as sharp-tongued as her mother.

ฝรั่งคนนั้นร้องเพลงลูกทุ่งไม่แพ้คนไทย

fa-rùng kon nún rórng playng lôok tÔOng mâi páir kon tai

That farang sings *luk tung* (Thai folk songs) songs just as well as a Thai.

6.5.3 | *Interrogative comparisons*

Questions involving comparisons follow the pattern QUESTION WORD + ADJECTIVE + **gwàh gun?**:

ที่ไหนไกลกว่ากัน

têe nǎi glai gwàh gun?

Which is further?

ใครเก่งกว่ากัน
krai gèng gwàh gun?
Who is the cleverer?

เล่มไหนถูกกว่ากัน
lêm năi tòok gwàh gun?
Which book is cheaper?

6.5.4 | *Negative comparisons*

Basic negative comparison can be made by the pattern, X + **sôo** + Y + **mâi dâi:** ('X can't beat Y'):

แกงเขียวหวานร้านนี้สู้ของแม่ไม่ได้
gairng kĕe-o wăhn ráhn née sôo kŏrng mâir mâi dâi:
The green curry at this restaurant isn't as good as Mum's.

ระบอบการรักษาพยาบาลสู้ที่โน้นไม่ได้
ra-bòrp gahn rúk-săh pa-yah-bahn sôo têe nóhn mâi dâi:
Hospital treatment isn't as good as over there.

More specific negative comparisons using adjectives (e.g. Western food is not as spicy as Thai food) are often reversed to produce a positive comparison (Thai food is spicier than Western food).

6.5.5 | *Excessives*

Excessive ('too . . .') constructions follow the pattern ADJECTIVE + (**gern**) **bpai** ('too much') with **gern** frequently omitted, especially in conversational Thai:

แพง(เกิน)ไป
pairng (gern) bpai
It's too expensive.

ไกล(เกิน)ไป
glai (gern) bpai
It's too far.

รองเท้าคับ(เกิน)ไป
rorng táo: kúp (gern) bpai
The shoes are too tight.

Excessive constructions can be intensified ('much too . . .') using the pattern,
ADJECTIVE + **mâhk** ('much') + **(gern) bpai**:

แพงมาก(เกิน)ไป
pairng mâhk (gern) bpai
much too expensive

นานมาก(เกิน)ไป
nahn mâhk (gern) bpai
much too long a time

Excessive constructions, with **gern** normally omitted, can be modified by
the addition of the degree adverbs, **nòy** ('a little'), **nít-nòy** ('a little bit') or
měu-un gun ('moderately') after **bpai**:

ช้าไปหน่อย
cháh bpai nòy
a little too late

เผ็ดไปนิดหน่อย
pèt bpai nít-nòy
a little bit too spicy

ไกลไปเหมือนกัน
glai bpai měu-un gun
somewhat too far

6.5.6 | *Superlatives*

Superlative constructions follow the pattern ADJECTIVE + **têe sÒOt**
('most'):

เธอเป็นนักร้องดังที่สุดของไทย
ter bpen núk rórng dung têe sÒOt kŏrng tai
She is Thailand's most famous singer.

อันไหนถูกที่สุด
un nǎi tòok têe sÒOt?
Which is the cheapest one?

ไม่บอกดีที่สุด
mâi bòrk dee têe sÒOt
Best not to tell.

ที่สำคัญที่สุดคือ ...
têe sǔm-kun têe sÒOt keu: ...
The most important thing is ...

Chapter 7

Adverbs and adverbial constructions

7.1 Adverbs of manner

Adverbs of manner are indistinguishable in form from adjectives; thus **dee** means both 'good' and 'well' and **cháh** both 'slow' and 'slowly'.

For simplicity, the term 'adjective' is used in this chapter when describing the structure of adverbial phrases.

Verbs are modified according to the following main patterns:

1 VERB (PHRASE) + ADJECTIVE
2 VERB (PHRASE) + REDUPLICATED ADJECTIVE
3 VERB (PHRASE) + ADVERBIAL PHRASE
4 VERB (PHRASE) + **dâi** + ADJECTIVE
5 VERB (PHRASE) + **hâi** + ADJECTIVE

7.1.1 VERB (PHRASE) + ADJECTIVE

In the simplest adverbial constructions, the verb or verb phrase is followed by an adjective:

เขาเดินช้า
káo dern cháh
He walks slowly.

คุณพูดชัด
kOOn pôot chút
You speak clearly.

คุณขับรถเร็ว

kOOn kùp rót ray-o

You drive quickly.

เธอจัดห้องสวย

ter jùt hôrng sǒo-ay

She arranged the room nicely.

7.1.2 | VERB (PHRASE) + REDUPLICATED ADJECTIVE

As noted in the previous chapter (6.4), reduplication often moderates the meaning of an adjective:

เขาซื้อถูก ๆ

káo séu: tòok tòok

He bought cheap(ish)ly.

เขาเดินช้า ๆ

káo dern cháh cháh

He walks slow(ish)ly.

บ้านอยู่ใกล้ๆ

bâhn yòo glâi glâi

My house is nearby.

Sometimes, however, it is difficult to distinguish any real difference in meaning between a single and reduplicated form; in cases where the reduplicated form is preferred, it seems to be because it creates a rhythm that is more pleasing to the ear.

Reduplication is also commonly used in commands, either with or without **hâi** (see 7.1.5); commands can be made more polite by the addition of **nòy** at the end:

มาเร็ว ๆ

mah ray-o ray-o

Come quickly!

อยู่เงียบ ๆ

yòo ngêe-up ngêe-up

Stay quiet!

พูดดัง ๆ หน่อย
pôot dung dung nòy
Speak up!

Reduplication, sometimes with a different vowel in the second syllable, is also used as an onomatopoeic device, to imitate, for example, sounds of laughter, rain and animal cries:

เขาหัวเราะคิก ๆ
káo hǒo-a ró' kík kík
She giggled.

แมวร้องเมี้ยว ๆ
mair-o rórng mée-o mée-o
The cat miaowed.

ฝนตกเสียงเปาะแปะ
fǒn dtòk sěe-ung bpò' bpàir
The rain pitter-pattered.

7.1.3 | *VERB (PHRASE) + ADVERBIAL PHRASE*

Another common way of forming adverbial constructions involves the use of 'adverb formers' of which the most common are **yàhng** ('like, as'), **doy-ee** ('by'), **dôo-ay** ('with') and **bpen** ('is, as'); **yàhng** is followed by a verb or verb phrase, **doy-ee** by a verb or noun phrase, and **dôo-ay** and **bpen** by a noun phrase:

7.1.3.1 | VERB (PHRASE) + **yàhng** + VERB PHRASE

เขาพูดอย่างไม่สุภาพ
káo pôot yàhng mâi sOO-pâhp
He spoke impolitely.

เขายิ้มอย่างมีความสุข
káo yím yàhng mee kwahm sÒOk
She smiled happily.

111

ปัจจุบันเริ่มมีการแข่งขันอย่างเป็นทางการมากกว่าเมื่อก่อน

**bpùt-jOO-bun née rêrm mee gahn kàirng kǔn yàhng bpen tahng
gahn mâhk gwàh mêu-a gòrn**

Nowadays there are beginning to be more formal competitions than in
the past.

7.1.3.2 VERB (PHRASE) + **doy-ee** + VERB PHRASE

เขาพูดเสียงน่าเกลียดโดยไม่รู้ตัว

káo pôot sěe-ung nâh glèe-ut doy-ee mâi róo dtoo-a

He spoke in an unpleasant-sounding voice without realising it.

เขาสามารถซ่อมได้โดยไม่ยาก

káo sǎh-mâht sôrm dâi doy-ee mâi yâhk

He was able to repair it without difficulty.

เขาไปจีบน้องของเพื่อนโดยเปิดเผย

káo bpai jèep nórng kǒrng pêu-un doy-ee bpèrt pěr-ee

He openly pursued his friend's younger sister.

ทุกสิ่งทุกอย่างดำเนินไปโดยเรียบร้อย

tÓOk sìng tÓOk yàhng dum-nern bpai doy-ee rêe-up róy

Everything went smoothly.

For examples of VERB (PHRASE) + **doy-ee** + NOUN PHRASE, see 8.4.

7.1.3.3 VERB (PHRASE) + **dôo-ay** + NOUN PHRASE

เขาทำงานด้วยความยากลำบาก

káo tum ngahn dôo-ay kwahm yâhk lum-bàhk

He worked with difficulty.

เธอดูหนังด้วยความตั้งใจ

ter doo nǔng dôo-ay kwahm dtûng jai

She watched the film intently.

For further examples, see 8.4.

7.1.3.4 VERB (PHRASE) + bpen + NOUN PHRASE

เขาจ่ายเงินเป็นวัน ๆ

káo jài: ngern bpen wun wun

They pay daily.

เขาแบ่งเป็นชิ้นเล็ก ๆ

káo bàirng bpen chín lék lék

She divided it into small pieces.

Note that in some adverbial phrases, **bpen** is also followed by certain adjectives, such as **bpra-jum** ('regular'), **tum-ma-dah** ('ordinary'), **pí-sàyt** ('special') and **bâh** ('crazy'):

เขาสนใจประเทศจีนเป็นพิเศษ

káo sŏn jai bpra-tâyt jeen bpen pí-sàyt

He is especially interested in China.

เธอชอบดูการ์ตูนญี่ปุ่นเป็นบ้าเลย

ter chôrp doo gah-dtoon yêe-bpÒOn bpen bâh ler-ee

She's really crazy about watching Japanese cartoons.

7.1.4 VERB (PHRASE) + dâi: + ADJECTIVE

When describing how well someone can do something, the adjective follows the auxiliary verb **dâi**:

เขาพูดได้คล่อง

káo pôot dâi: klôrng

He speaks fluently.

คุณเขียนได้สวย

kOOn kĕe-un dâi: sŏo-ay

You write nicely.

เขาน่าจะทำได้ดีกว่านี้

káo nâh ja tum dâi: dee gwàh née

He ought to be able to do better than this.

7.1.5 VERB (PHRASE) + hâi + ADJECTIVE

When giving commands as to how someone should do something, the causative verb **hâi** can be used before the adjective:

กินให้หมด
gin hâi mòt
Eat everything up!

ทำให้เสร็จ
tum hâi sèt
Finish it off!

แต่งตัวให้เรียบร้อย
dtàirng dtoo-a hâi rêe-up-róy
Dress respectably!

เขียนให้ดี
kĕe-un hâi dee
Write nicely!

Such commands can be 'softened', or made less abrupt by adding **ná** at the end (see 10.3.4).

7.2 Modification of adverbs

Adverbs are modified in the same way as adjectives (see 6.2). A small number of modifiers occur in the pattern VERB (PHRASE) + MODIFIER + ADJECTIVE:

ผมเรียนไม่เก่ง
pŏm ree-un mâi gèng
I don't do well in my studies.

เขาพูดไม่ค่อยชัด
káo pôot mâi kôy chút
He doesn't speak very clearly.

ทำอาหารไทยค่อนข้างจะยุ่งยาก
tum a-hăhn tai kôrn kâhng ja yÔOng yâhk
Cooking Thai food is rather complicated.

Other adverbial modifiers follow the pattern, VERB (PHRASE) + ADJECTIVE + MODIFIER:

เขาพูดเร็วมาก
káo pôot ray-o mâhk
He speaks very quickly.

เขาแต่งตัวเรียบร้อยขึ้น
káo dtàirng dtoo-a rêe-up-róy kêun
He dresses more respectably.

7.3 Comparison of adverbs

The comparison of adverbs follows the same pattern as that of adjectives (6.5), but with a verb preceding the adjective.

The basic comparative form is VERB (PHRASE) + ADJECTIVE + **gwàh**:

แม่ทำอาหารอร่อยกว่าฉัน
mâir tum a-hăhn a-ròy gwàh chún
My mother is a better cook than me.
(mother – make – food – tasty – more than – me)

พี่ชายเรียนหนังสือเก่งกว่าผม
pêe-chai: ree-un núng-sěu: gèng gwàh pŏm
My older brother was a better student than me.

7.3.1 Equal comparisons

Equal comparisons can be expressed as follows:

7.3.1.1 X + VERB (PHRASE) + ADJECTIVE + **tâo (tâo) gùp/ por (por) gùp** + Y

ฉันฝึกมานานเท่า(ๆ)กับ/พอ(ๆ)กับพี่
chún fèuk mah nahn tâo (tâo) gùp/por (por) gùp pêe
I've been practising as long as my sister.

ภาษาไทยพูดยากเท่า(ๆ)กับ/พอ(ๆ)กับภาษาเขมร
pah-săh tai pôot yâhk tâo (tâo) gùp/por (por) gùp pah-săh ka-măyn
Thai is as difficult to speak as Cambodian.

7.3.1.2 X + **gùp** + Y + VERB (PHRASE) + ADJECTIVE +
tâo (tâo) gun/por (por) gun

ฉันกับพี่ฝึกมานานเท่า(ๆ)กัน/พอ(ๆ)กัน

chún gùp pêe fèuk mah nahn tâo (tâo) gun/por (por) gun

My sister and I have been practising as long as each other.

ภาษาไทยกับภาษาเขมรพูดยากเท่า(ๆ)กัน/พอ(ๆ)กัน

**pah-săh tai gùp pah-săh ka-măyn pôot yâhk tâo (tâo) gun/
  por (por) gun**

Thai and Cambodian are as difficult to speak as each other.

7.3.1.3 X + VERB (PHRASE) + ADJECTIVE + **měu-un** + Y

ลูกสาวแต่งตัวสวยเหมือนดาราหนัง

lôok săo: dtàirng dtoo-a sŏo-ay měu-un dah-rah nŭng

Her daughter dresses as beautifully as a film star.

เธอทำกับข้าวอร่อยเหมือนแม่ครัวมืออาชีพ

ter tum gùp kâo a-ròy měu-un mâir kroo-a meu: ah-chêep

She cooks as tasty dishes as a professional chef.

7.3.2 *Excessive*

The excessive construction is VERB (PHRASE) + ADJECTIVE + (gern) **bpai**:

เขาหมดความอดทนเร็ว(เกิน)ไป

káo mòt kwahm òt ton ray-o (gern) bpai

He loses patience too quickly.

ไม่ต้องพยายามมาก(เกิน)ไป

mâi dtôrng pa-yah-yahm mâhk (gern) bpai

There's no need to try too hard.

7.3.3 *Superlative*

The superlative construction is VERB (PHRASE) + ADJECTIVE + **têe sÒOt**:

เธอร้องเพลงฝรั่งเพราะที่สุด

ter rórng playng fa-rùng pró' têe sÒOt

She sings Western songs the best.

พี่มาลีทำส้มตำอร่อยที่สุด

pêe mah-lee tum sôm dtum a-ròy têe sÒOt

Malee makes the tastiest papaya salad.

7.3.4 | *'As ... as possible'*

The 'as ... as possible' construction can be expressed in two ways, the first involving the repetition of the adjective and the second using the verb **tum** ('to do') instead of the repeated adjective:

7.3.4.1 | VERB (PHRASE) + **yàhng** + ADJECTIVE + **têe sÒOt** + (**tâo**) **têe ja** + ADJECTIVE + **dâi**

เขาวิ่งอย่างเร็วที่สุด(เท่า)ที่จะเร็วได้

káo wîng yàhng ray-o têe sÒOt têe ja ray-o dâi

He ran as quickly as possible

7.3.4.2 | VERB (PHRASE) + **yàhng** + ADJECTIVE + **têe sÒOt** + (**tâo**) **têe ja** + **tum** + **dâi**:

ผมจะทำอย่างดีที่สุด(เท่า)ที่จะทำได้

pǒm ja tum yàhng dee têe sÒOt (tâo) têe ja tum dâi

I shall do it as well as possible.

7.4 Adverbs of time

Since verbs do not indicate tense in Thai, adverbs and adverbial phrases are essential to specify when events take place.

Common adverbial phrases of time include:

Present:	เดี๋ยวนี้	dĕe-o née	now, at this moment
	ตอนนี้	dtorn née	now
	ปัจจุบันนี้	bpùt-jÒO-bun née	nowadays
	ทุกวันนี้	tÓOk wun née	these days
Past:	เมื่อก่อน	mêu-a gòrn	before, formerly
	ตอนนั้น	dtorn nún	at that time
	เมื่อกี้นี้	mêu-a gêe née	a minute ago
Future:	พรุ่งนี้	prÔOng née	tomorrow
	วันหลัง	wun lǔng	another day, some other day
	ครั้งหน้า	krúng nâh	next time

These adverbial phrases can occur either before the verb or after:

ตอนนี้เขาไม่ว่าง
dtorn née káo mâi wâhng
He is not free at the moment.

เมื่อก่อนฉันไม่ชอบ
mêu-a gòrn chún mâi chôrp
Before, I did not like it.

ผมจะไปเยี่ยมวันหลัง
pǒm ja bpai yêe-um wun lǔng
I'll go to visit her another day.

A more extensive list of time expressions appears in 14.7.

Two important adverbs of time which do have a fixed position are, **yung** ('still') and **láir-o** ('already'). **yung** occurs before the main verb and **láir-o** after the main verb:

ฉันยังหิว
chún yung hěw
I'm still hungry.

เรายังคิดอยู่
rao yung kít yòo
We're still thinking about it.

เขาไปแล้ว
káo bpai láir-o
He's already gone.

ใช่ ผมรู้แล้ว
châi, pǒm róo láir-o
Yes, I (already) know.

7.5 Adverbs of frequency

The following adverbs of frequency occur only after a verb or verb phrase:

บ่อย ๆ	**bòy bòy**	often
เสมอ	**sa-měr**	always
เรื่อย ๆ	**rêu-ay rêu-ay**	continuously
เป็นประจำ	**bpen bpra-jum**	regularly
เป็นระยะ ๆ	**bpen ra-yá ra-yá**	periodically

เราไปเที่ยวเมืองไทยบ่อย ๆ
rao bpai têe-o meu-ung tai bòy bòy
We visit Thailand often.

เขาทำอาหารเผ็ดเสมอ
káo tum ah-hǎhn pèt sa-měr
She always makes spicy food.

ฉันไปดูหนังเป็นระยะ ๆ
chún bpai doo nǔng bpen ra-yá ra-yá
I go to the cinema occasionally.

The words **tum-ma-dah** ('normally, usually') and **bpòk-ga-dtì** ('normally, usually') both occur more commonly at the beginning of a sentence:

ธรรมดาผมไม่กินเหล้า
tum-ma-dah pǒm mâi gin lâo
Normally I don't drink alcohol.

ปกติมีคนมากกว่านี้
bpòk-ga-dtì mee kon mâhk gwàh née
Usually there are more people than this.

Other expressions of frequency, such as **bahng krúng** ('sometimes'), **tÓOk wun** ('daily'), **ah-tít la sǒrng krúng** ('twice a week'), can occur either at the beginning of a sentence or at the end:

บางครั้งผมรู้สึกเบื่อ
bahng krúng pǒm róo-sèuk bèu-a
Sometimes I feel bored.

ฉันมักจะโทรไปคุยกับคุณแม่ทุกวัน
chún múk ja toh bpai koo-ee gùp kOOn mâir tÓOk wun
I usually telephone my mother every day.

เขาไปเล่นดนตรีกับเพื่อนอาทิตย์ละสองครั้ง
káo bpai lên don-dtree gùp pêu-un ah-tít la sǒrng krúng
He goes to play music with his friends twice a week.

7.6 Adverbs of degree

The following adverbs of degree occur only after a verb or verb phrase:

มาก	**mâhk**	a lot, very much, really
บ้าง	**bâhng**	somewhat
เหมือนกัน	**měu-un gun**	somewhat, fairly/reasonably
นิดหน่อย	**nít-nòy**	a little (bit)
หน่อย	**nòy**	a little

เขาเมามาก
káo mao mâhk
He's really drunk.

ฉันหิวนิดหน่อย
chún hěw nít-nòy
I'm a bit hungry.

ทนหน่อยนะ
ton nòy ná
Be a little patient!

měu-un gun is widely used to express qualified or polite agreement or enthusiasm. It commonly occurs in the pattern, **gôr . . .** + VERB (PHRASE) + **měu-un gun** when a negative response would be tactless:

อาจารย์สอนดีไหม
ah-jahn sŏrn dee mái?
Is he a good teacher?

– ก็ . . . ดี เหมือนกัน
– **gôr . . . dee měu-un gun**
– Well . . . yes.

While **mâhk** and **nít-nòy** also occur as quantifiers (13.12), it is important to distinguish between the adverb **bâhng** and the similar-sounding quantifier **bahng**; with both words commonly glossed as 'some' in Thai-English dictionaries, they are easily confused by the learner.

As a quantifier, **bahng** ('some') is always followed by a classifier, although it is not always preceded by a noun:

ฉันชอบกินอาหารแขกบางอย่าง
chún chôrp gin ah-hăhn kàirk bahng yàhng
I like some kinds of Indian food.

บางคนดีบางคนไม่ดี
bahng kon dee bahng kon mâi dee
Some people are good, some are bad.

bâhng normally modifies a verb and conveys the sense of 'to some extent' or 'somewhat'. It also occurs in Wh- questions, where it anticipates a plural answer (12.2.13). **bâhng** never occurs with classifiers.

เขาพูดภาษาไทยได้บ้าง
káo pôot pah-săh tai dâi bâhng
He speaks some Thai.

ผมเล่นได้บ้าง

pǒm lên dâi bâhng

I can play a bit.

ฉันอยากไปกินอาหารแขกบ้าง

chún yàhk bpai gin ah-hǎhn kàirk bâhng

(I – like – go – eat – food – Indian – somewhat)

I'd like to eat some Indian food.

เขาพูดจริงบ้าง ไม่จริงบ้าง

káo pôot jing bâhng mâi jing bâhng

(he – speak – true – somewhat – not – true – somewhat)

Some of what he says is true, some isn't.

หัดพูดความจริงบ้างซิ

hùt pôot kwahm jing bâhng sí

(practise – speak – truth – somewhat – *command particle*)

Try telling the truth!

คุณพบกับใครบ้าง

kOOn póp gùp krai bâhng?

Who did you meet?

One curious usage of **bâhng** is in the expression **bâhng gôr . . . bâhng gôr . . .** ('some people . . . and some people . . .'), which is identical in meaning to **bahng kon**:

บ้างก็ดี บ้างก็ไม่ดี

bâhng gôr dee bâhng gôr mâi dee

Some people are good, some are bad.

บ้างก็ชอบ บ้างก็ไม่ชอบ

bâhng gôr chôrp bâhng gôr mâi chôrp

Some people like it, some don't.

Chapter 8

Location markers and other prepositions

An important function of prepositions is to indicate location. This chapter introduces the major location markers and then looks at a few of the different ways of dealing with the English prepositions, 'to', 'for', 'by', 'with' and 'from'.

8.1 Location: têe and yòo

The most basic location words are formed using the preposition **têe** ('at') followed by the demonstratives, **nêe, nûn** or **nôhn** (3.5.4):

ที่นี่	**têe nêe**	here
ที่นั่น	**têe nûn**	there
ที่โน่น	**têe nôhn**	over there

In a simple sentence stating the location of something, **têe** follows the verb **yòo** ('to be situated at'):

อยู่ที่นี่
yòo têe nêe
Here it is / It's here.

บ้านอยู่ที่โน่น
bâhn yòo têe nôhn
The house is over there.

têe is optional after the verb **yòo**, and frequently omitted:

ฉันอยู่เมืองไทยนาน
chún yòo meu-ung tai nahn
I have lived in Thailand a long time.

เขาอยู่บ้านตอนเย็น
káo yòo bâhn dtorn yen
He is at home in the evenings.

8.1.1 | kûng + PREPOSITION

The following prepositions can all be prefixed by **kûng** ('side'); although
it is written with a long vowel in the Thai script, it is normally pronounced
as a short vowel when it occurs before a preposition.

ใน	**nai**	in
นอก	**nôrk**	outside of
บน	**bon**	on, on top of; upstairs
ล่าง	**lâhng**	underneath; downstairs
หน้า	**nâh**	in front of
หลัง	**lǔng**	behind
ข้าง	**kâhng**	by the side of

However, when a noun or noun phrase follows the preposition, **kûng** is
usually dropped:

อยู่ในรถ
yòo nai rót
It's in the car.

จอดหลังบ้านได้ไหม
jòrt lǔng bâhn dâi mái?
Can I park behind the house?

But if no noun follows the preposition, **kûng** cannot be dropped:

อยู่ข้างนอก
yòo kûng nôrk
It's outside.

อยู่ข้างบน
yòo kûng bon
It's on top/upstairs.

วางไว้ข้างๆ เก้าอี้
wahng wái kûng kâhng gâo êe
I put it down by the side of the chair.

8.1.2 | pai: + *PREPOSITION*

Several of the prepositions above (8.1) can be prefixed by **pai:** ('side, part'):

ภายใน	**pai: nai**	within, internal, inner
ภายนอก	**pai: nôrk**	outside, external, outer
ภายใต้	**pai: dtâi:**	under, inferior position
ภายหน้า	**pai: nâh**	ahead, in the future
ภายหลัง	**pai: lǔng**	afterwards, later on

ภายในเจ็ดวัน
pai: nai jèt wun
within seven days

ภายใต้อิทธิพลของเขา
pai: dtâi: ìt-tí-pon kǒrng káo
under his influence

ความสัมพันธ์ภายนอก
kwahm sǔm-pun pai: nôrk
external relations

8.1.3 | tahng + right/left

tahng ('way') prefixes the words for **sái:** ('left') and **kwǎh** ('right') when describing locations; **meu:** ('hand') may optionally be added to the end of the phrase:

อยู่ทางขวา
yòo tahng kwǎh
It's on the right.

อยู่ทางซ้ายมือ
yòo tahng sái: meu:
It's on the left-hand side.

8.1.4 | *Non-prefixed prepositions*

Common location prepositions which do not take any prefix include:

ระหว่าง	**ra-wàhng**	between
ไกล	**glai**	far
ใกล้	**glâi**	near
ตรงข้าม	**dtrong kâhm**	opposite
ริม	**rim**	on the edge of
ตาม	**dtahm**	along

ไปรษณีย์อยู่ตรงข้ามวัด
bprai-sa-nee yòo dtrong kâhm wút
The post office is opposite a temple.

เดินไปตามถนนใหญ่จนถึงสี่แยก
dern bpai dtahm ta-non yài jon tĕung sèe yâirk
Walk along the main road until you reach the crossroads.

เพื่อนเช่าบ้านอยู่ริมคลองรังสิต
pêu-un châo bâhn yòo rim klorng rung-sìt
My friend is renting a house on the edge of Khlong Rangsit/Rangsit Canal.

เราจะไปซื้อตามตลาด
rao ja bpai séu: dtahm dta-làht*
We're going to go and buy one in the market.
*(note the use of **dtahm** 'along' rather than **nai** 'in')

8.2 'To'

Neither motion towards a place ('I went *to* Thailand'), nor the indirect object with 'to give' ('He gave it *to* me'; see 5.12) require prepositions in Thai; speaking *to* someone, uses the preposition **gùp** ('with'):

ผมเดินทางไปเมืองไทย
pǒm dern thang bpai meu-ung tai
I travelled to Thailand.

เขาให้หนังสือฉัน
káo hâi núng-sěu chún
He gave the book to me.

ฉันอยากจะพูดกับเขา
chún yàhk ja pôot gùp káo
I'd like to speak to him.

8.3 'For'

The Thai words most commonly used to translate 'for' are **hâi, pêu-a, sǔm-rùp** and **sòo-un**. While the distinctions are sometimes elusive and there is some overlap in usage, some broad principles can be applied:

8.3.1 hâi

hâi is used to express the idea of doing something for somebody, or getting somebody to do something for you; it is commonly used in polite requests (15.4.4).

เขาซื้อหนังสือให้ฉัน
káo séu: núng-sěu: hâi chún
He bought a book for me.

ผมจะบอก(เขา)ให้(คุณ)
pǒm ja bòrk (káo) hâi (kOOn)
I'll tell him for you.

ช่วยใส่กล่องกลับบ้านให้(ฉัน)ด้วย
chôo-ay sài glòrng glùp bâhn hâi (chún) dôo-ay
Please put it in a take-away box for me.

8.3.2 | pêu-a

pêu-a can be translated as 'for the sake of' and often conveys an idea of altruism or self-sacrifice; it also occurs in purpose clauses, meaning 'in order to' (9.2.4). Note also low-tone pèu-a, which is used when inviting someone to do something on one's behalf in expressions like *Have one (e.g. a beer) for me*:

ทุกสิ่งทุกอย่างผมทำเพื่อคุณ
tÓOk sìng tÓOk yàhng pŏm tum pêu-a kOOn
Everything I do is for you.

ฉันทำงานเพื่ออนาคตของเรา
chún tum ngahn pêu-a a-nah-kót kŏrng rao
I am working for our future.

เขาเสียสละตัวเองเพื่อประเทศชาติ
káo sĕe-a sa-là dtoo-a ayng pêu-a bpra-tâyt châht
He sacrificed himself for the nation.

เราซื้ออาหารเพื่อบริจาค
rao séu a-hăhn pêu-a bor-rí-jàhk
We bought food for donating.

กินเผื่อด้วยนะ
gin pèu-a dôo-ay ná
Eat some for me, too, OK?

8.3.3 | sŭm-rùp

sŭm-rùp means both 'for' and, at the beginning of a sentence, 'as for', 'as far as . . . is concerned' (see 9.1):

นี่สำหรับคุณ
nêe sŭm-rùp kOOn
This is for you.

สำหรับอาหารเย็นเราจะไปกินข้างนอก
sŭm-rùp ah-hăhn yen rao ja bpai gin kûng nôrk
As far as the evening meal is concerned, we will eat out.

8.3.4 sòo-un

sòo-un also means 'as for' and is used to introduce a statement (see 9.1):

ส่วนผมคิดว่าไม่ดีเลย
sòo-un pŏm kít wâh mâi dee ler-ee
As for me, I don't think it is good at all.

Two other common uses of 'for' in English are to express duration of time ('I have been studying Thai *for* three years') and to give reasons ('I am angry with him *for* gossiping about me'). Duration of time requires no preposition in Thai (14.7.5), while reason clauses are introduced by the relative pronoun **têe**:

ผมเรียนภาษาไทยมาสามปีแล้ว
pŏm ree-un pah-săh tai mah săhm bpee láir-o
I have been studying Thai for three years.

เราไปสองวันเท่านั้น
rao bpai sŏrng wun tâo-nún
We are only going for three days.

ฉันโกรธเขาที่(เขา)นินทาฉัน
chún gròht káo têe (káo) nin-tah chún
I am angry with him for gossiping about me.

ขอโทษที่ผมมาช้า
kŏr-tôht têe pŏm mah cháh
I am sorry for being late.

8.4 'By'

The two Thai words most commonly used to translate 'by' are **doy-ee** and **dôo-ay**; both are used to indicate the means of doing something.

ฉันไปโดยรถเมล์
chún bpai doy-ee rót may*
I went by bus.

* Note, however, that while **doy-ee** can be used with all means of transportation, in practice it is commonly avoided. Instead, travelling somewhere as a passenger in a vehicle is expressed by the pattern, **nûng** ('to sit') + VEHICLE + **bpai/mah** + PLACE:

คุณทำด้วย/โดยวิธีไหน

kOOn tum dôo-ay/doy-ee wí-tee năi?

How did you do it? (you – do – by – method – which?)

คุณทำด้วยมือหรือ

kOOn tum dôo-ay meu: lěr?

You did it by hand, then?

เขาเขียนด้วยความยากลำบาก

káo kěe-un dôo-ay kwahm yâhk lum-bàhk

He writes with difficulty.

ฉันนั่งรถเมล์ไปเชียงใหม่

chún nûng rót may bpai chee-ung mài

I went to Chiangmai by bus.

To indicate that someone drove the vehicle, **nûng** is replaced by an appropriate verb meaning 'to drive' – **kùp** (for cars), **kèe** (for motorcycles, horses, bicycles) or **tèep** (for pedal trishaws):

ผมขับรถมา

pŏm kùp rót mah

I came by car (as the driver)/I drove here.

เราขี่มอเตอร์ไซค์ไปหัวหิน

rao kèe mor-dter-sai bpai hŏo-a hĭn

We drove to Hua Hin by motorcycle.

'By' in English is also used to indicate (i) the agent in a passive sentence (He was hit *by* a car: 5.8), (ii) place (It is *by* the television) and (iii) time limitation (I must finish *by* Friday). As a location word, 'by' can be translated as **glâi glâi** ('near') or **kûng kâhng** ('next to, beside'); time limit can be conveyed by **gòrn** ('before') or **pai: nai** ('within'):

อยู่ใกล้ ๆ / ข้าง ๆ ทีวี

yòo glâi glâi / kûng kâhng tee wee

It is by the TV.

ฉันจะทำให้เสร็จก่อนพรุ่งนี้

chún ja tum hâi sèt gòrn prÔOng-née

I shall finish it by tomorrow.

เราต้องตัดสินใจภายในวันศุกร์

rao dtôrng dtùt sĭn jai pai: nai wun sÒOk

We have to decide by Friday.

8.5 'With'

'With' in English is used mainly to indicate (i) accompaniment (I went *with* a friend) and (ii) instrument (She hit her husband *with* a stick). Accompaniment, in Thai, is conveyed by **gùp**:

ฉันไปกับเพื่อน

chún bpai gùp pêu-un

I went with a friend.

Instrument is less clear-cut. **dôo-ay** can be used in the pattern, SUBJECT + VERB (PHRASE) + **dôo-ay** + INSTRUMENT, but it often sounds unnatural; instead, many native speakers favour the pattern, SUBJECT + **chái** ('to use') + INSTRUMENT + VERB (PHRASE):

เขาเคยมาเมืองไทยด้วยทุน AFS

káo ker-ee mah meu-ung tai dôo-ay tOOn AFS

He's been to Thailand with/on an AFS scholarship.

เธอใช้ไม้ตีผัว

ter chái mái: dtee pŏo-a

She hit her husband with a stick.

เราต้องใช้มือกิน

rao dtôrng chái meu: gin

We shall have to eat with our fingers.

And **gùp** is also sometimes used to indicate instrument in the expressions **hĕn gùp dtah** ('to see with one's own eyes') and **fung gùp hŏo** ('to hear with one's own ears').

'From'

'From' can most frequently be translated by **jàhk**:

เขามาจากเชียงใหม่

káo mah jàhk chee-ung mài

He comes from Chiangmai.

ฉันได้จดหมายจากแม่

chún dâi jòt-mǎi: jàhk mâir

I got a letter from my mother.

เรานั่งรถเมล์จากหัวหินไปกรุงเทพ ๆ

rao nûng rót may jàhk hǒo-a hǐn bpai grOOng-tâyp

We went from Hua Hin to Bangkok by bus.

When 'from' identifies the beginning of a period of time, **dtûng-dtàir** ('since') is used, either in the pattern, **dtûng-dtàir** + TIME WORD + **tĕung** ('till') + TIME WORD, or **dtûng-dtàir** + TIME WORD + **mah**:

ตั้งแต่เช้าถึงเย็น

dtûng-dtàir cháo: tĕung yen

from morning till evening

ตั้งแต่ปีสองพันห้าร้อยสี่สิบมา

dtûng-dtàir bpee sŏrng pun hâh róy sèe sìp mah

from the year 2540/since 2540

ตั้งแต่วันนั้นมา

dtûng-dtàir wun nún mah

from that day

Chapter 9

Clauses and sentences

Word order and topicalisation

Word order in a sentence generally follows the pattern, SUBJECT + VERB + OBJECT:

subject	verb	object
พ่อ	ซื้อ	รถ
pôr	**séu:**	**rót**
Father	bought	a car
ฉัน	รัก	คุณ
chún	**rúk**	**kOOn**
I	love	you

In spoken Thai it is common for the subject noun to be followed immediately by its pronoun. The beginner needs to be alert to distinguish this noun-pronoun apposition from similar-looking possessive phrases (3.5.12):

พ่อเขาซื้อรถ
pôr káo séu: rót
(father – he – buy – car)
Father bought a car.

ครูเขาไม่มา
kroo káo mâi mah
(teacher – he – not – come)
The teacher didn't come.

รถมันติด

rót mun dtìt

(cars – they – stuck)

The traffic is jammed.

However, either subject or object, or even both, may be omitted when they are understood from the context. In the following sentence, for example, subject, direct object, and indirect object are not stated, leaving just a sequence of four verbs (5.13):

ต้องรีบไปซื้อให้

dtôrng rêep bpai séu hâi

(must – hurry – go – buy – for)

I must rush off and buy some for her.

Another extremely common pattern, known as topicalisation, involves placing a word or phrase other than the subject at the beginning of the sentence, so that it becomes the 'topic' of the sentence (i.e. what the sentence is 'about').

เสื้อเก่าๆ จะเอาไปบริจาคพรุ่งนี้

sêu-a gào gào ja ao bpai bor-ri-jàhk prÔOng née

(clothes – old – old – will – take – donate – tomorrow)

I'll give away the old clothes tomorrow.

อาหารที่เหลือเราจะเก็บไว้กินพรุ่งนี้

ah-hăhn têe lĕu-a rao ja gèp wái gin prÔOng née

(food – which – remains – we – will – keep – eat – tomorrow)

We'll save the food that's left over and eat it tomorrow.

คนไทยที่แต่งงานกับฝรั่งเดียวนี้มีเยอะ

kon tai têe dtàirng ngahn gùp fa-rùng dĕe-o née mee yér

(Thais – who – marry – with – Westerners – now – there are – many)

Now there are lots of Thais who are married to Westerners.

ผู้หญิงคนนั้นคิดว่าคงเป็นคนญี่ปุ่น

pôo-yĭng kon nún kít wâh kong bpen kon yêe-bpÒOn

(girl – *classifier* – that – (I) – think – that – is – bound to be – person – Japanese)

I think that girl is probably Japanese.

ความรักไม่มีใครเข้าใจได้

kwahm rúk mâi mee krai kâo jai dâi:

(love – there is not – anyone – understand – can)

No one can understand love.

ค่ารถจากสุรินทร์มาแต่ละที สมจิตก็ออกให้แม่

kâh rót jàhk sŎO-rin mah dtàir la tee sŏm-jìt gôr òrk hâi mâir

(bus fare – from – Surin – come – each time – Somjit – then – pays for –
mother)

Every time, Somjit pays her mother's bus fare from Surin.

เงินเดือนสมจิตเดือนละ ๘๐๐ นั้น แม่ยังคงมาเอาไป
หมดเหมือนเดิม

**ngern deu-un sŏm-jìt deu-un la sèe pun nún mâir yung kong mah
ao bpai mòt mĕu-un derm**

(salary – Somjit – per month – 4,000 – the – mother – still – bound to –
come – take – all – like before)

Her mother is still sure to come and take all of Somjit's 4,000 (baht)
monthly salary.

A topic may be introduced by **rêu-ung** ('about, concerning'), **sòo-un** ('as
for') or **sŭm-rùp** ('as for'). In spoken Thai, the particle **nâ/nâh** is often
used at the end of the topic phrase (10.3.5), while in written Thai the end
of a topic clause is often marked by **nún** and the verb in the following
clause introduced by **gôr** ('so, therefore, well, then'):

เรื่องทรงผมนักเรียนนะ มันมาจากรัฐเผด็จการ

rêu-ung song pŏm núk ree-un ná mun mah jàhk rút pa-dèt-gahn

As for school children's hairstyles, they come from a dictatorial state.

เรื่องผู้หญิงในชีวิตของผม ยังไม่จบแน่นอน เพราะใน
บทนี้เขียนเรื่องแม่เท่านั้น

**rêu-ung pôo-yĭng nai chee-wít kŏrng pŏm yung mâi jòp nâir-norn
pró' nai bòt née kĕe-un rêu-ung mâir tâo-nún**

As for women in my life, that's not the end, of course, because in this
chapter I've written only about my mother.

ส่วนหนังสือ English-Thai Dictionary ก็ได้เขียนเสร็จเมื่อปี
พ.ศ. ๒๕๐๘

sòo-un núng-sĕu: English-Thai Dictionary **gôr dâi kĕe-un sèt mêu-a
bpee por sŏr sŏrng pun hâh róy bpàirt**

As for the *English-Thai Dictionary*, he finished writing it in BE 2508.

ส่วนกรรมวิธีและมารยาทในการดื่มไวน์ก็ยิ่งเต็มไปด้วย
ความสลับซับซ้อน

**sòo-un gum-ma-wí-tee lair mah-ra-yâht nai gahn dèu:m wai gôr
yîng dtem bpai dôo-ay kwahm sa-lùp súp sórn**

As for the procedure and etiquette in drinking wine, it is even more full
of complexities.

สำหรับปัญหาด้านการเงินนั้น เขาบอกว่า แม้จะมีปัญหา
บ้าง แต่ไม่เคยถือว่าเป็นความทุกข์

**sŭm-rùp bpun-hăh dâhn gahn ngern nún káo bòrk wâh máir ja mee
bpun-hăh bâhng dtàir mâi ker-ee tĕu: wâh bpen kwahm tÓOk**

As for money problems, he said that although there were some problems,
he had never regarded himself as being unhappy.

สำหรับกรณีของเสรีไทยในอังกฤษ ดูจะซับซ้อนกว่าใน
กรณีของสหรัฐ

**sŭm-rùp go-ra-nee kŏrng sáy-ree tai nai ung-grìt doo ja súp sórn
gwàh nai go-ra-nee kŏrng sa-hà-rút**

As for the case of the Seri Thai [WWII resistance group] in England,
it appears it was more complex than the case in America.

9.2   Subordinate clauses

Subordinate clauses frequently occur before the main clause. Some
subordinate and main clauses are linked by paired conjunctions, one at
the beginning of each clause. **gôr** (see 9.1), although often optional, is used
extensively in introducing the main clause. Some common examples of
paired conjunctions are:

ถ้า(หากว่า)...ก็...   **tâh (hâhk wâh)...gôr...**
                        if...then...(9.2.1)

(การ)ที่...ก็...   **gahn têe...gôr...**
                        the fact that...so/therefore...(9.2.2)

(ถึง)แม้ว่า...แต่...   **tĕung máir wâh...dtàir...**
                        although...but...(9.2.3)

นอกจาก(นั้นแล้ว)ยัง   **nôrk jàhk (nún láir-o)...yung...**
                        apart from (that)...still...(9.2.5)

ยิ่ง...(ก็)ยิ่ง...   **yîng...(gôr) yîng...**
                        the more...the more...(9.2.6)

9.2.1 | *Conditional clauses: 'if'*

Conditional sentences can be formed by the pattern, **tâh...gôr** + VERB
('If..., then...'); alternative words for 'if' are **tâh hâhk wâh, hâhk wâh,
hâhk dtàir wâh**:

ถ้า(หากว่า)ฝนตกฉันก็ไม่ไป
tâh (hâhk wâh) fŏn dtòk chún gôr mâi bpai
If it rains, I'm not going / If it had rained, I wouldn't have gone, etc.

Often, however, the 'if' word is omitted, and in abrupt speech, even **gôr**, too:

ฝนตกฉัน(ก็)ไม่ไป
fŏn dtòk chún (gôr) mâi bpai
If it rains, I'm not going / If it had rained, I wouldn't have gone, etc.

ไม่มีกิจห้ามเข้า
mâi mee gìt hâhm kâo
(not – have – business – forbidden – to enter)
No entry to unauthorised persons.

The conditional clause and main clause may be linked by **lá gôr**, in which
case the verb normally follows:

(ถ้าคุณ)ไม่รีบละก็ไม่ทัน
(tâh kOOn) mâi rêep lá gôr mâi tun
If you don't hurry, you won't be in time.

Frustratingly elusive for most beginners are expressions consisting of the
same verb in the pattern VERB + **gôr** + VERB, with **tâh** omitted:

ไปก็ไป
bpai gôr bpai
If we're going, then let's go.

กินก็กิน
gin gôr gin
If you're going to eat, then go ahead and eat.

ซื้อก็ซื้อ
séu: gôr séu:
If you're going to buy it, then go ahead and buy it.

9.2.2 | Reason clauses: 'the fact that/because', 'owing to'

Reason clauses commonly involve the expression, **gahn têe** ('the fact that'), which can be used in two patterns:

(a) **gahn têe . . . gôr + prór wâh . . .** ('The fact that . . . is because . . .')

In this pattern, the consequence is stated first and the reason or cause given in the second clause:

การที่ผมไม่ได้บอกเขาตรงไปตรงมาก็เพราะว่าผมกลัว
**gahn têe pǒm mâi dâi bòrk káo dtrong bpai dtrong mah gôr
    prór wâh pǒm gloo-a**
The fact that I didn't tell him frankly was because I was scared.

การที่คนขับรถวิ่งหนีก็คงเพราะว่าเขาเมา
gahn têe kon kùp rót wîng něe gôr kong prór wâh káo mao
The fact that the driver ran away was probably because he was drunk.

(b) **gahn têe . . . gôr + VERB (PHRASE)** (The fact that/Because . . . so . . .)

In this pattern, the reason or cause is stated in the first clause and the consequence or conclusion follows in the second:

การที่คุณไปอ่านประวัติศาสตร์ประเทศนั้นเป็นของดี
แต่อย่าเชื่อเขาทีเดียวนัก
**gahn têe kOOn bpai àhn bpra-wùt-sàht bpra-tâyt nún bpen
    kǒrng dee; dtàir yàh chêu-a káo tee dee-o núk**
The fact that you went and read the history of the country is good; but
    don't believe everything they say.

การที่เพื่อนนักโทษการเมืองต้องสูญเสียชีวิตไปถึงหก
คนในชั่วระยะเวลาเพียงหกสัปดาห์ ทำลายขวัญ
นักโทษการเมืองที่เหลืออยู่อย่างยิ่ง

**gahn têe pêu-un núk tôht gahn meu-ung dtôrng sĕe-a chee-wít
bpai tĕung hòk kon nai chôo-a rá-yá way-lah pee-ung hòk sùp-
bpa-dàh tum lai: kwŭn núk tôht gahn meu-ung têe lĕu-a yòo
yàhng yîng**

The fact that as many as six of their fellow political prisoners died within
the space of just six weeks thoroughly destroyed the morale of the
remaining political prisoners.

In both pattern (a) and (b) it is not unusual for **gahn** to be dropped and
the sentence to begin with **têe:**

ที่ผมพูดอย่างนั้นก็เพราะว่าโกรธ

têe pŏm pôot yàhng nún gôr prór wâh gròht

The fact that I spoke like that was because I was angry.

ที่เขายังไม่กลับมาฉันก็ต้องรออยู่

têe káo yung mâi glùp mah chún gôr dtôrng ror yòo

The fact he hasn't come back yet, I shall have to wait.

'Owing/due to . . .' sentences follow a similar pattern but are prefaced by
nêu-ung jàhk, or the rather more formal-sounding **nêu-ung (mah) jàhk gahn
têe . . .** ('owing to the fact that . . .'):

เนื่องจากประเทศอเมริกากว้างใหญ่ไพศาล พลเมืองที่อยู่
ในภาคต่างๆ ก็มีค่านิยมและวิถีดำเนินชีวิตแตกต่างกัน
ออกไป

**nêu-ung jàhk bpra-tâyt a-may-ri-gah gwâhng yài pai-săhn pon-la-
meu-ung têe yòo nai pâhk dtàhng dtàhng gôr mee kâh ní-yom
láir wí-tĕe dum-nern chee-wít dtàirk dtàhng gun òrk bpai**

Due to the fact that America is a vast country, its citizens who live in
different regions have differing values and ways of life.

9.2.3 | Concessive clauses: 'although'

Concessive clauses concede or admit a fact and begin with either **(tĕung) máir wâh . . . dtàir . . .** ('although') or **túng túng têe** ('although'); the main clause counters or contradicts that fact and frequently begins with **dtàir** ('but'):

(ถึง)แม้ว่าฉันใส่น้ำปลาเยอะแต่ยังไม่อร่อย

(tĕung) máir wâh chún sài núm bplah yér dtàir yung mâi a-ròy

Although I put a lot of fish sauce in, it still doesn't taste good.

ทั้ง ๆ ที่ฝนยังตกหนักอยู่แต่เรา(ก็)ยังคิดจะไป

túng túng têe fŏn yung dtòk nùk yòo dtàir rao (gôr) yung kít ja bpai

Although it's still raining heavily, we're still planning to go.

Another kind of concessive clause is formed by the pattern, **mâi wâh ja** ('regardless, no matter') + VERB + QUESTION WORD; the main clause may be introduced by **gôr**.

ไม่ว่าจะแพงแค่ไหน(ก็)ยังรู้สึกคุ้ม

mâi wâh ja pairng kâir năi gôr yung róo-sèuk kÓOm

Regardless of how expensive it was, I still think it was worth it.

ไม่ว่าจะเดินไปไหนก็จะเห็นแต่คนหน้าบึ้ง

mâi wâh ja dern bpai năi gôr ja hĕn dtàir kon nâh bêung

No matter where you walk, you see only people with sullen faces.

ไม่ว่าจะบอกกี่ครั้งเขาก็คงไม่ยอมฟัง

mâi wâh ja bòrk gèe krúng káo gôr kong mâi yorm fung

No matter how many times you tell him, he won't listen.

9.2.4 | Purpose clauses: 'in order to'

Purpose clauses often begin with **pêu-a (têe) ja** ('in order to'):

เขากินอาหารถูก ๆ เพื่อ(ที่)จะประหยัดเงิน

káo gin ah-hăhn tòok tòok pêu-a (têe) ja bpra-yùt ngern

He eats cheap food in order to economise.

ผมทำอย่างนั้นเพื่อ(ที่)จะช่วยเพื่อน

pŏm tum yàhng nún pêu-a (têe) ja chôo-ay pêu-un

I did that in order to help a friend.

เราจะเดินทางกลางคืนเพื่อจะได้ไม่เสียเวลา
rao ja dern thang glahng keu:n pêu-a ja dâi mâi sĕe-a way-lah
We'll travel overnight so as not to waste time.

9.2.5 | Additive clauses: 'apart from'

A common pattern for giving additional information is, **nôrk jàhk (nún láir-o) . . . yung . . . (dôo-ay)** ('apart from (that) . . . still . . .'):

นอกจากเชียงใหม่แล้วเรายังไปเที่ยวลำปางด้วย
nôrk jàhk chee-ung mài láir-o rao yung bpai têe-o lum-bpahng dôo-ay
Apart from Chiangmai, we went to Lampang.

นอกจากจะกินน้ำมันเยอะแล้วค่าซ่อมยังแพงด้วย
**nôrk jàhk ja gin núm mun yér láir-o kâh sôrm yung pairng
    dôo-ay**
Apart from using a lot of petrol, the repair costs are expensive too.

นอกจากนั้นแล้วยังมีสาเหตุอีกหลายอย่าง
nôrk jàhk nún láir-o yung mee sǎh-hàyt èek lǎi: yàhng
Apart from that, there are many other reasons.

9.2.6 | 'the more . . . the more . . .'

'The more . . . , the more . . .' is expressed by the pattern **yîng . . . (gôr)
yîng . . . :**

ยิ่งฟังก็ยิ่งไม่เข้าใจ
yîng fung gôr yîng mâi kâo jai
The more I listen, the more I don't understand/the less I understand.

ยิ่งแม่รู้ว่าสมจิตมีเงินเดือนแน่นอน แม่ก็ยิ่งเห็นว่า
    สามารถจะทำบุญได้บ่อยขึ้น
**yîng mâir róo wâh sǒm-jìt mee ngern deu-un nair-norn mâir gôr
    yîng hĕn wâh sǎh-mâht ja tum bOOn dâi bòy kêun**
The more her mother realised that Somjit had a steady income, the more
    she thought she could make merit more often.

9.2.7 | *Time clauses*

Some common time clause expressions include:

พอ ...ปุ๊บ ...	por ...bpÓOp ...	no sooner ... than ...
...ปุ๊บ ...ปั๊บ	...bpÓOp ...bpúp	no sooner ... than ...
เมื่อ ...(ก็) ...	mêu-a ...(gôr) ...	when (past) ...
เวลา ...(ก็) ...	way-lah ...(gôr) ...	when ...
หลังจากที่ ...(ก็) ...	lŭng jàhk têe ... (gôr) ...	after ...
ก่อนที่จะ ...(ก็) ...	gòrn têe ...(gôr) ...	before ...
ขณะที่ ...(ก็) ...	ka-nà têe ...(gôr) ...	while ...
ตอนที่ ...(ก็) ...	dtorn têe ...(gôr) ...	while ...
ในระหว่างที่ ...(ก็) ...	nai ra-wàhng têe ... (gôr) ...	while ...

พอนั่งลงหน้าทีวีปุ๊บก็หลับ
por nûng long nâh tee wee bpÓOp gôr lùp
No sooner does he sit down in front of the TV than he falls asleep.

กินปุ๊บอิ่มปั๊บ
gin bpÓOp ìm bpúp
As soon as I (start to) eat, I feel full.

เมื่อเรียนจบแล้ว ฉันก็ไปสมัครงานเป็นครู
mêu-a ree-un jòp láir-o chún gôr bpai sa-mùk ngahn bpen kroo
When I graduated, I went and applied for a job as a teacher.

ก่อนที่จะถอนเงินได้ผมก็ต้องปรึกษากับแฟน
gòrn têe ja tŏrn ngern dâi: pŏm gôr dtôrng bprèuk-săh gùp fairn
Before I can withdraw the money, I'll have to discuss it with my wife.

ขณะที่ผมคุยโทรศัพท์อยู่ก็มีคนมาบอกข่าว
ka-nà têe pŏm koo-ee toh-ra-sùp yòo gôr mee kon mah bòrk kào:
While I was chatting on the phone, someone came and told me the news.

9.3 Direct and indirect speech

Both direct and indirect speech are introduced by **wâh** (5.9). When pronouns are omitted in the second clause, direct and indirect speech become identical in form. **wâh** plays the role of inverted commas in direct speech and 'that' in indirect speech:

เขาบอกว่า (เขา)จะไม่ไป
káo bòrk wâh (káo) ja mâi bpai
He said that he's not going.

เขาบอกว่า (ผม)จะไม่ไป
káo bòrk wâh (pǒm) ja mâi bpai
He said, 'I'm not going.'

For indirect questions, see 12.4.

9.4 Imperatives

A simple verb or verb phrase is the most basic form of command. This can sound abrupt and is normally softened by adding a mild command particle, **sí** or **tèr**, or the more insistent particle, **sêe** (10.3.9, 10.3.10). Commands can be further softened by adding polite particles (10.2).

Commands can also be expressed by the patterns, VERB (PHRASE) + REDUPLICATED ADJECTIVE (7.1.2), VERB + **hâi** + ADJECTIVE (7.1.5) and VERB + **sěe-a** (5.7.12).

jong is an imperative which appears in written instructions, as for example, at the top of an examination paper:

จงตอบคำถาม
jong dtòrp kum tǎhm
Answer the (following) questions.

Negative imperatives follow the pattern, **yàh** ('Don't') + VERB (PHRASE), or **hâhm** ('It's forbidden to . . .') + VERB (PHRASE) (11.8).

For requesting someone to do/not do something, see 15.4.4 and 15.4.5.

9.5 Exemplification

Examples are commonly enclosed within the 'wrap-around' pattern,
chên . . . bpen dtôn (for example, . . .): however, either **chên . . .** or **. . . bpen
dtôn** may be omitted:

ต้องทำหลายอย่างเช่นซักผ้าหุงข้าวตัดหญ้าเป็นต้น
**dtôrng tum lǎi: yàhng chên súk pâh hǒOng kâo: dtùt yâh bpen
dtôn**

I have to do lots of things, such as washing, cooking and cutting the grass.

'To give an example' is **yók** ('to raise') **dtoo-a yàhng** ('example'):

ขอยกตัวอย่างหนึ่ง
kǒr yók dtoo-a yàhng nèung

Let me give an example.

9.6 Exclamatory particles

อ้าว	**âo:**	Contradicting, chiding; disappointment; *Hey!*; *Oh!* (Is that so?)
เอ๊	**áy**	Thinking or wondering; *Ermm . . .*
ต๊าย	**dtái:**	Shock, horror; *Good Lord!* More common in female speech; variations include **dtái: dtai:, dtai: láir-o** and **dtai: jing**
เอ๊ะ	**é**	Surprise. *Eh?*; *What?*
เฮ้ย	**hêr-ee**	Calling attention: *Hey! Hold on a minute!*
แหม	**mǎir**	Surprise; *Goodness!*
โอ้โฮ	**ôh hoh**	Surprise; indignation; *Wow! Oh yeah?*
อุ๊ย	**óo-ee**	Pain or mishap; *Ouch!*; *Oops!*
อ้อ	**ôr**	Realisation; *Ah!* (Now I understand.)

Chapter 10

Sentence particles

Sentence particles occur at the end of an utterance and serve a grammatical or communicative function. They can be divided into three main groups: (a) question particles, (b) polite particles and (c) mood particles.

10.1 Question particles

Question particles are relatively straightforward. They are few in number and all occur at the end of an utterance to transform it into a question which requires a 'yes/no' answer. They are dealt with in 12.1.

10.2 Polite particles

Polite particles are added to the end of an utterance to show respect to the addressee. The most common are **krúp**, used by males at the end of statements and questions, and **kâ** used by females at the end of statements and **ká**, also used by females, but at the end of questions.

ไปไหนครับ
bpai năi krúp?
Where are you going? (male asking)

– กลับบ้านค่ะ
– **glùp bâhn kâ**
– I'm going home. (female responding)

อร่อยไหมคะ

a-ròy mái ká?

Is it tasty? (female asking)

– อร่อยครับ

– **a-ròy krúp**

– Yes. (male responding)

Polite particles are also used as response particles to mean 'yes', or, when preceded by the negative particle **mâi**, 'no'.

Polite particles are used after someone's name to call their attention; the female particles **ká?** and **já?** are sometimes pronounced **kǎh** and **jǎh** respectively, the change of tone and vowel-lengthening signalling the speaker's closeness or desired closeness to the person she is addressing:

คุณแม่ขา

kOOn mâir kǎh?

Mummy? (daughter speaking)

–- จ๋า

– **jǎh**

– Yes (dear)? (mother responding)

| **10.2.1** | **krúp** (ครับ) |

Used by male speakers only, at the end of both statements and questions as a sign of politeness; used after a name to attract that person's attention; used as a response when one's name is called (when the vowel is often lengthened to **kráhp**); used in isolation as a 'yes' response (12.1.2; 12.1.4); used, often repetitively, to reassure the speaker of one's attention, for example on the telephone (**krúp ... krúp ... krúp**); used after **mâi** to mean 'no'. In Bangkok speech the **r** is typically lost and **krúp** becomes **kúp**.

| **10.2.2** | **krúp pǒm** (ครับผม) |

Used by male speakers only; interchangeable with **krúp** (above) except it is not used in isolation with the negative **mâi**. Often used humorously as a sign of exaggerated deference or politeness.

10.2.3 ká (คะ)

Used by female speakers only, at the end of questions as a sign of politeness; used after a name to attract that person's attention; used as a response when one's name is called; used after the particle sí/sêe (10.3.9).

10.2.4 kâ, kâh, kà (ค่ะ)

Used by female speakers only, at the end of statements as a sign of politeness; used as a response when one's name is called (when the vowel is often lengthened to kâh); used in isolation as a 'yes' response; used to reassure the speaker of one's attention (kâ . . . kâ . . . kâ) when the vowel may also be lengthened to kâh; used after mâi to mean 'no'; often pronounced kà with a low tone and short vowel.

10.2.5 kǎh? (ขา)

Used by female speakers only after a name to attract the person's attention; can also be used as a response when one's name is called.

10.2.6 há (ฮะ)

Used by male speakers as an informal substitute for krúp; used by female speakers as an informal substitute for ká; male pronunciation is characterised by a distinctive final glottal stop not associated with female usage.

10.2.7 hâ (ฮ่ะ)

Used by female speakers as an informal substitute for kâ.

10.2.8 já (จ๊ะ)

Used by adult male and female speakers at the end of questions when talking to children, servants or people of markedly lower social status; used as a 'sweet-talk' question particle between males and females or a 'best friends' question particle between females; used after the name of a child, servant or inferior to attract that person's attention; used in polite requests after the particle **sí**.

10.2.9 | jâ, jâh (จ๊ะ)

Used by adult male and female speakers at the end of a statement when speaking to children, servants and people of inferior status; between males and females denotes anything from easy familiarity to 'sweet talk'; between females signals 'best friends talk'; used as a response when one's name is called (when the vowel is often lengthened to **jâh**); used in isolation as a 'yes' response; used to reassure speaker of one's attention (**jâh ... jâh ... jâh**) when the vowel is normally lengthened; used after **mâi**, to mean 'no'.

10.2.10 | jăh (จ๋า)

Used by older or senior male and female speakers after a younger or junior person's name to attract that person's attention (e.g. parents or adults calling children); similarly used between equals as a sign of affection; can also be used as a response, more typically by females, when one's name is called.

10.2.11 | wá/wâ/wóy-ee (วะ/ว่ะ/โว้ย)

An impolite or informal particle, used to indicate rudeness, anger and aggressiveness when speaking to strangers, or intimacy with close friends of equal status; **wá** is used with questions and **wâ/wóy-ee** with statements; more common in male speech but can be used by females; it is the particle favoured by baddies on the big screen, used by drinking friends as the evening progresses, and the one to snarl, in the expression **tum a-rai wá?** ('What the hell are you doing?') – if you have the misfortune to encounter an intruder in your house.

10.2.12 | yá/yâ (ยะ/ย่ะ)

An impolite or informal particle, similar to **wá/wâ** (above), but used only by female speakers.

10.2.13 | pâ-yâ-kâ *(พ่ะย่ะค่ะ)* / pay-ká *(เพคะ)*

Polite particles used when speaking to royalty; male speakers use **pâ-yâ-kâ** and female speakers **pay-ká**.

10.3 Mood particles

Mood particles represent a major obstacle for the serious learner. Their function is often conveyed in English purely by intonation, so they cannot easily be translated; to complicate matters one particle may have several variant forms, involving a change in tone or vowel length, with each form reflecting a subtle difference.

Many basic language courses deliberately omit mood particles for the sake of simplicity and it is possible to avoid using them and get by quite adequately. But without mood particles, statements often sound incomplete, abrupt or even impolite. They are best learnt by imitation; everyday conversation, television, dialogue in novels and interviews in newspapers and magazines all provide a ready supply of examples, although the written form of a particle does not always reflect its normal pronunciation. This section discusses some of the most common particles; for a more detailed treatment, see Cooke (1989).

10.3.1 | dôo-ay *(ด้วย)*

This particle is typically used in polite requests, apologies and cries for help:

ขอโทษด้วย
kŏr-tôht dôo-ay
Sorry!

เช็คบิลด้วย
chék bin dôo-ay
Can I have the bill, please?

ช่วยด้วย
chôo-ay dôo-ay
Help!

149

10.3.2 lá/la (ละ)

A contracted form of **láir-o** ('already'), one use of **lá** is to indicate that a state has been reached:

พอละ

por lá

That's enough.

ดีละ

dee lá

That's fine.

ถูกละ

tòok lá

That's right/correct.

เอาละ

ao lá

OK!; Right, then!

It can also be used to indicate that a situation is about to change (probably representing a contraction of **ja . . . láir-o** ('to be about to . . .')):

ผมกลับบ้านละ

pŏm glùp bâhn lá

I'm going home.

ไปละ

bpai lá

I'm leaving.

จะกินละ

ja gin lá

I'm going to eat.

Another use is with **èek** ('again') to show mild irritation:

มาอีกละ

mah èek lá

He's back again.

สมชายอีกละ

sŏm-chai: èek lá

It's Somchai again.

10.3.3 lâ (ล่ะ)

This particle occurs commonly in questions, as a way of pressing for an answer; in the following two examples, it is common to hear **lâ** reduced to **â**:

ทำไมล่ะ
tum-mai lâ?
Why?

ไปไหนล่ะ
bpai nǎi lâ?
Where are you going?

Sometimes the particle conveys a sense of irritation, similar to English 'why on earth . . . ?':

ทำไมต้องไปบอกเขาล่ะ
tum-mai dtôrng bpai bòrk káo lâ?
Why on earth did you have to go and tell her?

เอาไปซ่อนไว้ที่ไหนล่ะ
ao bpai sôrn wái têe-nǎi lâ?
Where on earth have you gone and hidden it?

It is also used in the pattern **láir-o . . . lâ?** ('And how about . . . ?, What about . . . ?') to change the focus or topic of conversation:

แล้วคุณล่ะ
láir-o kOOn lâ?
And how about you?

แล้วพรุ่งนี้ล่ะ
láir-o prÔOng née lâ?
And how about tomorrow?

10.3.4 ná (นะ)

This particle often serves to make a sentence milder or less abrupt by seeking approval, agreement or compromise. Commands are similarly made

milder and convey a sense of coaxing and urging; **ná** often corresponds to
the use of '. . . , OK?' or '. . . , right?' in English.

ไปละนะ
bpai lá ná
I'm going now, OK?

ฉันไม่ว่านะ
chún mâi wâh ná
I don't mind, OK?

อย่าบอกเธอนะ
yàh bòrk ter ná
Don't tell her, OK?

ná is also used after question words when requesting someone to repeat
a piece of information, similar to English 'What was that again?':

อะไรนะ
a-rai ná?
Pardon? What was that again?

ใครนะ
krai ná?
Who was that again?

คุณกลับเมื่อไรนะ
kOOn glùp mêu-rài ná?
When was it that you said you were going back?

Note also the use of **ná** as a question particle when seeking agreement
(12.1.4).

10.3.5 | nâ/nâh (น่ะ/น่า)

This particle is used when persuading somebody to do something or accept
an idea when they are reluctant (cf. 'Oh, come on, . . .').

อย่าไปน่า
yàh bpai nâh
Oh, come on, don't go.

It is also used to highlight the topic of a sentence, in much the same way that some speakers of English use 'right':

ผู้หญิงน่ะก็เป็นอย่างนั้น

pôo-yǐng nâ gôr bpen yàhng nún

Women, right, are like that.

ตอนครูสอนอยู่น่ะ ผมฟังไม่รู้เรื่องเลย

dtorn kroo sǒrn yòo nâ pǒm fung mâi róo rêu-ung ler-ee

When the teacher is teaching, right, I don't understand a word.

10.3.6 nòy (หน่อย)

Polite request particle, basically meaning 'just a little'; used to minimise degree of imposition on listener; similar in function to **tee** (10.3.11), but used much more widely; commonly occurs in requests that begin with **kǒr** or **chôo-ay**.

พูดช้า ๆ หน่อยได้ไหม

pôot cháh cháh nòy dâi mái?

Could you speak slowly, please?

ขอดูหน่อย

kǒr doo nòy

Could I have a look, please?

ช่วยปิดทีวีหน่อย

chôo-ay bpìt tee wee nòy

Please turn the TV off.

10.3.7 ngai (ไง)

Often used as a response to a statement or question to show that the respondent thinks the answer is self-evident:

เขาไม่ยอมฆ่ามัน

káo mâi yorm kâh mun

He wouldn't kill it.

– ก็เป็นบาปไงล่ะ

– gôr bpen bàhp ngai lâ

– Well, it's sinful, of course.

153

เสื้อฉันหายไปไหน
sêu-a chún hăi: bpai năi?
Where's my shirt disappeared to?

– นี่ไง อยู่ตรงนี้เอง
– nêe ngai yòo dtrong née ayng
– Here it is. Right here.

It is also used in the Thai equivalent of 'here you are', used when giving
something to someone:

นี่ไงล่ะครับ/ค่ะ
nêe ngai lâ krúp/kâ
Here you are!

10.3.8 ròrk/lòrk *(หรอก)*

Occurs most commonly at the end of negative statements to contradict the
addressee's statement or belief:

ไม่ต้องหรอก
mâi dtôrng ròrk
There's no need. (when declining an offer)

แพงครับ
pairng krúp
It's expensive.

– ไม่แพงหรอกค่ะ
– mâi pairng ròrk kâ
– No it isn't.

In positive statements it can convey a qualified or somewhat hesitant
acceptance of the addressee's statement or belief:

ก็จริงหรอก
gôr jing lòrk
That's true (but ...)

เขาพูดไทยเก่ง

káo pôot tai gèng

He speaks Thai well.

– ก็เก่งหรอก แต่ยังเขียนไม่เป็น

– gôr gèng lòrk dtàir yung kěe-un mâi bpen

– Yes ... but he can't write yet.

It can also be used, with the appropriate tone of voice, to indicate irony or sarcasm, saying one thing but meaning the opposite:

เขาเป็นพลเมืองดีหรอก

káo bpen pon-la-meu-ung dee lòrk

He's a good citizen.

or mild annoyance:

ผมพูดได้เองหรอก

pǒm pôot dâi ayng lòrk

I can speak for myself.

10.3.9 sí/sì/see/sêe *(ซิ/สิ/ซี/ซี่)*

This particle is most commonly used in commands. When pronounced with a short vowel and followed by a polite particle it does not convey any sense of abruptness and is widely used in polite requests ('Do sit down, please'); more insistent requests and commands are conveyed when the particle is pronounced with a falling tone and longer vowel ('Sit down!').

เชิญนั่งซิคะ

chern nûng sí ká

Please sit down.

ดูซิครับ

doo sí krúp

Look!, Take a look!

พูดอีกทีซิคะ

pôot èek tee sí ká

Please say that again.

นั่งซี่

nûng sêe

Sit down! (and listen)

ปิดประตูซี่

bpìt bpra-dtoo sêe

Shut the door! (I've told you once already)

Another use of this particle is to emphasise a positive response to a question;
note that the tone of the female particle (**ká**) is high after **see**.

ไปไหมครับ

bpai mái krúp?

Shall we go?

– ไปซีคะ

– bpai see ká

– Yes, let's.

อยากลองไหม

yàhk lorng mái?

Do you want to try it?

– อยากซีคะ

– yàhk see ká

– Yes, I would.

It is also used to contradict negative statements:

เขาคงไม่มา

káo kong mâi mah

He probably won't come.

– มาซี

– mah see

– Oh yes he will!

ฉันพูดอังกฤษไม่เก่ง

chún pôot ung-grìt mâi gèng

I don't speak English well.

– เก่งซี

– gèng see

– Oh yes you do!

10.3.10 tèr/hèr (เถิด/เถอะ/เหอะ)

A mild, 'urging' particle, used in suggestions, invitations, requests and mild commands; can often be conveyed in English by 'you'd/we'd better . . .', 'why don't you/we . . .', 'go ahead and . . .', 'let's . . .', depending on the context; when it is used to urge someone to do something, a reason is often given, too; when joint activity is being suggested, it is often preceded by **gun** ('together'); often reduced to **hèr** in informal speech.

กลับบ้านเถอะ ดึกแล้ว
glùp bâhn tèr dèuk láir-o
You'd better go home. It's late.

ไปกินกันเถอะ
bpai gin gun tèr
Let's go and eat.

เดี๋ยวเหอะ
dĕe-o hèr
Steady on!/Not so fast!

10.3.11 tee (ที)

Polite request particle, basically meaning 'just this once'; used to minimise degree of imposition on listener; similar in function to **nòy** but much more restricted in use; note the idiomatic **kŏr tee**.

ขอโทษที
kŏr-tôht tee
Sorry!

ขอพูดที
kŏr pôot tee
Can I say something/get a word in?

ช่วยปิดทีวีที
chôo-ay bpìt tee wee tee
Please turn the TV off.

ขอที
kŏr tee
Must you? (sense of exasperation)

157

Chapter 11

Negation

Negative words in Thai are (a) **mâi** ('not, no'), widely used in negative sentences and negative responses to questions; (b) **mí**, a variant of **mâi**; (c) **yàh** ('don't') and (d) **hâhm** ('to forbid'), both used in negative commands and prohibitions; (e) **bplào:** ('no'), a negative response, which contradicts the assumption in the question, and (f) **yung** ('not yet'), used only as a negative response to . . . **réu yung?** questions (12.1.6).

11.1 Negating main verbs

Verbs are generally negated by the pattern, **mâi** + VERB (PHRASE):

ฉันไม่ไป
chún mâi bpai
I'm not going.

อาหารไม่อร่อย
ah-hăhn mâi a-ròy
The food isn't tasty.

Verb compounds (5.3) also follow this pattern:

ผมไม่เปลี่ยนแปลง
pŏm mâi bplèe-un bplairng
I'm not changing.

ฉันไม่ดูแลเขา
chún mâi doo lair káo
I don't look after them.

For negation of 'to be', see 5.1.

11.2   Negating resultative verbs

Combinations of verb + resultative verb (5.4) are superficially similar to
verb compounds, but are negated by the pattern VERB + (OBJECT) + **mâi**
+ RESULTATIVE VERB.

เรานอนไม่หลับ
rao norn mâi lùp
We didn't sleep.

เขาหาไม่เจอ
káo hǎh mâi jer
He can't find it.

ฉันคิดไม่ออก
chún kít mâi òrk
I can't work it out.

เขาอ่านไม่เข้าใจ/ไม่รู้เรื่อง
káo àhn mâi kâo jai/mâi róo rêu-ung
He doesn't understand (what he is reading).

ผมฟังไม่ทัน
pǒm fung mâi tun
I can't follow what they're saying. (i.e. they're speaking too fast)

บอกไม่ถูก
bòrk mâi tòok
It's hard to put into words.

ฉันดูหนังไม่จบ
chún doo nǔng mâi jòp
I didn't see the film through to the end.

ลูกกินข้าวไม่หมด
lôok gin kâo: mâi mòt
My kids don't eat up all their rice.

The word **yung** can be added, either immediately before **mâi**, or immediately before the main verb, to convey the sense that the action has not yet produced the intended result:

ฉันดูหนังยังไม่จบ/ฉันยังดูหนังไม่จบ

chún doo nǔng yung mâi jòp/chún yung doo nǔng mâi jòp
I haven't finished watching the film yet.

เขาทำงานยังไม่เสร็จ/เขายังทำงานไม่เสร็จ

káo tum ngahn yung mâi sèt/káo yung tum ngahn mâi sèt
He hasn't finished work yet.

11.3 Negating auxiliary verbs

There are three patterns for negating auxiliary verbs; note the difference in meaning of **dtôrng** ('have to, must') in the examples in 11.3.1 and 11.3.2:

11.3.1 mâi + AUXILIARY VERB + VERB (PHRASE)

A relatively small number of auxiliary verbs follow this pattern, the most common being:

ต้อง	dtôrng	have to, must
เคย	ker-ee	used to do/be, to have ever done/been
ควร(จะ)	koo-un (ja)	should/ought
น่า(จะ)	nâh (ja)	should/ought
อยาก(จะ)	yàhk (ja)	want to, would like to

คุณไม่ต้องบอกเขา

kOOn mâi dtôrng bòrk káo
There's no need to tell him. / You don't have to tell him.

ฉันไม่เคยกิน

chún mâi ker-ee gin
I've never eaten it.

คุณไม่ควร(จะ)ซื้อ

kOOn mâi koo-un (ja) séu:
You shouldn't have bought it.

เราไม่อยาก(จะ)กลับบ้าน
rao mâi yàhk (ja) glùp bâhn
We don't want to go home.

11.3.2 AUXILIARY VERB + mâi + VERB (PHRASE)

Auxiliary verbs which follow this pattern include:

อาจ(จะ)	**àht (ja)**	may/might
ดูเหมือน(จะ)	**doo měu-un (ja)**	look like/as though
ต้อง	**dtôrng**	have to, must
เห็น(จะ)	**hěn (ja)**	seem that
จะ	**ja**	future time marker
คง(จะ)	**kong (ja)**	will probably, sure to
มัก(จะ)	**múk (ja)**	tend to, usually
ท่า(จะ)	**tâh (ja)**	might, it could be
ท่าทาง(จะ)	**tâh thang (ja)**	look like/as though
แทบ(จะ)	**tâirp (ja)**	almost, nearly
ย่อม(จะ)	**yôrm (ja)**	likely to

ผมอาจจะไม่ไป
pǒm àht ja mâi bpai
I might not go.

คุณต้องไม่บอกเขา
kOOn dtôrng mâi bòrk káo
You must not tell him.

คุณคงจะไม่สนใจ
kOOn kong ca mâi sǒn jai
You probably won't be interested.

เขามักจะไม่ชอบ
káo múk ja mâi chôrp
She usually doesn't like it.

11.3.3 VERB (PHRASE) + mâi + AUXILIARY VERB

This pattern occurs with the modal verbs expressing ability and permission, **bpen, dâi:** and **wǎi** (5.6.2):

เขาพูดไทยไม่ เป็น
káo pôot tai mâi bpen
He can't speak Thai.

คุณไปไม่ได้
kOOn bpai mâi dâi:
You can't go.

ฉันทนไม่ไหว
chún ton mâi wǎi
I can't stand it.

11.4 mâi dâi + VERB (PHRASE)

The pattern, **mâi dâi** + VERB (PHRASE) is used as follows:

11.4.1 To form a negative past with verbs of motion, action, utterance, etc.

It is not used with stative verbs or pre-verbs (5.7.7):

เพื่อนไม่ได้มา
pêu-un mâi dâi mah
My friend didn't come.

เราไม่ได้ซื้อ
rao mâi dâi séu:
We didn't buy it.

เขาไม่ได้บอก
káo mâi dâi bòrk
He didn't say.

To contradict an assumption

It does not indicate any particular tense and may refer to the past or present:

บ้านอยู่กรุงเทพฯหรือ
bâhn yòo grOOng-tâyp lěr?
Your house is in Bangkok, then?

– เปล่าไม่ได้อยู่กรุงเทพฯ
– bplào: mâi dâi yòo grOOng-tâyp
– No, it's not in Bangkok.

เขาเป็นแฟนหรือ
káo bpen fairn lěr?
She's your girlfriend, then?

– เปล่า ไม่ได้เป็น
– bplào: mâi dâi bpen
– No, she's not.

คุณสอนภาษาอังกฤษหรือ
kOOn sǒrn pah-sǎh ung-grìt lěr?
You taught English, then?

– เปล่า ไม่ได้สอน
– bplào: mâi dâi sǒrn
– No, I didn't.

To negate the verbs chêu ('to be named') and bpen ('to be'). (See 5.1)

เขาไม่ได้ชื่อต้อย
káo mâi dâi chêu dtǒy
Her name isn't Toi.

ผมไม่ได้เป็นคนอเมริกัน
pǒm mâi dâi bpen kon a-may-ri-gun
I'm not an American.

11.5 mâi châi + NOUN

mâi châi + NOUN negates phrases consisting of the verb **bpen** ('to be') +
NOUN (5.1); it is often interchangeable with **mâi dâi bpen** + NOUN (11.4.3).

นี่ไม่ใช่บ้านเขา
nêe mâi châi bâhn káo
This isn't his house.

ฉันเป็นครูไม่ใช่หมอ
chún bpen kroo mâi châi mǒr
I'm a teacher, not a doctor.

เขาไม่ใช่เพื่อน
káo mâi châi pêu-un
He's not a friend.

'It is neither . . . , nor . . .', is expressed by the pattern, NOUN 1 + **gôr mâi
châi** + NOUN 2 + **gôr mâi cherng**:

สีม่วงก็ไม่ใช่ชมพูก็ไม่เชิง
sěe môo-ung gôr mâi châi, chom-poo gôr mâi cherng
It's neither purple, nor pink.

จะว่าเป็นของใหม่ก็ไม่ใช่ ของแปลกก็ไม่เชิง
ja wâh bpen kǒrng mài gôr mâi châi, kǒrng bplàirk gôr mâi cherng
You can't say it's either something new or something unusual.

11.6 mâi mee

mâi mee ('there isn't/aren't') is placed before a noun to form the negative
quantifier 'not any' and 'no':

ไม่มีรถเมล์
mâi mee rót may
There aren't any buses.

ไม่มีเพื่อนมาเยี่ยมฉัน
mâi mee pêu-un mah yêe-um chún
No friends came to visit me.

mâi mee is also used to negate the indefinite pronouns **krai** ('anyone') **a-rai** ('anything') and **têe-năi** ('anywhere'):

ไม่มีใครรู้

mâi mee krai róo

No one knows.

ไม่มีอะไรเกิดขึ้น

mâi mee a-rai gèrt kêun

Nothing happened.

ไม่มีที่ไหนที่ดีกว่านี้

mâi mee têe-năi têe dee gwàh née

There's nowhere better than this.

11.7 Modifying negatives: intensifying and softening

Negative statements are intensified or softened by using a 'wrap-around' construction in which the verb occurs between the negative word and the modifier: **mâi** + VERB (PHRASE) + INTENSIFIER/SOFTENER.

Common negative intensifiers are:

ไม่ . . . เลย	**mâi . . . ler-ee**	not at all . . .
ไม่ . . . แน่	**mâi . . . nâir**	not . . . for sure
ไม่ . . . เด็ดขาด	**mâi . . . dèt kàht**	absolutely not . . .

ฉันไม่ชอบเลย

chún mâi chôrp ler-ee

I don't like it at all.

เขาไม่มาแน่

káo mâi mah nâir

He's not coming for sure.

เราไม่ไป เด็ดขาด

rao mâi bpai dèt kàht

We're absolutely not going.

A more elaborate pattern is **mâi . . . máir dtàir** + CLASSIFIER + **dee-o** ('not . . . , not even a single . . .'):

ผมไม่รู้จักใครแม้แต่คนเดียว
pǒm mâi róo-jùk krai máir dtàir kon dee-o
I don't know even a single person.

เขาไม่สนใจแม้แต่นิดเดียว
káo mâi sǒn jai máir dtàir nít dee-o
He is not even the slightest bit interested.

Common softeners are:

ไม่(ค่อย) . . . เท่าไหร่	**mâi (kôy) . . . tâo-rài**	not very . . .
ไม่(ค่อย) . . . นัก	**mâi (kôy) . . . núk**	not very . . .
ไม่(สู้) . . . นัก	**mâi (sôo) . . . núk**	not very . . .

หนังไม่ค่อยสนุกเท่าไหร่
nǔng mâi kôy sa-nÒOk tâo-rài
The film wasn't very much fun.

บ้านนี้อยู่ไม่ไกลจากบ้านเรานัก
bâhn née yòo mâi glai jàhk bâhn rao núk
This house wasn't very far from our house.

เรื่องเงินทำให้สัมพันธภาพระหว่างลูกหลานไม่ค่อยดีนัก
rêu-ung ngern tum hâi sǔm-pun-ta-pâhp ra-wàhng lôok lǎhn mâi kôy dee núk
The issue of money made relations among the children and grandchildren not very good.

mâi (kôy) also commonly occurs without **tâo-rài** or **núk**:

ฉันไม่ค่อยชอบ
chún mâi kôy chôrp
I don't like it very much.

11.8 Negative imperatives

Negative commands follow the pattern, **yàh** ('Don't') + VERB (PHRASE), or **hâhm** ('It's forbidden to . . .') + VERB (PHRASE); both can be made

more emphatic ('absolutely not, under no circumstances, don't ever . . .')
by adding **bpen un kàht** or **dèt kàht** after the verb or verb phrase, or
modified in various other ways by the addition of mood particles (10.3).
See also 15.4.5.

อย่า/ห้ามบอกเขา(นะ)
yàh/hâhm bòrk káo (ná)
Don't tell him (right)?

อย่า/ห้ามโทรมาอีกเป็นอันขาด
yàh/hâhm toh mah èek bpen un kàht
Don't ever, under any circumstances, ring me again.

The pattern, **yàh pêrng** + VERB (PHRASE) conveys the sense that it is the
wrong time for doing something:

อย่าเพิ่งปิดแอร์นะ
yàh pêrng bpìt air ná
Don't turn the air-conditioning off just yet, OK?

อย่าเพิ่งบอกเขานะ
yàh pêrng bòrk káo ná
Don't tell him just yet, OK?

อย่าเพิ่ง
yàh pêrng
Not now!

11.9 Negative causatives

Causative constructions (5.11) are negated according to the following
patterns:

11.9.1 SUBJECT (human/non-human) + mâi + tum + (inanimate OBJECT) + VERB

ขอยืมหน่อย จะไม่ทำเสีย
kŏr yeu:m nòy ja mâi tum sĕe-a
Can I borrow it? I won't damage it.

ผมไม่ได้ทำแตกครับ

pŏm mâi dâi tum dtàirk krúp

I didn't break it.

11.9.2 | *SUBJECT (human) + mâi + hâi + (animate OBJECT) +*
VERB (PHRASE)

เขาไม่ให้ภรรยาทำงาน

káo mâi hâi pun-ra-yah tum ngahn

He doesn't let his wife work.

พ่อไม่ให้ลูกกลับบ้านดึก

pôr mâi hâi lôok glùp bâhn dèuk

The father doesn't let his children come home late.

เราไม่ให้แมวเข้าบ้าน

rao mâi hâi mair-o kâo bâhn

We don't let the cat come inside the house.

When **hâi** is preceded by a specifying verb, such as **bòrk** ('to tell'), the negative can take two distinct forms and meanings (11.9.3, 11.9.4), depending on whether it is **hâi** or the specifying verb which is being negated.

11.9.3 | *SUBJECT (human) + specifying verb + mâi + hâi +*
(animate OBJECT) + VERB (PHRASE)

เขาบอกไม่ให้ฉันใช้เงินมาก

káo bòrk mâi hâi chún chái ngern mâhk

He told me not to spend a lot of money.

เมียเตือนไม่ให้กลับบ้านดึก

mee-a dtèu-un mâi hâi káo glùp bâhn dèuk

His wife warned him not to come home late.

พ่อห้ามไม่ให้ฉันกินเหล้า

pôr hâhm mâi hâi chún gin lâo

My father forbids me to drink alcohol.

หัวหน้าปฏิเสธไม่ให้ผมลาป่วย

hŏo-a nâh bpà-dtì-sàyt mâi hâi pŏm lah bpòo-ay

My boss refuses to let me take sick leave.

Alternatively, the object can occur after the specifying verb and before **mâi hâi**:

เขาบอกฉันไม่ให้ใช้เงินมาก
káo bòrk chún mâi hâi chái ngern mâhk
He told me not to spend a lot of money.

พ่อห้ามฉันไม่ให้กินเหล้า
pôr hâhm chún mâi hâi gin lâo
My father forbids me to drink alcohol.

Note that in negative causative constructions, the verbs **hâhm** ('to forbid') and **bpà-dtì-sàyt** ('to refuse') occur with **mâi hâi** (and not **hâi** on its own), creating an apparent 'double negative' ('forbid not to let', 'refuse not to let'). It should also be noted that **hâhm** can occur without **hâi**, both in simple causative sentences and in negative imperatives (11.8):

พ่อห้ามฉันกินเหล้า
pôr hâhm chún gin lâo
My father forbids me to drink alcohol.

ห้ามเปิดประตู
hâhm bpèrt bpra-dtoo
Don't open the door!

11.9.4 | SUBJECT (human) + mâi + specifying verb + hâi + (animate OBJECT) + VERB (PHRASE)

แม่ไม่อนุญาตให้ลูกไปดูหนัง
mâir mâi a-nÓO-yâht hâi lôok bpai doo nǔng
The mother doesn't allow her children to go to see films.

ฉันไม่ยอมให้เขาทำอย่างนั้น
chún mâi yorm hâi káo tum yàhng nún
I don't let him do that.

เขาไม่ได้เตือนให้ระวังขโมย
káo mâi dâi dteu-un hâi rao ra-wung ka-moy-ee
He didn't warn us to watch out for burglars.

11.9.5 *SUBJECT (human or non-human) + mâi + tum hâi + (OBJECT) + VERB (PHRASE)*

แต่กลับไปอยู่บ้านเกิดไม่ได้ทำให้เธอมีความสุขมากขึ้น
dtàir glùp bpai yòo bâhn gèrt mâi dâi tum hâi ter mee kwahm sÒOk mâhk kêun
But going back to live in her place of birth did not make her happier.

ที่ต้องไป ๆ มา ๆ บ่อย ๆ อย่างนี้ ไม่ได้ทำให้ฉันเดือดร้อน
têe dtôrng bpai bpai mah mah bòy bòy yàhng née mâi dâi tum hâi chún dèu-ut rórn
The fact that I have to go back and forth often like this doesn't make things difficult for me.

11.10 Negative questions

Negative questions ('You didn't . . . did you?') are formed according to the following patterns:

(a) **mâi** + VERB + **lěr?**
(b) **mâi** + VERB + **châi mái?**
(c) SUBJECT + VERB + **mâi châi lěr?**

Note that the question particle **mái?** (12.1.1) is not used in negative questions.

Negative questions present a problem for English speakers in that yes/no answers are reversed in Thai: where in English we say 'No (I didn't)' and 'Yes (I did)', Thai has 'Yes, that's right (I didn't)' and 'No, that's right (I did)'. In replying to negative questions, providing additional clarification to a yes/no response (shown in brackets in the following examples) can pre-empt misunderstandings:

คุณไม่ซื้อหรือ
kOOn mâi séu: lěr?
You're not buying it, right?

– ครับ(ไม่ซื้อ)/ซื้อซีคะ
– krúp (mâi séu)/séu see ká
– No (I'm not)/Yes, I am.

คุณไม่รู้ใช่ไหม
kOOn mâi róo châi mái?
You don't know, right?

– ใช่(ไม่รู้)/ไม่ใช่(รู้)
– châi (mâi róo)/mâi châi (róo)
– No (I don't)/Yes (I do).

นี่รถของคุณไม่ใช่หรือ
nêe rót kǒrng kOOn mâi châi lěr?
This is your car, isn't it?

– ใช่(ของผม)/ไม่ใช่
– châi (kǒrng pǒm)/mâi châi
– Yes (it's mine)/No.

For negative why? questions ('why didn't you . . . ?') see 12.2.7.

11.11 Negative conditional clauses

Negative conditional clauses ('unless, otherwise, if . . . not') are introduced by **mâi yàhng nún** ('otherwise') – often shortened in speech to **mâi yung nún**, **mâi ngún** or **ngún**, **mí-chà-nún** ('otherwise') or simply **mâi**; as in positive conditional clauses (9.2.1), the word **tâh** ('if') is frequently omitted:

ไม่อย่างนั้นเราจะไปรับ
mâi yàhng nún rao ja bpai rúp
Otherwise we'll go and pick her up.

มิฉะนั้นผมไม่ไป
mí-chà-nún pǒm mâi bpai
Otherwise I'm not going.

ไม่อยากไปก็ไม่ต้อง
mâi yàhk bpai gôr mâi dtôrng
If you don't want to go, you don't have to.

ไม่บอกก็ช่วยไม่ได้
mâi bòrk gôr chôo-ay mâi dâi
Unless you tell me, then I can't help.

ไม่ใช่วันนี้ก็ต้องเป็นพรุ่งนี้

mâi châi wun née gôr dtôrng bpen prÔOng née

If not today, then it must be tomorrow.

11.12 Saying 'no'

The negative answer to a yes/no question is determined by the question particle. Thus, for example, a 'no' answer to a question that ends in ... **mái?** is **mâi** + VERB, while for a question ending in ... (**láir-o**) **réu yung?**, it is **yung**. Yes/no answers are dealt with in more detail in 12.1, but the following chart provides a basic summary of the most likely negative responses:

Questions ending in:	NO answer
... **mái?**	**mâi** + VERB
... **lĕr?**	**mâi** (+ POLITE PARTICLE)
	mâi + VERB
	bplào:
... **châi mái?**	**mâi châi**
	mâi cherng
... **láir-o réu yung?**	**yung** (+ POLITE PARTICLE)
	yung + VERB
... **réu bplào:?**	**mâi** + VERB
	bplào:
... **ná**	**mâi** + VERB

Note also, the more qualified 'no' response, **mâi cherng** ('not really, not exactly, I wouldn't say that'):

น่าเบื่อมากไหม

nâh bèu-a mâhk mái?

Was it very boring?

– ก็ไม่เชิง

– **gôr mâi cherng**

– Well, not exactly.

11.13 Useful negative expressions

ไม่เป็นไร	**mâi bpen rai**	Never mind!
ไม่มีทาง	**mâi mee tahng**	No way!
ไม่มีวัน	**mâi mee wun**	Never!
ไม่มีปัญหา	**mâi mee bpun-hăh**	No problem!; without question
ใช้ไม่ได้	**chái mâi dâi**	(it's) no good
ไม่เป็นเรื่อง	**mâi bpen rêu-ung**	(it's) nonsense
ไม่เข้าเรื่อง	**mâi kâo rêu-ung**	(it's) irrelevant
ไม่เอาไหน	**mâi ao năi**	(it's) useless, good-for-nothing
เป็นไปไม่ได้	**bpen bpai mâi dâi**	(it's) impossible
ไม่เกี่ยว	**mâi gèe-o**	(it's) irrelevant

เขาพูดไม่เป็นเรื่อง
káo pôot mâi bpen rêu-ung
He's talking nonsense.

เขาเป็นคนไม่เอาไหน
káo bpen kon mâi ao năi
He's a good-for-nothing.

11.14 Two further negatives: mí and hăh ... mâi

Two other negative forms to be aware of, which are most likely to be encountered in written Thai, are **mí**, a polite, rather formal variant of **mâi**, and the 'wrap-around' expression, **hăh** + VERB (PHRASE) + **mâi**, which can seriously mislead the unsuspecting learner:

เขาทำโดยมิได้หวังประโยชน์อะไร
káo tum doy-ee mí dâi wăng bpra-yòht a-rai
He did it without hoping for any benefit.

จะเรียกว่าอย่างอื่นให้โก้หร่านกว่านี้หาได้ไม่
ja rêe-uk wâh yàhng èun hâi gôh ràhn gwàh née hăh dâi mâi
You couldn't call it anything fancier than this.

Chapter 12

Questions

12.1 Yes/no questions

Statements are transformed into questions that require a simple yes/no answer by adding the question particles, **mái?**, **lěr?**, **châi mái?**, **ná**, **réu bplào:?** or **(láir-o) réu yung?**, to the end of the statement:

Statement	Question
อาหารญี่ปุ่นแพง	อาหารญี่ปุ่นแพงไหม
ah-hǎhn yêe-bpÒOn pairng	**ah-hǎhn yêe-bpÒOn pairng mái?**
Japanese food is expensive.	Is Japanese food expensive?
เขาเป็นเพื่อน	เขาเป็นเพื่อนใช่ไหม
káo bpen pêu-un	**káo bpen pêu-un châi mái?**
He's a friend.	He's a friend, isn't he?

There is no single word for 'yes' and for 'no'; the appropriate way of saying yes/no is determined by the question particle used.

12.1.1 ...mái? questions

mái? questions are neutral: they do not anticipate either a positive or negative response. Answers to simple **mái?** questions are formed as follows:

Yes: VERB
No: **mâi** + VERB

ไกลไหม	– ไกล/ไม่ไกล
glai mái?	– **glai/mâi glai**
Is it far?	– Yes/No.

If the question includes more than one verb, the first verb is normally used in responses:

อยากไปดูหนังไหม
yàhk bpai doo nǔng mái?
Would you like to go and see a film?

– อยาก/ไม่อยาก
– **yàhk/mâi yàhk**
– Yes/No.

Although the question particle **mái?** is written in Thai script as if it had a rising tone, in normal speech it is pronounced with a high tone. Note that **mái?** is not used in negative questions (11.10).

| 12.1.2 | **. . . lěr/rěu:? questions** |

lěr? questions are not neutral: they make an assumption and seek confirmation of that assumption. Answers to **lěr?** questions are formed as follows:

Yes: **krúp/kâ** (+ VERB)
        or
        VERB + **krúp/kâ**

No: **mâi** + VERB
        or
        bplào: + **krúp/kâ** (+ **mâi** + VERB)*

* **bplào:** conveys a stronger sense of denying the assumption made in the question; to avoid abruptness, it may be followed by a further clarifying statement.

เขาชอบหรือ
káo chôrp lěr?
He likes it, does he?

– ครับ ชอบ/ไม่ชอบ
– **krúp chôrp/mâi chôrp**
– Yes/No.

– เปล่าค่ะ ไม่ชอบเลย
– **bplào: kâ mâi chôrp ler-ee**
– No, he doesn't like it at all.

lĕr? commonly occurs in negative questions (11.10) and in isolation, where it means 'Really?'; it is written in Thai script as if it were pronounced rĕu:, although this pronunciation is seldom heard.

12.1.3 ...châi mái? *questions*

châi mái? is similar to lĕr? (12.1.2), in that it seeks confirmation for the assumption made in the question. Answers to châi mái? questions are formed as follows:

Yes: **châi**
No: **mâi châi**

แม่เป็นคนไทยใช่ไหม
mâir bpen kon tai châi mái?
Your mother is Thai, isn't she?

– ใช่/ไม่ใช่
– **châi/mâi châi**
– Yes/No.

châi mái? also commonly occurs in negative questions (11.10).

12.1.4 ...ná *questions*

ná? questions are invitations to agree with the preceding comment (e.g. It's a nice day today, isn't it?), rather than to confirm whether or not it is true. It is commonly used in conversation-initiating questions. (For other uses of ná, see 10.3.4.) Answers to ná? questions are formed as follows:

Yes: **krúp/kâ** or VERB + **krúp/kâ**
No: **mâi** + VERB + **krúp/kâ**

วันนี้ร้อนนะ
wun née rórn ná?
It's hot today, isn't it?

– ครับ/ค่ะ / ไม่ร้อนครับ/ค่ะ
– **krúp/kâ / mâi rórn krúp/kâ**
– Yes/No.

12.1.5 ...réu bplào:? *questions*

réu bplào:? questions, although not as brusque as the English translation
('... or not?') suggests, require a straight answer. Answers to **réu bplào:?**
questions are formed as follows:

If the question refers to the present or future:

Yes: VERB

No: **mâi** + VERB
       or
       bplào: (+ **mâi** + VERB)

คุณจะไปหรือเปล่า
kOOn ja bpai réu bplào:?
Are you going or not?

– ไป/ไม่ไป
– **bpai/mâi bpai**
– Yes/No.

เขาเบื่อหรือเปล่า
káo bèu-a réu bplào:?
Is he bored or not?

– เบื่อ/ไม่เบื่อ or เปล่า ไม่เบื่อ
– **bèu-a/mâi bèu-a** or **bplào: mâi bèu-a**
– Yes/No.

If the question refers to the past, stative verbs (5.2) behave differently to
other verbs:

Yes: VERB + **láir-o**
       or
       STATIVE VERB (+ **krúp/kâ**)

No: **mâi dâi** + VERB
       or
       bplào: + **krúp/kâ** (+ **mâi dâi** + VERB)
       or
       mâi + STATIVE VERB
       or
       bplào: + **krúp/kâ** (+ **mâi** + STATIVE VERB)

คุณบอกเขาหรือเปล่า

kOOn bòrk káo réu bplào:?

Did you tell him (or not)?

– บอกแล้ว/ไม่ได้บอก

– bòrk láir-o/mâi dâi bòrk

– Yes/No.

คุณเบื่อหรือเปล่า

kOOn bèu-a réu bplào:?

Were you bored (or not)?

– เบื่อ/ไม่เบื่อ or เปล่าครับ/ค่ะ ไม่เบื่อ

– bèu-a/mâi bèu-a or **bplào: krúp/kâ mâi bèu-a**

– Yes/No.

As an alternative to **réu bplào:?**, '. . . or not?' questions can also be formed using **réu mâi?**; answers follow the same pattern as for **réu bplào:?** questions:

คุณจะไปหรือไม่

kOOn ja bpai réu mâi?

Are you going or not?

Note that **réu** in **réu bplào:?** and **réu yung?** (12.1.6) is pronounced with a high tone, but spelt as if it were pronounced with a rising tone, **rěu:**.

12.1.6 . . . (láir-o) réu yung? *questions*

(láir-o) réu yung? questions ask whether something has happened yet; the word **láir-o** ('already') is often omitted in spoken Thai. Answers to **(láir-o) réu yung?** questions are formed as follows, with the negative response **yung** often expanded to avoid sounding too abrupt:

Yes: VERB + **láir-o**

No: **yung krúp/kâ** expanded by
either
yung mâi dâi + VERB
or
yung mâi + STATIVE VERB

กินข้าว(แล้ว)หรือยัง

gin kâo: (láir-o) réu yung?

Have you eaten yet?

– กินแล้ว/ยังค่ะ ยังไม่ได้กิน

– **gin láir-o/yung kâ yung mâi dâi gin**

– Yes/No, I haven't.

พอ(แล้ว)หรือยัง

por (láir-o) réu yung?

Is that enough?

– พอแล้ว/ยังครับ ยังไม่พอ

– **por láir-o/yung krúp yung mâi por**

– Yes/No.

(**láir-o**) **réu yung?** questions are also used to ask whether someone is married or has children:

คุณแต่งงาน(แล้ว)หรือยัง

kOOn dtàirng ngahn (láir-o) réu yung?

Are you married?

– แต่งแล้ว/ยังครับ ยังไม่แต่ง

– **dtàirng láir-o/yung krúp yung mâi dtàirng**

– Yes/No, I'm not.

เขามีลูก(แล้ว)หรือยัง

káo mee lôok (láir-o) réu yung?

Do they have any children?

– มีแล้ว/ยังค่ะ ยังไม่มี

– **mee láir-o/yung kâ yung mâi mii**

– Yes/No, they don't.

Note that หรือ is here pronounced **réu** (with a short vowel and high tone) rather than **rěu:** (with a long vowel and rising tone) as the spelling suggests.

| 12.1.7 | **ja . . . réu yung?** *questions* |

Superficially similar to (**láir-o**) **réu yung?** questions (see 12.1.6), are those that have the pattern **ja** + VERB + **réu yung?** This construction refers not to past actions, but conveys the meaning 'Do you want to . . . yet?' or 'Are you ready to . . . yet?' Answers to **ja** + VERB + **réu yung?** questions are formed as follows:

Yes: VERB
    or
    ja + VERB + **láir-o**

No: **yung krúp/kâ**
    or
    yung mâi + VERB

จะกินหรือยัง
ja gin réu yung?
Are you ready to eat yet?

– กิน or จะกินแล้ว/ยังครับ ยังไม่กิน
– gin or **ja gin láir-o/yung krúp yung mâi gin**
– Yes/No, not yet.

จะกลับบ้านหรือยัง
ja glùp bâhn réu yung?
Are you ready to go home yet?

– กลับ or จะกลับแล้ว/ยังค่ะ ยังไม่กลับ
– glùp or **ja glùp láir-o/yung kâ yung mâi glùp**
– Yes/No, not yet.

12.2 Wh- questions

In English the Wh- question words (who?, what?, where?, why?, when?, which? how?) normally occur at the beginning of the question. In Thai the position of some question words varies according to their grammatical function in the sentence, while others have a fixed position.

Most Wh- questions are answered by substituting the response word in the position in the sentence that the question word occupies.

Many of the Wh- question words also function as indefinite pronouns ('anyone', 'anything', etc., see 4.8).

12.2.1 Who? questions

The position of the question word **krai?** ('who?') is determined by its grammatical function in the sentence; if the question pattern is VERB + **krai?**, then the answer will be (VERB) + PERSON, while if the question is **krai?** + VERB, the answer will be PERSON + (VERB):

คุณไปกับใคร
kOOn bpai gùp krai?
Who are you going with?

– (ไป)กับเพื่อน
– (bpai) gùp pêu-un
– With a friend.

ใครสอน
krai sŏrn?
Who taught you?

– อาจารย์มานัส(สอน)
– ah-jahn mah-nút (sŏrn)
– Acharn Manat (did).

12.2.2 Whose? questions

Whose? questions are formed by the pattern NOUN + (**kŏrng**) + **krai?** (see also 3.5.12); when there is a preceding noun, **kŏrng** ('of') is often omitted; if there is no preceding noun, however, it may not be omitted:

บ้าน(ของ)ใคร
bâhn (kŏrng) krai?
Whose house?

– บ้าน(ของ)เรา/ของเรา
– bâhn (kŏrng) rao/kŏrng rao
– Our house/Ours.

นี่ของใคร
nêe kŏrng krai?
Whose is this?

– ของผม
– kŏrng pŏm
– It's mine.

12.2.3 *What? questions*

What? questions are formed using the pattern, VERB (PHRASE) + **a-rai?** ('what?'); note, however, that **a-rai?** occurs before the aspect marker **yòo** (5.7.3) and directional verbs (5.5):

เขาชื่ออะไร
káo chêu a-rai?
What's her name?

– ชื่อต๋อย
– chêu dtŏy
– Her name is Toi.

คุณทำอะไรอยู่
kOOn tum a-rai yòo?
What are you doing?

– ดูทีวีอยู่
– doo tee wee yòo
– Watching TV.

คุณซื้ออะไรมา
kOOn séu: a-rai mah?
What did you buy?

เกิดอะไรขึ้น
gèrt a-rai kêun?
What's happening?

Note also the common idiomatic expression:

อะไรกัน
a-rai gun?
What's up?

Thai uses **yung-ngai?** ('How?') rather than **a-rai** (see 12.2.8) for some questions where English uses 'What?'

12.2.4 Which? questions

Which? questions are formed using the pattern, VERB + (NOUN) + CLASSIFIER + **năi?** ('which?'):

เอาหนังสือเล่มไหน
ao núng-sěu lêm năi?
Which book do you want?

– (เอา) เล่มนั้น
– **(ao) lêm nún**
– I want that one.

คุณคุยกับคนไหน
kOOn koo-ee gùp kon năi?
Which person did you chat with?

– (คุยกับ) ผู้หญิงคนญี่ปุ่น
– **(koo-ee gùp) pôo-yǐng kon yêe-bpÒOn**
– (I chatted with) the Japanese girl.

เขากลับวันไหน
káo glùp wun năi?
Which day is he returning?

– (กลับ) วันอาทิตย์
– **(glùp) wun ah-tít**
– (He is returning) on Sunday.

| 12.2.5 | *Where? questions* |

Where? questions are formed using the pattern, VERB (PHRASE) + **têe năi?** ('where?'); **têe năi?** always occurs at the end of a sentence. Answers follow the pattern, (VERB (PHRASE) +) **têe** + LOCATION:

คุณพักอยู่ที่ไหน
kOOn púk yòo têe năi?
Where are you staying?

– (พักอยู่) ที่โรงแรมรีโน
– (púk yòo) têe rohng rairm ree-noh
– (I'm staying) at the Reno Hotel.

เขาเกิดที่ไหน
káo gèrt têe năi?
Where was he born?

– (เกิด) ที่กรุงเทพฯ
– (gèrt) têe grOOng-tâyp
– (He was born) in Bangkok.

In both questions and answers, **têe** is normally dropped when the preceding verb is **bpai** ('to go') or **mah jàhk** ('to come from'); in spoken Thai **têe** is also often dropped when the preceding verb is **yòo** ('to be situated at'):

ไปไหน
bpai năi?
Where are you going?

– ไปซื้อของ
– bpai séu: kŏrng
– I'm going shopping.

เขามาจากไหน
káo mah jàhk năi?
Where does he come from?

– (มาจาก) เชียงใหม่
– (mah jàhk) chee-ung mài
– (He comes from) Chiangmai.

บ้านอยู่ไหน

bâhn yòo nǎi?

Where is your house?

– (อยู่)ถนนสุขุมวิท

– **(yòo) ta-nǒn sŎO-kŎOm-wít**

– It's on Sukhumwit Road.

12.2.6	**When? questions**

When? questions are formed using the pattern, VERB (PHRASE) + **mêu-rài?** ('when?'); answers follow the pattern (VERB (PHRASE) +) EXPRESSION OF TIME. **mêu-rài?** normally occurs at the end of a sentence, but may occur at the beginning for emphatic effect:

คุณกลับเมื่อไร

kOOn glùp mêu-rài?

When are you returning?

– (กลับ) อาทิตย์หน้า

– **(glùp) ah-tít nâh**

– (I'm returning) next week.

คุณจะบอกเขาเมื่อไร

kOOn ja bòrk káo mêu-rài?

When are you going to tell him?

เมื่อไรคุณจะบอกเขา

mêu-rài kOOn ja bòrk káo?

When are you going to tell her?

For asking the time and how long something takes, see 14.8.5.

12.2.7	**Why? questions**

Why? questions are formed using the basic pattern, **tum-mai?** ('why?') + (SUBJECT) + **(těung)** + VERB (PHRASE); the word **těung**, a colloquial variant of **jeung** ('therefore') is optional but extremely common in spoken Thai.

Negative why? questions (Why doesn't he . . . ?) follow a similar pattern: **tum-mai** + (SUBJECT) + **(těung)** + **mâi** ('not') + VERB (PHRASE).

Why? questions are answered by **pró' (wâh)** ('because') + VERB:

ทำไมถึงซื้อ

tum-mai tĕung séu:?

Why did you buy it?

– เพราะ(ว่า)ถูกดี

– pró' (wâh) tòok dee

– Because it was nice and cheap.

ทำไมเขาถึงไม่กิน

tum-mai káo tĕung mâi gin?

Why didn't he eat it?

– เพราะ(ว่า) เผ็ดไป

– pró' (wâh) pèt bpai

– Because it was too spicy.

tum-mai? can also occur at the end of the sentence, usually in an informal context:

บอกทำไม

bòrk tum-mai?

Why did you tell her?

To ask 'Why?' in response to a statement, the final particle **lâ?** (see 10.3.3) is frequently added:

ฉันเปลี่ยนใจแล้ว

chún bplèe-un jai láir-o

I've changed my mind.

– ทำไมล่ะ

– tum-mai lâ?

– Why?

12.2.8 *How? questions: manner*

How? questions in English can be divided into those of manner ('How did you get there?') and those of degree ('How long is it?'); the latter are dealt with in section 12.2.9.

Questions of manner follow the pattern, VERB (PHRASE) + **yung-ngai?** ('how?'); **yung-ngai?** is written as if it were spelt **yàhng-rai**, but in informal speech the pronunciation may be reduced further to simply **ngai?**.

กินอย่างไร
gin yung-ngai?
How do you eat it?

เขียนอย่างไร
kĕe-un yung-ngai?
How do you write it?

เป็นอย่างไร
bpen ngai?
How are things?

yung-ngai? is sometimes used when English uses 'What?':

คุณว่าอย่างไร
kOOn wâh yung-ngai?
What do you think?

คุณจะทำอย่างไร
kOOn ja tum yung-ngai?
What will you do?

| 12.2.9 | *How? questions: degree* |

Some questions of degree, such as How tall? How long (in time)?, How long (in measurement)? and How wide? follow the pattern, MEASURE WORD + **tâo-rài?** ('how much?'); such questions anticipate a specific numerical response, such as '1.65 metres', '2 hours', etc.

คุณไปนานเท่าไหร่
kOOn bpai nahn tâo-rài?
How long are you going for?

หนักเท่าไหร่
nùk tâo-rài?
How heavy is it?

สูงเท่าไหร่
sŏong tâo-rài?
How tall is it?

How? questions which do not necessarily anticipate a precise numerical quantification in the response can be formed by the pattern, VERB (PHRASE) + **mâhk kâir năi?** ('to what extent?'):

เบื่อมากแค่ไหน
bèu-a mâhk kâir năi?
How bored were you?

– เบื่อมากจริง ๆ
– bèu-a mâhk jing jing
– I was really bored.

สวยมากแค่ไหน
sŏo-ay mâhk kâir năi?
How pretty is she?

– ก็ . . . สวยเหมือนกัน
– gôr . . . sŏo-ay měu-un gun
– Well . . . quite pretty.

แพงมากแค่ไหน
pairng mâhk kâir năi?
How expensive is it?

– แพงมากอย่างไม่น่าเชื่อ
– pairng mâhk yàhng mâi nâh chêu-a
– Unbelievably expensive.

12.2.10 | *How much? questions*

How much? questions are formed using the pattern, VERB (PHRASE) + **tâo-rài?** ('how much?'); **tâo-rài?** always occurs at the end of the question:

นี่เท่าไหร่
nêe tâo-rài?
How much is this?

คุณซื้อเท่าไหร่

kOOn séu: tâo-rài?

How much did you buy it for?

เขาขายบ้านเท่าไหร่

káo kăi: bâhn tâo-rài?

How much did they sell the house for?

Questions which ask 'how much per . . . ?', are formed using the pattern, (NOUN +) CLASSIFIER + **la tâo-rài?** (see also 13.11):

ส้มโลละเท่าไหร่

sôm loh la tâo-rài?

How much are oranges a kilo?

เดือนละเท่าไหร่

deu-un la tâo-rài?

How much a month?

คนละเท่าไหร่

kon la tâo-rài?

How much per person?

12.2.11 How many? questions

How many? questions follow the pattern VERB + (NOUN) + **gèe** ('how many?') + CLASSIFIER; the answer normally consists of NUMBER + CLASSIFIER:

เอากาแฟกี่ถ้วย

ao gah-fair gèe tôo-ay?

How many cups of coffee do you want?

– สองถ้วย

– **sŏrng tôo-ay**

– Two.

มีลูกกี่คน

mee lôok gèe kon?

How many children do you have?

– สามคน

– **săhm kon**

– Three.

189

ไปกี่วัน

bpai gèe wun?

How many days are you going for?

– เจ็ดวัน

– jèt wan

– Seven.

| 12.2.12 | *Wh- questions + dee* |

The pattern VERB + WH- QUESTION + **dee** is used for asking for advice:

กินอะไรดี

gin a-rai dee?

What shall I/we eat?

ไปเมื่อไรดี

bpai mêu-rài dee?

When shall I/we go?

ทำอย่างไรดี

tum yung-ngai dee?

What shall I/we do?

พูดอย่างไรดี

pôot yung-ngai dee?

How shall I say it?/What shall I say?

| 12.2.13 | *Wh- questions + bâhng* |

The pattern VERB (PHRASE) + WH- QUESTION + **bâhng** anticipates a list of things, people, places, etc. in the response; the list is normally expressed as, X + Y + **láir-o gôr** ('and') + Z:

เขาซื้ออะไรบ้าง

káo séu: a-rai bâhng?

What (plural) did he buy?

– (ซื้อ) ผัก ขิง แล้วก็ปลา
– (séu:) pùk kǐng láir-o gôr bplah
– (He bought) vegetables, ginger and fish.

เจอใครบ้าง
jer krai bâhng?
Who (plural) did you meet?

– (เจอ) นก อู๊ดแล้วก็ เจี๊ยบ
– (jer) nók óot láir-o gôr jée-up
– (I met) Nok, Oot and Jiap.

คุณไปเที่ยวที่ไหนบ้าง
kOOn bpai têe-o têe nǎi bâhng?
Where (plural) did you go?

– (ไปเที่ยว) ลาว พม่า แล้วก็จีน
– (bpai têe-o) lao: pa-mâh láir-o gôr jeen
– (I went to) Laos, Burma and China.

The question **bpen yung-ngai bâhng?** ('How are things?') when used as a greeting, requires a simple formulaic response, such as 'Fine', and not a list of grumbles; it is, often reduced to **bpen ngai bâhng?** or **bpen ngai?**:

เป็นอย่างไรบ้าง
bpen yung-ngai bâhng?
How are things?

– สบายดีครับ/ค่ะ
– sa-bai: dee krúp/kâ
– Fine.

| 12.2.14 | **How/what about . . . ? questions**

How/What about . . . ? is used as a non-initiating question when the topic of conversation is defined and the kind of information to be supplied is understood by both parties; it is formed by the pattern: **láir-o + NOUN + lâ?**

แล้วคุณล่ะ
láir-o kOOn lâ?
And how/what about you?

แล้วเพื่อนล่ะ

láir-o pêu-un lâ?

And how/what about your friend?

แล้วพรุ่งนี้ล่ะ

láir-o prÔOng née lâ?

And how/what about tomorrow?

12.3 Alternative questions

Alternative questions ('Do you want tea *or* coffee?') link two phrases with **rěu:** ('or') which in spoken Thai is usually pronounced **réu**, with a short vowel and high tone:

ไปดูหนังหรือกลับบ้าน

bpai doo nǔng réu glùp bâhn?

Shall we see a film or go home?

เอาน้ำชาหรือกาแฟ

ao núm chah réu gah-fair?

Do you want tea or coffee?

To reply to such questions, you repeat the appropriate phrase, e.g. **glùp bâhn** 'Go home'; **ao gah-fair** ('I'll have coffee').

A much-contracted form of alternative question common in spoken Thai omits **réu**, and follows the pattern, VERB + **mâi** + VERB:

ไปไม่ไป

bpai mâi bpai?

Are you going or not? (lit. go – not – go)

ซื้อไม่ซื้อ

séu: mâi séu:?

Are you going buy it or not? (lit. buy – not – buy)

These could be expanded using **réu** to **ja bpai réu ja mâi bpai?** (will – go – or – will – not – go) and **ja séu: réu ja mâi séu:?** (will – buy – or – will – not – buy).

12.4 Indirect questions

Indirect questions are formed by the pattern: SUBJECT + **tǎhm** ('to ask')
+ (DIRECT OBJECT) + **wâh** ('that') + DIRECT QUESTION:

Direct question

จะกลับคืนนี้ไหม
ja glùp keu:n née mái?
Will you be back tonight?

Indirect question

เขาถามว่า จะกลับคืนนี้ไหม
káo tǎhm wâh ja glùp keu:n née mái?
He asked if I'd be back tonight.

Direct question

มีแฟนหรือยัง
mee fairn réu yung?
Do you have a boyfriend?

Indirect question

ผมถามเขาว่ามีแฟนหรือยัง
pǒm tǎhm káo wâh mee fairn réu yung?
I asked her if she had a boyfriend.

For indirect speech, see 5.9 and 9.3.

Chapter 13

Numbers, measurement and quantification

There are several different words for 'number' in Thai. The most common is **lâyk**, which in certain cases is followed by **têe** and in other cases prefixed by **mǎi:**. The word **ber**, from English 'number', has a more restricted usage, most commonly with telephone numbers, room numbers and clothes and shoes sizes.

เลข	**lâyk**	numeral, figure, odd/even numbers, Thai/Arabic numbers, house numbers
เลขที่	**lâyk têe**	house numbers, passport number
หมายเลข	**mǎi: lâyk**	bank accounts, contestants on game shows, beauty contests
เบอร์	**ber**	telephone numbers, email addresses, room numbers, shoe/clothes sizes, players' numbers on sports shirts
สาย	**sǎi:**	bus numbers/routes
ป้าย	**bpâi:**	car number plates
จำนวน	**jum-noo-un**	quantity, amount

เลขเก้า
lâyk gâo
number nine

บ้านเลขที่เจ็ด
bâhn lâyk têe jèt
house no. 7

หมายเลขบัญชีธนาคาร
măi: lâyk bun-chee ta-na-kahn
bank account number

ห้องเบอร์ยี่สิบสาม
hôrng ber yêe sìp săhm
room no. 23

เบอร์โทรศัพท์
ber toh-ra-sùp
telephone number

ใส่เบอร์อะไร
sài ber a-rai?
What size do you take?

เสื้อเบอร์เจ็ดเป็นใคร
sêu-a ber jèt bpen krai?
Who's the number 7? / Who's wearing the number 7 shirt?

รถเมล์สาย ๑๓๗
rót may săi: nèung săhm jèt
the number 137 bus

เงินจำนวนหนึ่ง
ngern jum-noo-un nèung
an amount of money

13.1 Cardinal numbers

Both Thai and Arabic numbers are in common everyday use. Thai script numerals are identical to those found in the Cambodian script, while the Lao script employs some but not all of the same number symbols.

0	ศูนย์	๐	**sŏon**
1	หนึ่ง	๑	**nèung**
2	สอง	๒	**sŏrng**
3	สาม	๓	**săhm**

4	สี่	๔	sèe
5	ห้า	๕	hâh
6	หก	๖	hòk
7	เจ็ด	๗	jèt
8	แปด	๘	bpàirt
9	เก้า	๙	gâo:
10	สิบ	๑๐	sìp

Numbers 12 to 19 are formed regularly using **sìp** + unit; 11 is irregular, using **èt** instead of **nèung**:

11	สิบเอ็ด	๑๑	sìp-èt
12	สิบสอง	๑๒	sìp-sŏrng
13	สิบสาม	๑๓	sìp-săhm
14	สิบสี่	๑๔	sìp-sèe

Multiples of ten up to 90 use **sìp** ('ten') as a suffix and are regular with the exception of 'twenty', which uses **yêe** instead of **sŏrng**.

20	ยี่สิบ	๒๐	yêe-sìp
30	สามสิบ	๓๐	săhm-sìp
40	สี่สิบ	๔๐	sèe-sìp
50	ห้าสิบ	๕๐	hâh-sìp
60	หกสิบ	๖๐	hòk-sìp
70	เจ็ดสิบ	๗๐	jèt-sìp
80	แปดสิบ	๘๐	bpàirt-sìp
90	เก้าสิบ	๙๐	gâo:-sìp

Numbers between 10 and 100 are formed in a regular way with the exception of 21, 31, 41, etc. where the word for 'one' is **èt** and not **nèung**. In numbers 21–29, **yêe-sìp** is often contracted to **yêep** in informal spoken Thai:

21	ยี่สิบเอ็ด	๒๑	yêe-sìp èt (yêep èt)
22	ยี่สิบสอง	๒๒	yêe-sìp sǒrng (yêep sǒrng)
23	ยี่สิบสาม	๒๓	yêe-sìp sǎhm (yêep sǎhm)
31	สามสิบเอ็ด	๓๑	sǎhm-sìp èt
32	สามสิบสอง	๓๒	sǎhm-sìp sǒrng
33	สามสิบสาม	๓๓	sǎhm-sìp sǎhm
41	สี่สิบเอ็ด	๔๑	sèe-sìp èt
42	สี่สิบสอง	๔๒	sèe-sìp sǒrng
51	ห้าสิบเอ็ด	๕๑	hâh-sìp èt

Numbers from 100 upwards are also formed regularly, but in addition to words for 'thousand' and 'million', there are also specific words for 'ten thousand' and 'hundred thousand':

100	(หนึ่ง) ร้อย	๑๐๐	(nèung) róy
101	(หนึ่ง) ร้อยเอ็ด	๑๐๑	(nèung) róy èt
102	(หนึ่ง) ร้อยสอง	๑๐๒	(nèung) róy sǒrng
1000	(หนึ่ง) พัน	๑๐๐๐	(nèung) pun
1002	(หนึ่ง) พัน(กับ)สอง	๑๐๐๒	(nèung) pun (gùp) sǒrng
1200	(หนึ่ง) พันสอง(ร้อย)	๑๒๐๐	(nèung) pun sǒrng (róy)
10,000	(หนึ่ง) หมื่น	๑๐๐๐๐	(nèung) mèu:n
100,000	(หนึ่ง) แสน	๑๐๐๐๐๐	(nèung) sǎirn
1,000,000	(หนึ่ง) ล้าน	๑๐๐๐๐๐๐	(nèung) láhn

Numbers, including the year, are read as in the following examples; years may be prefaced by **bpee** ('year'):

1986   (ปี) หนึ่งพันเก้าร้อยแปดสิบหก
(bpee) nèung pun gâo: róy bpàirt-sìp hòk

2541   (ปี) สองพันห้าร้อยสี่สิบเอ็ด
(bpee) sŏrng pun hâh róy sèe-sìp èt

75,862   เจ็ดหมื่นห้าพันแปดร้อยหกสิบสอง
jèt mèu:n hâh pun bpàirt róy hòk-sìp sŏrng

432,925   สี่แสนสามหมื่นสองพันเก้าร้อยยี่สิบห้า
sèe săirn săhm mèu:n sŏrng pun gâo: róy yêe-sìp hâh

When a cardinal number occurs with a noun, the appropriate classifier must also be used (3.5.1, 3.5.5, 3.5.8).

13.2   Cardinal numbers with sùk and dtûng

sùk + CARDINAL NUMBER + CLASSIFIER conveys the sense of 'as little/ few as', 'merely' or 'just', and is often reinforced by **tâo-nún** ('only') at the end of the phrase; sometimes it simply conveys the idea of approximation. When sùk occurs before a classifier with no number word, it is understood that 'one' has been omitted.

ผมจะไปสักห้าวัน
pŏm ja bpai sùk hâh wun
I'm going for five days or so.

เราคุยกันสักชั่วโมงเท่านั้น
rao koo-ee gun sùk chôo-a-mohng tâo-nún
We chatted for just an hour.

เขาอยากมีลูกสักคนสองคน
káo yàhk mee lôok sùk kon sŏrng kon
They would like to have a child or two.

dtûng + CARDINAL NUMBER + CLASSIFIER conveys the idea of 'as much/many as':

เขาคุยกันตั้งสามชั่วโมง
káo koo-ee gun dtûng săhm chôo-a-mohng
They chatted for as long as three hours.

เขาเรียนตั้งห้าปีแล้ว

káo ree-un dtûng hâh bpee láir-o

He has studied for as long as five years.

Both **sùk** and **dtûng** can be used with other, non-numerical quantifier words such as 'a little' and 'a long time':

รออีกสักหน่อยได้ไหม

ror èek sùk nòy dâi: mái?

Can you wait a little longer?

ผมไม่ได้พบเขาตั้งนาน

pŏm mâi dâi póp káo dtûng nahn

I haven't met him for a long time.

13.3 Ordinal numbers

Ordinal numbers in Thai are formed by the pattern, **têe** + CARDINAL NUMBER:

ที่หนึ่ง	**têe nèung**	first
ที่สอง	**têe sŏrng**	second
ที่สาม	**têe sǎhm**	third

When an ordinal number occurs with a noun, the appropriate classifier must also be used (3.5.3, 3.5.9).

The word **râirk** also means 'first', but in a historical sense rather than in rank order. It is therefore not always interchangeable with **têe nèung**:

ครั้งที่หนึ่ง/ครั้งแรก

krúng têe nèung/krúng râirk

the first time

But:

รางวัลที่หนึ่ง

rahng-wun têe nèung

the first (top) prize

รางวัล(ครั้ง)แรก

rahng-wun (krúng) râirk

the inaugural prize

Note that in the expression **tee râirk** ('at first'), the word **tee** ('time') is a noun, pronounced with a mid-tone, not the location marker **têe** ('at'):

ทีแรกฉันไม่ชอบเขา

tee râirk chún mâi chôrp káo
At first I didn't like him.

'Firstly', 'secondly', and so on, used in putting forward numbered points in a reasoned argument, follow the pattern **bpra-gahn** ('item, sort, kind') + ORDINAL NUMBER:

| ประการที่หนึ่ง | **bpra-gahn têe nèung** | firstly |

or

ประการแรก	**bpra-gahn râirk**	
ประการที่สอง	**bpra-gahn têe sǒrng**	secondly
ประการที่สาม	**bpra-gahn têe sǎhm**	thirdly

13.4 Sanskrit numbers

The Sanskrit numbers **àyk** ('one'), **toh** ('two') and **dtree** ('three') are used to distinguish between academic degrees and military ranks, and in the names of tones and tone marks (2.5.2):

ปริญญาเอก/โท/ตรี

bpa-rin-yah àyk/toh/dtree
PhD/MA, MSc etc./BA, BSc etc.

พล(ตำรวจ)เอก/โท/ตรี

pon (dtum-ròo-ut) àyk/toh/dtree
(police) general/lieutenant-general/major-general

The word **toh** is also used instead of **sǒrng** when giving telephone numbers, which are read as if each unit is a single digit:

เบอร์โทรศัพท์โท-สี่-ห้า-สาม-โท-เก้า-แปด

ber toh-ra-sùp toh – sèe – hâh – sǎhm – toh – gâo: – bpàirt
telephone number, two – four – five – three – two – nine – eight

Other Sanskrit numbers appear in the words for 'decade', 'decathlon' and 'century':

ทศวรรษ	**tót-sa-wút**	decade
ทศกรีฑา	**tót-sa-gree-tah**	decathlon
ศตวรรษ	**sà-dta-wút**	century

13.5 Once, twice …

'Once', 'twice' and so on, are formed using CARDINAL NUMBER + **krúng** or **hǒn**, both of which mean 'time' or 'occasion':

หนึ่งครั้ง/หน	**nèung krúng/hǒn**	once, one time
สองครั้ง	**sǒrng krúng**	twice
สามครั้ง	**sǎhm krúng**	three times

When **nèung** occurs after **krúng** it is less emphatic; **dee-o** ('single') may also be used instead of **nèung** for greater emphasis:

ครั้งหนึ่ง	**krúng nèung**	once, on one occasion
ครั้งเดียว	**krúng dee-o**	(just) once, on a single occasion

krúng and **hǒn** are also used with ordinal numbers to mean 'first time', 'second time' and so on:

ครั้งที่หนึ่ง	**krúng têe nèung**	the first time

or

ครั้งแรก	**krúng râirk**	
ครั้งที่สอง	**krúng têe sǒrng**	the second time
ครั้งที่สาม	**krúng têe sǎhm**	the third time

201

Fractions, decimals, percentages, multiples and averages

13.6.1 *Fractions*

Fractions, other than 'half', are expressed by the pattern **sàyt** ('numerator') + NUMBER + **sòo-un** ('denominator') + NUMBER:

เศษหนึ่งส่วนสี่   **sàyt nèung sòo-un sèe**   quarter

เศษสามส่วนสี่   **sàyt săhm sòo-un sèe**   three quarters

However, in expressions like 'three quarters of the population . . .', **săhm nai sèe** (three-in-four) is more common:

ประชาชนสามในสี่
bpra-chah-chon săhm nai sèe
three quarters of the population

krêung ('half') behaves like other number words in occurring after a noun and before a classifier:

เหล้าครึ่งขวด
lâo krêung kòo-ut
half a bottle of whisky

ครึ่งวัน
krêung wun
half a day

krêung also occurs after a classifier in the pattern, NOUN + (NUMBER +) CLASSIFIER + **krêung** to mean 'NUMBER and a half'; if no number word appears, the phrase conveys the idea of 'one and a half':

เหล้าสองขวดครึ่ง
lâo sŏrng kòo-ut krêung
two and a half bottles of whisky

เราไปเดือนครึ่ง
rao bpai deu-un krêung
We went for a month and a half.

13.6.2 Decimals

Decimal numbers are read as NUMBER + jÒOt ('point') + NUMBER; decimals behave like other numbers in being followed by a classifier (see 2.4):

สี่จุดห้า
sèe jÒOt hâh
4.5

ยาวหกจุดห้าสามนิ้ว
yao: hòk jÒOt hâh sǎhm néw
6.53 inches long

13.6.3 Percentages

Percentages can be expressed either using the English word **bper-sen** ('per cent') in the pattern, NOUN + NUMBER + **bper-sen,** or in the pattern NOUN + **róy la** ('per hundred') + NUMBER (+ CLASSIFIER):

ประชาชนห้าสิบเปอร์เซ็นต์
bpra-chah-chon hâh-sìp bper-sen
Fify per cent of the people

อัตราดอกเบี้ยร้อยละสองจุดห้า
ùt-dtrah dòrk bêe-a róy la sǒrng jÒOt hâh
2.5% interest rate

13.6.4 Multiples

'x times more . . .' is expressed by the pattern, ADJECTIVE/ADVERB + **gwàh** + NUMBER + **tâo:**

ใหญ่กว่าสามเท่า
yài gwàh sǎhm tâo
three times bigger

สนุกกว่าพันเท่า
sa-nÒOk gwàh pun tâo
a thousand times more fun

203

| 13.6.5 | *Averages* |

When 'average' refers to a numerical calculation or estimate, **cha-lèe-a** ('average') or ('on average') **doy-ee cha-lèe-a** is used.

เงินเดือนเฉลี่ยสำหรับงานประเภทนี้คือ ๒-๓๐,๐๐๐ บาท
ngern deu-un cha-lèe-a sŭm-rùp ngahn bpra-pâyt née keu: sŏrng
  tĕung săhm meu:n bàht
The average salary for this kind of work is 20–30,000 baht per month.

ต้องทำงานกลางคืนเดือนละสี่วันโดยเฉลี่ย
dtôrng tum ngahn glahng keu:n deu-un la sèe wun doy-ee
  cha-lèe-a
She has to work four nights a month on average.

Note that **bpahn glahng**, not **cha-lèe-a**, is used to mean 'average' in the sense of 'moderate' or 'ordinary':

ฝีมือปานกลาง
fĕe meu: bpahn glahng
average (moderate) skill

คุณภาพปานกลาง
kOOn-na-pâhp bpahn glahng
average (ordinary) quality

13.7 Collective numbers

The collective numbers **kôo** ('pair') and **lŏh** ('dozen') behave like classifiers and occur in the pattern, NOUN + NUMBER + COLLECTIVE NUMBER:

รองเท้าสามคู่
rorng táo: săhm kôo
three pairs of shoes

ไข่ครึ่งโหล
kài krêung lŏh
half a dozen eggs

13.8 Some idiomatic expressions involving numbers

săirn ('one hundred thousand') or **săirn ja** or **săirn têe ja** is used before certain adjectives to mean 'extremely', 'ever so . . .':

แสนไกล
săirn glai
extremely far

แสนจะสนุก
săirn ja sa-nòOk
ever such fun

róy bpàirt ('one hundred and eight') means 'all kinds of', and often mirrors the use of '101' in English; it is sometimes intensified by the addition of **pun** ('thousand'):

ร้อยแปดคำที่คนไทยมักใช้ผิด
róy bpàirt kum têe kon tai múk chái pìt
'108 words which Thais tend to use incorrectly' (book title)

ปัญหาร้อยแปด(พัน)ประการ
bpun-hăh róy bpàirt (pun) bpra-gahn
all kinds of problems

hâh róy ('five hundred'), curiously, is added to the word **john** ('bandit, thief') but to no other noun; it does not indicate plurality, nor intensify the scale of thievery, nor reflect the speaker's attitude:

โจรห้าร้อย
john hâh róy
bandit, thief

săhm-sìp sŏrng ('thirty-two') is used with the word **ah-gahn** ('state, condition, sign') in the expression **ah-gahn króp săhm-sìp sŏrng** ('to be perfectly normal'). Literally, it means 'the full thirty-two conditions' and is a reference to the traditional belief that the body comprised thirty-two integral parts, including hair, teeth, skin, fingernails, limbs and internal organs. The expression is used to describe newly born children or those escaping injury in an accident; it is used in negative statements – with **ah-gahn** often omitted – to describe a person who behaves in an irrational, usually bad way.

อาการครบสามสิบสอง
ah-gahn króp sǎhm-sìp sǒrng
to be perfectly normal

คนนั้นไม่ครบสามสิบสอง
kon nún mâi króp sǎhm-sìp sǒrng
That person's not all there.

gâo: ('nine') is regarded as lucky because it is identical in pronunciation (but not spelling) to a part of the word for 'to progress' (**gâo: nâh**):

| เก้า | **gâo:** | nine |
| ก้าวหน้า | **gâo: nâh** | to progress |

13.9 Measurements

Measurements, such as 'three metres *wide*', 'two hours *long*' and 'six feet *tall*' follow the pattern, TYPE OF MEASUREMENT (i.e. length, weight, etc.) + NUMBER + UNIT OF MEASUREMENT:

ยาวเจ็ดนิ้ว
yao: jèt néw
seven inches long

หนักห้าสิบกิโล
nùk hâh-sìp gi-loh
fifty kilos in weight

Area is expressed as NUMBER + **dtah-rahng** ('square') + UNIT OF MEASUREMENT:

สิบตารางเมตร
sìp dtah-rahng máyt
ten square metres

Plots of land are normally measured in **dtah-rahng wah** (square *waa*; 1 sq. *waa* = 4 sq. metres) or **râi** (*rai*; 1 *rai* = 1600 sq. metres or 400 sq. *waa*; 2.53 *rai* = 1 acre); note that **wah** is a linear measurement and is therefore preceded by **dtah-rahng**, but **râi** is itself an area measurement and so does not occur with **dtah-rahng**:

สี่สิบตารางวา
sèe sìp dtah-rahng wah
forty square *waa*

ขายที่ดิน ๑๐ไร่
kăi: têe din sìp râi
Land for sale: 10 *rai*

13.10 Distances

The distance between two places can be expressed by the pattern, PLACE
A + **yòo** ('to be located') + **glai jàhk** ('far from') + PLACE B + NUMBER
+ UNIT OF MEASUREMENT:

หัวหินอยู่ไกลจากกรุงเทพฯสองร้อยกิโลเมตร
hŏo-a hĭn yòo glai jàhk grOOng-tâyp sŏrng róy gi-loh-mét
Hua Hin is 200 kilometres from Bangkok.

hàhng jàhk ('far from') can be used as an alternative to **glai jàhk**:

ไปรษณีย์อยู่ห่างจากบ้านไม่กี่นาที
bprai-sa-nee yòo hàhng jàhk bâhn mâi gèe nah-tee
The post office is a few minutes from my house.

13.11 Distribution: 'per'

Expressions like '500 baht per person', 'six times per week' and 'how much
per kilo?' involve the use of **la** ('per'); the word order in Thai is the opposite to English (e.g. person – per – 500 baht), with the number expression
or question occurring after **la**:

คนละห้าร้อยบาท
kon la hâh róy bàht
500 baht per person

อาทิตย์ละหกครั้ง
ah-tít la hòk krúng
six times a week

โลละเท่าไหร่

loh la tâo-rài?

How much per kilo?

Note the idiomatic expressions **kon la rêu-ung (gun)** ('a different matter') and **kon la yàhng (gun)** ('a different kind') where **kon** does not mean 'person'.

เป็นคนละเรื่อง(กัน)

bpen kon la rêu-ung (gun)

That's a different matter.

เป็นคนละอย่าง(กัน)

bpen kon la yàhng (gun)

They're (two) different kinds.

In public notices and formal written Thai, **dtòr** is often used instead of **la** to mean 'per':

ค่าใช้จ่ายต่อเดือนไม่เกิน ๕ พันบาท

kâh chái jài: dtòr deu-un mâi gern hâh pun bàht

monthly expenses not in excess of 5,000 baht

๓,๐๐๐ บาทต่อตารางวา

săhm pun bàht dtòr dtah-rahng wah

three thousand baht per square *waa*

๒ เที่ยวต่อวัน

sŏrng têe-o dtòr wun săhm

two departures per day

13.12 Quantifiers

The following quantifiers occur in the pattern, (NOUN +) QUANTIFIER + CLASSIFIER (3.5.2). They occupy the same position between nouns and classifiers as cardinal numbers (3.5.1) and can therefore be thought of as 'number words'. All, with the exception of **mâhk**, can occur before a classifier without a preceding noun:

ทุก	**tÓOk**	every, all
แต่ละ	**dtàir la**	each

บาง	**bahng**	some
หลาย	**lǎi:**	several, many
ไม่กี่	**mâi gèe**	not many
น้อย	**nóy**	few
มาก	**mâhk**	many

งานแต่ละชิ้น
ah-hǎhn dtàir la chín
each piece of work

ช่วงเวลาหลายเดือน
chôo-ung way-lah lǎi: deu-un
a period of several/many months

อาหารบางอย่าง
ah-hǎhn bahng yàhng
some kinds of food

คนไทยไม่กี่คน
kon tai mâi gèe kon
not many Thai people

In phrases involving **nóy** ('few'), the classifier is commonly omitted:

เขามีโอกาสน้อย(ครั้ง)
káo mee oh-gàht nóy (krúng)
He has few opportunities.

A small number of quantifiers, including **yér** ('many'), **yáir** ('many'), **yér yáir** ('many'), **mâhk*** ('many'), **mâhk-mai:** ('many'), **nít-nòy** ('a little') and **lék nóy** ('few, little') follow a noun, but do not occur with classifiers:

เธอมีเพื่อนคนไทยเยอะแยะ
ter mee pêu-un kon tai yér yáir
She's got lots of Thai friends.

* **mâhk** may occasionally be encountered with a following classifier in rather stylised Thai.

ไม่อยากกินอาหารมากวันนี้

mâi yàhk gin ah-hǎhn mâhk wun née

I don't want to eat a lot of food today.

ใส่น้ำตาลนิดหน่อย

sài núm dtahn nít-nòy

Put a little sugar in.

มีข้าวเหลือเล็กน้อย

mee kâo: lěu-a lék nóy

There's a little rice left over.

The quantifiers **mâhk** and **nít-nòy** also function as adverbs of degree (7.6). For a note on the difference between the quantifier **bahng** and the adverb of degree **bâhng**, see 7.6.

13.13 Negative quantification

Negative quantities are expressed by the pattern **mâi mee** ('there is/are not', 'not have') + NOUN:

ไม่มีโอกาส

mâi mee oh-gàht

There's no opportunity.

ไม่มีน้ำปลา

mâi mee núm bplah

There's no fish sauce.

13.14 Approximation: 'about'

Approximation is expressed using **bpra-mahn** or **rao:** (both of which mean 'about') + NUMBER + CLASSIFIER:

นักท่องเที่ยวประมาณร้อยคน

núk tôrng têe-o bpra-mahn róy kon

about 100 tourists

ราวหกชั่วโมง

rao: hòk chôo-a mohng

about six hours

Two consecutive numbers also convey approximation:

สองสามวัน
sŏrng săhm wun
two or three days

ห้าหกคน
hâh hòk kon
five or six people

A range of numbers ('from . . . to . . .') is expressed by NUMBER + **tĕung** ('to') + NUMBER + CLASSIFIER:

สิบถึงสิบห้าคน
sìp tĕung sìp-hâh kon
(from) ten to fifteen people

Lower limits can be expressed by **yàhng nóy têe sÒOt** ('at least') + NUMBER + CLASSIFIER:

อย่างน้อยที่สุดสามวัน
yàhng nóy têe sÒOt săhm wun
at least three days

Upper limits ('at the most') follow a similar pattern using **mâhk** ('much') instead of **nóy**:

อย่างมากที่สุดหมื่นบาท
yàhng mâhk têe sÒOt mèu:n bàht
at the most 10,000 baht

13.15 Restriction: 'only'

There are several different words for 'only . . .' and they can occur in various combinations:

(a) NOUN (PHRASE) + NUMBER + CLASSIFIER + **tâo-nún**
(b) NOUN (PHRASE) + **pee-ung** + NUMBER + CLASSIFIER (+ **tâo-nún**)
(c) NOUN (PHRASE) + (**pee-ung**) + **dtàir** + NUMBER + CLASSIFIER (+ **tâo-nún**)
(d) NOUN (PHRASE) + (**pee-ung**) + **kâir** + NUMBER + CLASSIFIER (+ **tâo-nún**)

211

Note, however, that the order NUMBER + CLASSIFIER is normally reversed when the number is 'one' (see 3.5.1) and the word **dee-o** ('single') is commonly used instead of **nèung** ('one'). The use of **dtàir** ('but') to mean 'only' is mirrored in the archaic English usage of 'but' in statements like, 'I have *but* three daughters fair.'

เขามีลูกสองคนเท่านั้น

káo mee lôok sŏrng kon tâo-nún

They only have two children.

เขามีเพื่อนสนิทคนเดียวเท่านั้น

káo mee pêu-un sa-nìt kon dee-o tâo-nún

He has only one close friend.

เงินเหลือเพียงสี่ร้อยบาท(เท่านั้น)

ngern lĕu-a pee-ung sèe róy bàht (tâo-nún)

There are only four hundred baht left.

มีแต่ใบละยี่สิบใบเดียว(เท่านั้น)

mee dtàir bai la yêe-sìp bai dee-o (tâo-nún)

I've only got one 20 baht note.

ฉันไปเที่ยวเชียงใหม่แค่สามวัน(เท่านั้น)

chún bpai têe-o chee-ung mài kâir săhm wun (tâo-nún)

I went to Chiangmai for only three days

13.16 'More than'

'More than . . .' is usually expressed using the word **gwàh** ('more than, -er than'); its position in relation to the number and classifier varies.

13.16.1 NOUN (PHRASE) + NUMBER + gwàh + CLASSIFIER

This pattern tends to be used when dealing with multiples of ten and round numbers:

เธอมีรองเท้าร้อยกว่าคู่

ter mee rorng táo: róy gwàh kôo

She owns more than a hundred pairs of shoes.

ฉันได้เงินเดือนสองหมื่นกว่าบาท

chún dâi ngern deu-un sŏrng mèu:n gwàh bàht

I get a monthly salary of more than 20,000 baht.

เราเดินทางยี่สิบกว่าชั่วโมง

rao dern tahng yêe-sìp gwàh chôo-a mohng

We travelled for more than twenty hours.

13.16.2 | NOUN (PHRASE) + gwàh + NUMBER + CLASSIFIER

This pattern is also used only with large round numbers:

ประชาชนที่เดินขบวนต่อต้านสงครามมีกว่าเจ็ดแสนคน

**bpra-chah-chon têe dern ka-boo-un dtòr dtâhn sŏng-krahm mee
gwàh jèt săirn kon**

More than 700,000 people demonstrated against the war.

เขาซื้อบ้านกว่าห้าสิบล้าน

káo séu: bâhn gwàh hâh sìp láhn

He bought a house for more than 50 million.

13.16.3 | NOUN (PHRASE) + mâhk gwàh + NUMBER + CLASSIFIER

This pattern can be used generally and with non-round numbers:

หนังสือมากกว่าสิบห้าเล่ม

núng-sĕu: mâhk gwàh sìp hâh lêm

more than fifteen books

เขากินเบียร์มากกว่าหกขวด

káo gin bee-a mâhk gwàh hòk kòo-ut

He drank more than six bottles of beer.

mâhk gwàh can be substituted by either **gern** ('in excess of') or **gern gwàh**:

นักเรียนเกิน(กว่า)สามสิบห้าคน

núk ree-un gern (gwàh) săhm-sìp hâh kon

more than thirty pupils

213

13.16.4 NOUN (PHRASE) + NUMBER + CLASSIFIER + gwàh

This pattern is used to convey the idea of a fraction – but not a whole
unit – more; **gwàh** is sometimes reduplicated, with the first element pronounced **gwa**, with a mid-tone and a shortened vowel:

ฉันรอสองชั่วโมงกว่า

chún ror sŏrng chôo-a mohng gwàh

I waited over two hours.

บ่ายสี่โมงกว่า ๆ

bài: sèe mohng gwa gwàh

a little after 4 p.m.

Note the difference between

เขากินเบียร์สองขวดกว่า

káo gin bee-a sŏrng kòo-ut gwàh

He has drunk over two bottles of beer (but not as many as three).

and

เขากินเบียร์มากกว่าสองขวด

káo gin bee-a mâhk gwàh sŏrng kòo-ut

He has drunk more than two bottles of beer (i.e. at least three).

13.17 'Less than'

'Less than ...' can be expressed most simply by the pattern (NOUN
(PHRASE) +) **nóy gwàh** ('less than') + NUMBER + CLASSIFIER:

ผู้ใหญ่น้อยกว่าสิบคน

pôo-yài nóy gwàh sìp kon

less than ten adults

เขาพูดน้อยกว่าห้านาที

káo pôot nóy gwàh hâh nah-tee

He spoke for less than five minutes.

The negative form of the 'as many as' construction (13.18), NOUN (PHRASE) + **mâi tĕung** + NUMBER + CLASSIFIER, is also commonly used to express 'less than':

เขาได้เงินเดือนไม่ถึงหมื่นบาท
káo dâi ngern deu-un mâi tĕung mèu:n bàht
He gets a monthly salary of less than 10,000 baht.

13.18 'As many as'

'As many as . . .' or 'up to . . .' is expressed by the pattern NOUN (PHRASE) + **tĕung** ('to reach') + NUMBER + CLASSIFIER:

มีคนสมัครถึงพันคน
mee kon sa-mùk tĕung pun kon
There were as many as a thousand applicants.

For the negative form, see 13.17.

Chapter 14
Time

Days of the week are normally prefaced by the word **wun** ('day'); no preposition, corresponding to English 'on', is used:

วันจันทร์	**wun jun**	Monday
วันอังคาร	**wun ung-kahn**	Tuesday
วันพุธ	**wun pÓOt**	Wednesday
วันพฤหัส*	**wun pa-réu-hùt**	Thursday
วันศุกร์	**wun sÒOk**	Friday
วันเสาร์	**wun săo**	Saturday
วันอาทิตย์	**wun ah-tít**	Sunday

* Note the alternative, very formal spelling and pronunciation:

วันพฤหัสบดี
wun pa-réu-hùt-sa-bor-dee

เราจะกลับมาวันพุธ
rao ja glùp mah wun pÓOt
We'll be back on Wednesday.

วันเสาร์(วัน)อาทิตย์ไปเที่ยวที่ไหนบ้าง
wun săo (wun) ah-tít bpai têe-o têe năi bâhng?
Where did you go at the weekend?

14.2 Parts of the day

Words like **cháo:** ('morning') and **bài:** ('afternoon') are commonly prefixed with the word **dtorn** ('period of time') to express the idea 'in the morning', 'in the afternoon', etc.:

(ตอน)เช้า	**(dtorn) cháo:**	morning
(ตอน)บ่าย	**(dtorn) bài:**	afternoon
(ตอน)เย็น	**(dtorn) yen**	(early) evening
(ตอน)กลางคืน	**(dtorn) glahng keun**	night-time
(ตอน)กลางวัน	**(dtorn) glahng wun**	daytime

เรานัดพบกันตอนเย็น
rao nút póp gun dtorn yen
We've arranged to meet in the evening.

ตอนบ่ายฉันไม่ว่าง
dtorn bài: chún mâi wâhng
I'm not free in the afternoon.

ไปเช้ากลับเย็น
bpai cháo: glùp yen
We'll go in the morning and return in the evening.

14.3 Months

Months with 31 days end in **-kom**, those with 30 days in **-yon** and February in **-pun**. In normal speech, the word **deu-un** ('month') is often prefixed and the final syllable omitted; no preposition corresponding to English 'in' is used:

มกราคม	**mók-ga-rah-kom**	January
กุมภาพันธ์	**gOOm-pah-pun**	February
มีนาคม	**mee-nah-kom**	March
เมษายน	**may-săh-yon**	April

พฤษภาคม	préut-sa-pah-kom	May
มิถุนายน	mí-tOO-nah-yon	June
กรกฎาคม	ga-rúk-ga-dah-kom	July
สิงหาคม	sǐng-hǎh-kom	August
กันยายน`	gun-yah-yon	September
ตุลาคม	dtOO-lah-kom	October
พฤศจิกายน	préut-sa-jìk-gah-yon	November
ธันวาคม	tun-wah-kom	December

เขาไปเดือนสิงหาฯ
káo bpai deu-un sǐng-hǎh
He's going in August.

14.4   Years

The year is calculated according to the Buddhist Era (BE) (**pÓOt-ta-sùk-ka-ràht**, or **por sǒr** for short), which dates from the birth of the Buddha, 543 years before the birth of Christ. To convert Thai years to AD (**krít-ta-sùk-ka-ràht**, or **kor sǒr** for short), subtract 543; thus, 2500 BE is 1957 AD, while 2000 AD is 2543 BE.

To express the idea that something happened or will happen in a certain year, the word **bpee** ('year') is used before the number; the preposition **nai** ('in') may preface **bpee** but this is more common in formal written Thai than in the spoken language:

เขาแต่งงาน(ใน)ปี ๒๕๔๑
káo dtàirng ngahn (nai) bpee sǒrng pun hâh róy sèe-sìp èt
He got married in 2541 (1998).

Most Thais are also aware of their birth year in the twelve-year cycle in which each year is named after an animal. This animal term is specific to the year and is not used to refer to the living creature. The animal year is normally prefaced by the word **bpee**.

ปีชวด	bpee chôo-ut	Year of the Rat (1948, '60 …)
ปีฉลู	bpee cha-lŏo	Year of the Ox (1949, '61 …)
ปีขาล	bpee kăhn	Year of the Tiger (1950, '62 …)
ปีเถาะ	bpee tò!	Year of the Rabbit (1951, '63 …)
ปีมะโรง	bpee ma-rohng	Year of the Dragon (1952, '64 …)
ปีมะเส็ง	bpee ma-sĕng	Year of the Snake (1953, '65 …)
ปีมะเมีย	bpee ma-mee-a	Year of the Horse (1954, '66 …)
ปีมะแม	bpee ma-mair	Year of the Goat (1955, '67 …)
ปีวอก	bpee wôrk	Year of the Monkey (1956, '68 …)
ปีระกา	bpee ra-gah	Year of the Cock (1957, '69 …)
ปีจอ	bpee jor	Year of the Dog (1958, '70 …)
ปีกุน	bpee gOOn	Year of the Pig (1959, '71 …)

A twelve-year cycle is called **rôrp bpee**; the 'completion of five cycles' (**króp hâh rôrp**), that is the sixtieth birthday, is traditionally celebrated as a major milestone in a person's life.

In addition to the Western New Year (**bpee mài**) both the traditional Thai New Year (**sŏng-grahn**) in mid-April and the Chinese New Year (**dtrÒOt jeen**) in January or February are widely celebrated. Thailand adopted the international convention of beginning the new year on 1 January 1941.

14.5 Dates

Dates are expressed using the pattern **wun** ('day') + ORDINAL NUMBER + MONTH (+ YEAR):

วันที่ ๑๔ ตุลาฯ (2516)
wun têe sìp-sèe dtOO-lah (sŏrng pun hâh róy sìp hòk)
14 October (2516)

วันที่ ๑๕ เดือนหน้า
wun têe sìp-hâh deu-un nâh
The 15th of next month.

'What date . . . ?' questions use the expression, **wun têe tâo-rài?**

วันนี้(เป็น)วันที่เท่าไหร่
wun née (bpen) wun têe tâo-rài?
What is the date today?

ไปวันที่เท่าไหร่
bpai wun têe tâo-rài?
What date are you going?

14.6 Seasons

There are three seasons in Thailand, the cool season (November to February), the hot season (March to June) and the rainy season (July to October). The formal word for 'season' is **reu-doo**, but **nâh** is more commonly used in speech. 'Spring/autumn' literally translate as 'season – leaves – come into bud/fall'.

หน้า(ฤดู)หนาว	**nâh (reu-doo) năo:**	cool season
หน้าร้อน	**nâh rórn**	hot season
หน้าฝน	**nâh fŏn**	rainy season
ฤดูใบไม้ผลิ	**reu-doo bai mái: plì**	spring
ฤดูใบไม้ร่วง	**reu-doo bai mái: rôo-ung**	autumn

14.7 Useful expressions of time

In this section common expressions of time are listed at some length because of some unpredictable irregularities in the patterns. **mêu-a** ('when') occurs in expressions of past time; where **née** ('this') appears in brackets, it is optional.

14.7.1 'Today', 'tomorrow', 'yesterday'

วันนี้   **wun née**
today

พรุ่งนี้   **prôOng née**
tomorrow

มะรืน

ma-reun
the day after tomorrow

เมื่อวาน(นี้)

mêu-a wahn (née)
yesterday

เมื่อวานซืน(นี้)

mêu-a wahn seu:n (née)
the day before yesterday

เช้านี้

cháo: née
this morning

บ่ายนี้

bài: née
this afternoon

เย็นนี้

yen née
this evening

คืนนี้

keun née
tonight

เมื่อวาน(นี้)ตอนเช้า
or เช้าวานนี้

**mêu-a wahn (née) dtorn cháo:
cháo: wahn née**
yesterday morning

เมื่อวาน(นี้)ตอนบ่าย
or บ่ายวานนี้

**mêu-a wahn (née) dtorn bài:
bài: wahn née**
yesterday afternoon

เมื่อวาน(นี้)ตอนเย็น
or เย็นวาน นี้

**mêu-a wahn (née) dtorn yen
yen wahn née**
yesterday evening

เมื่อคืน(นี้)

mêu-a keun (née)
yesterday night

พรุ่งนี้เช้า

prÔOng née cháo:
tomorrow morning

พรุ่งนี้บ่าย

prÔOng née bài:
tomorrow afternoon

พรุ่งนี้เย็น

prÔOng née yen
tomorrow evening

คืนพรุ่งนี้

keun prÔOng née
tomorrow night

14.7.2 'This', 'next', 'last ...'

The words **née** ('this'), **nâh** ('next') and **têe láir-o** ('last') can occur after any unit of time. (**mêu-a**) ... may optionally be used with **têe láir-o** in 'last week/month/year'. **bpee glai:** and (**wun**) **rÔOng kêun** are fixed expressions:

อาทิตย์นี้	**ah-tít née**	this week
เดือนหน้า	**deu-un nâh**	next month
(เมื่อ)ปีที่แล้ว	**(mêu-a) bpee têe láir-o**	last year
ปีกลาย	**bpee glai:**	last year
(วัน)รุ่งขึ้น	**(wun) rÔOng kêun**	the next day

14.7.3 'Beginning', 'during', 'middle', 'end'

14.7.3.1 'Beginning': **dtôn**

ต้นปีที่แล้ว
dtôn bpee têe láir-o
the beginning of last year

14.7.3.2 'During': **ra-wàhng**

ระหว่างเดือนเมษาฯ
ra-wàhng deu-un may-săh
during April

14.7.3.3 'Middle': **glahng**

กลางเดือนหน้า
glahng deu-un nâh
the middle of next month

14.7.3.4 'End': **sîn/bplai:**

สิ้น/ปลายปีนี้

sîn/bplai: bpee née

the end of this year

14.7.4 'Ago', 'in ... time', 'within', 'since'

14.7.4.1 'Ago': **(mêu-a) ... gòrn/têe láir-o/mah láir-o/mah née**

'Ago' is normally expressed using **(mêu-a)** + NUMBER + UNIT OF TIME + *either* **gòrn** *or* **têe láir-o** *or* **mah láir-o** *or* **mah née**, which can be used interchangeably; note, however, that 'a moment ago' is a set phrase which does not follow this pattern.

(เมื่อ)ห้าปีก่อน

(mêu-a) hâh bpee gòrn

five years ago

(เมื่อ)เจ็ดเดือนที่แล้ว

(mêu-a) jèt deu-un têe láir-o

seven months ago

(เมื่อ)สามวันมาแล้ว

(mêu-a) sǎhm wun mah láir-o

three days ago

(เมื่อ)สองสามนาทีมานี้

(mêu-a) sǒrng sǎhm nah-tee mah née

two or three minutes ago

เมื่อกี้นี้(เอง)/เมื่อตะกี้นี้(เอง)

mêu-a gêe née (ayng)/mêu-a dta-gêe née (ayng)

(just) a moment ago

14.7.4.2 'In ... time': èek

อีกหกวัน
èek hòk wun
in six days' time

14.7.4.3 'Within': pai: nai

ภายในสามเดือน
pai: nai sǎhm deu-un
within three months

14.7.4.4 'Since': dtûng-dtàir

ตั้งแต่เมื่อวาน
dtûng-dtàir mêu-a wahn
since yesterday

14.7.5 Duration of time

Duration of time (I'm going *for* two weeks) is most commonly expressed by the pattern, VERB (PHRASE) + EXPRESSION OF TIME; there is no preposition in Thai corresponding to English 'for':

ผมไปสองอาทิตย์
pǒm bpai sǒrng ah-tít
I'm going for two weeks.

เธอเรียนภาษาไทยสามปี
ter ree-un pah-sǎh tai sǎhm bpee
She studied Thai for three years.

Two alternative patterns for expressing duration of time are, (a) VERB + **bpen way-lah** + EXPRESSION OF TIME, and (b) VERB + **dâi:** + EXPRESSION OF TIME; the latter is used only when referring to the past:

เขาจะเรียนที่มหาวิทยาลัยเป็นเวลาสามปี
káo ja ree-un têe ma-hǎh-wít-ta-yah-lai bpen way-lah sǎhm bpee
He will study at university for three years.

ฉันเคยมาเที่ยวเป็นเวลา ๓ เดือนเมื่อ ๘ ปีที่แล้ว

**chún ker-ee mah têe-o bpen way-lah sǎhm deu-un mêu-a bpàirt
  bpee têe láir-o**

I visited here for three months eight years ago.

หนูไปโรงเรียนที่อุตรดิตถ์ได้ปีกว่า

nǒo bpai rohng ree-un têe ÒOt-dta-ra-dìt dâi: bpee gwàh

I went to school in Uttaradit for over a year.

ออกจากร้านก๋วยเตี๋ยวได้ไม่นาน หนูก็ไปอยู่ร้านขายเสื้อผ้า

**òrk jàhk ráhn gǒo-ay dtěe-o dâi: mâi nahn nǒo gôr bpai yòo ráhn
  kǎi: sêu-a pâh**

Not long after leaving the noodle shop I went to (work) at a shop selling
clothes.

14.8 Telling the time

14.8.1 *Hours*

Telling the time in Thai is complicated by the fact that the hour word,
equivalent to 'o'clock' in English, varies according to the time of day, and
with it, the position of the hour number:

dtee + NUMBER	I a.m. – 5 a.m.
NUMBER + **mohng cháo:**	6 a.m. – II a.m.
bài: + NUMBER + **mohng**	I p.m. – 4 p.m.
NUMBER + **mohng yen**	5 p.m. – 6 p.m.
NUMBER + **tÔOm**	7 p.m. – II p.m.

The hours from 6 a.m. to 11 a.m. can be counted using numbers 6–11 +
mohng cháo:, or in an alternative way based on a division of the day in to
six-hour periods, starting from 7 a.m., whereby 8 a.m. becomes '2 o'clock
in the morning', 9 a.m. '3 o'clock . . .' and so on:

midnight	เที่ยงคืน	**têe-ung keun**
I a.m.	ตีหนึ่ง	**dtee nèung**
2 a.m.	ตีสอง	**dtee sǒrng**
3 a.m.	ตีสาม	**dtee sǎhm**

4 a.m.	ตีสี่	dtee sèe
5 a.m.	ตีห้า	dtee hâh
6 a.m.	หกโมงเช้า	hòk mohng cháo:
7 a.m.	เจ็ดโมงเช้า	jèt mohng cháo:
or	โมงเช้า	mohng cháo:
8 a.m.	แปดโมงเช้า	bpàirt mohng cháo
or	สองโมงเช้า	sŏrng mohng cháo
9 a.m.	เก้าโมงเช้า	gâo mohng cháo
or	สามโมงเช้า	săhm mohng cháo
10 a.m.	สิบโมงเช้า	sìp mohng cháo
or	สี่โมงเช้า	sèe mohng cháo
11 a.m.	สิบเอ็ดโมงเช้า	sìp-èt mohng cháo
or	ห้าโมงเช้า	hâh mohng cháo
midday	เที่ยงวัน	têe-ung wun
1 p.m.	บ่ายโมง	bài: mohng
2 p.m.	บ่ายสองโมง	bài: sŏrng mohng
3 p.m.	บ่ายสามโมง	bài: săhm mohng
4 p.m.	บ่ายสี่โมง	bài: sèe mohng
5 p.m.	ห้าโมงเย็น	hâh mohng yen
6 p.m.	หกโมงเย็น	hòk mohng yen
7 p.m.	ทุ่มหนึ่ง	tôOm nèung
8 p.m.	สองทุ่ม	sŏrng tôOm
9 p.m.	สามทุ่ม	săhm tôOm
10 p.m.	สี่ทุ่ม	sèe tôOm
11 p.m.	ห้าทุ่ม	hâh tôOm

Note: **dtee** and **bài:** appear before the number; **dtee** and **tÔOm** do not occur with **mohng**.

A traditional way of counting the hours of darkness, still used among elderly people in Bangkok and in rural areas, uses the word **yahm** ('a three-hour watch period'):

9 p.m.	ยามหนึ่ง	**yahm nèung**
midnight	สองยาม	**sŏrng yahm**
3 a.m.	สามยาม	**săhm yahm**

14.8.2 Half hours

Half past the hour is expressed as HOUR TIME + **krêung** ('half'). However, the words **cháo:** (6 a.m. to 11 a.m.) and **yen** (4–5 p.m.) are normally omitted:

3.30 a.m.	ตีสามครึ่ง	**dtee săhm krêung**
7.30 a.m.	เจ็ดโมงครึ่ง	**jèt mohng krêung**
11.30 a.m.	สิบเอ็ดโมงครึ่ง	**sìp-èt mohng krêung**
2.30 p.m.	บ่ายสองโมงครึ่ง	**bài: sŏrng mohng krêung**
5.30 p.m	ห้าโมงครึ่ง	**hâh mohng krêung**
10.30 p.m	สี่ทุ่มครึ่ง	**sèe tÔOm krêung**

14.8.3 Quarter hours and minutes past/to the hour

There is no special word for 'quarter past' or 'quarter to' the hour. Minutes past the hour are expressed as HOUR TIME + NUMBER + **nah-tee** ('minute'):

10.15 a.m.	สิบโมงสิบห้านาที	sìp mohng sìp-hâh nah-tee
2.10 p.m.	บ่ายสองโมงสิบนาที	bài: sŏrng mohng sìp nah-tee
9.15 p.m.	สามทุ่มสิบห้านาที	săhm tÔOm sìp-hâh nah-tee

Minutes to the hour are expressed as èek ('further', 'more') + NUMBER + nah-tee ('minute') + HOUR TIME:

10.45 a.m.   อีกสิบห้านาทีสิบเอ็ดโมงเช้า
               èek sìp-hâh nah-tee sìp-èt mohng cháo

5.40 p.m.   อีกยี่สิบนาทีหกโมงเย็น
               èek yêe-sìp nah-tee hòk mohng yen

11.55 p.m.   อีกห้านาทีเที่ยงคืน
               èek hâh nah-tee têe-ung keun

14.8.4   *The 24-hour clock system*

In the 24-hour clock system hours are expressed as NUMBER + nah-li-gah ('clock, o'clock'). Minutes past the hour, including half past the hour, follow the pattern, NUMBER + nah-li-gah + NUMBER + nah-tee; minutes to the hour are expressed as èek + NUMBER + nah-tee + NUMBER + nah-li-gah:

16.00   สิบหกนาฬิกา
        sìp-hòk nah-li-gah

20.30   ยี่สิบนาฬิกาสามสิบนาที
        yêe-sìp nah-li-gah sǎhm-sìp nah-tee

22.55   อีกห้านาทียี่สิบสามนาฬิกา
        èek hâh nah-tee yêe-sìp sǎhm nah-li-gah

14.8.5   *Asking the time/how long something takes*

To ask the time, gèe mohng láir-o? or way-lah tâo-rài láir-o? is used; to ask what time something happens, the pattern VERB (PHRASE) + gèe mohng? is used:

กี่โมงแล้ว / เวลาเท่าไหร่แล้ว
gèe mohng láir-o? / way-lah tâo-rài láir-o?
What time is it?

รถออกกี่โมง
rót òrk gèe mohng?
What time does the bus leave?

To ask how long it takes to do something, the pattern **chái way-lah** ('use time') (+ VERB (PHRASE)) + **gèe** ('how many?') + TIME EXPRESSION is used:

ใช้เวลากี่ชั่วโมง
chái way-lah gèe chôo-a mohng?
How many hours does it take?

ใช้เวลาเดินทางกี่ชั่วโมง
chái way-lah dern tahng gèe chôo-a mohng?
How many hours does the journey take?

ใช้เวลาเรียนกี่ปี
chái way-lah ree-un gèe bpee
How many years does it take to study?

Chapter 15

Thai speech conventions

15.1 Politeness

Politeness can be conveyed verbally in Thai by the appropriate choice of vocabulary, such as polite final particles (10.2), deferential pronouns (4.1) and formal vocabulary. As in most languages, the pitch and volume of voice can also be used to convey politeness. Speaking Thai softly and undemonstratively can be both a mark of politeness (reflecting the speaker's unwillingness to be too assertive) and a sign of authority and high status (reflecting the speaker's lack of need to be assertive); the foreigner who assumes these to be signs of weakness and indecision is likely to become culturally lost very quickly.

15.2 Thanks

The most widely used word for thank you is **kòrp-kOOn**; when speaking to children or subordinates, **kòrp-jai** may be used instead. **kòrp-pra-kOOn** is used when speaking to those of higher social status, or when wishing to be especially polite. All of these forms can be intensified by adding **mâhk** ('much') or its reduplicated form **mâhk mâhk**:

ขอบคุณ (มาก) ครับ/ค่ะ
kòrp-kOOn (mâhk) krúp/kâ
Thank you (very much).

ขอบพระคุณ
kòrp-pra-kOOn
Thank you (especially polite and to superiors).

ขอบใจ

kòrp-jai

Thank you (to children and subordinates).

Thanking someone for doing something is expressed by the pattern, **kòrp-kOOn + têe + VERB (PHRASE)**:

ขอบคุณที่บอกล่วงหน้า

kòrp-kOOn têe bòrk lôo-ung nâh

Thank you for telling me in advance.

Thanking someone for something is expressed by the pattern, **kòrp-kOOn + sǔm-rùp ('for') + NOUN (PHRASE)**:

ขอบคุณสำหรับทุกสิ่งทุกอย่าง

kòrp-kOOn sǔm-rùp tÓOk sìng tÓOk yàhng

Thank you for everything.

Thanks can be acknowledged (a) silently, with a smile or a nod, (b) by **krúp** (male speakers) or **kâ** (female speakers), or (c) by **mâi bpen rai** ('never mind' / 'that's alright' / 'don't mention it'):

ขอบคุณมากครับ

kòrp-kOOn mâhk krúp

Thank you very much.

– ไม่เป็นไรค่ะ

– mâi bpen rai kâ

– That's alright.

15.3 Apologies

The essential word for apologising is **kǒr-tôht**; in informal situations it is often shortened to **'tôht**. In more formal situations, **kǒr a-pai** may be used, or even more formally, **kǒr bpra-tahn tôht**. **kǒr-tôht** can be intensified by **mâhk mâhk** or **jing jing**:

ขอโทษครับ/ค่ะ

kǒr-tôht krúp/kâ

Sorry; please excuse me.

ขอโทษมากๆ/จริงๆ

kǒr-tôht mâhk mâhk/jing jing

I'm ever so sorry.

ขออภัย

kǒr a-pai

Sorry; please excuse me (formal).

ขอประทานโทษ

kǒr bpra-tahn tôht

Sorry; please excuse me (very formal).

In everyday speech, **kǒr-tôht** is commonly followed by the mood particles
tee or **dôo-ay ná** (10.3); '**tôht tee** is used to apologise for tiny errors, while
kǒr-tôht dôo-ay ná conveys a stronger sense of apology:

(ขอ)โทษที

(kǒr) 'tôht tee

Sorry.

ขอโทษด้วยนะ

kǒr-tôht dôo-ay ná

Sorry.

Apologising for doing something, is expressed by the pattern, **kǒr-tôht têe**
+ VERB (PHRASE):

ขอโทษที่รบกวน

kǒr-tôht têe róp-goo-un

Sorry for disturbing you.

Note that **têe** here has a falling tone and is not to be confused with the
final particle tee in '**tôht tee**.

The expression **sěe-a jai** ('I'm sorry') is an expression of sympathy or regret
rather than an apology (15.6.3).

15.4 Polite requests

15.4.1 *Requests for information*

Basic requests for information can be prefaced by **kǒr-tôht krúp/kâ** ('excuse
me') for politeness:

ขอโทษครับ/ค่ะ รถออกกี่โมง
kǒr-tôht krúp/kâ, rót òrk gèe mohng?
Excuse me, what time does the train leave?

ขอโทษครับ/ค่ะ ไปรษณีย์อยู่ที่ไหน
kǒr-tôht krúp/kâ, bprai-sa-nee yòo têe-nǎi?
Excuse me, where is the post office?

<hr>

15.4.2 *Requests for something*

Requests for something are expressed by the pattern, **kǒr** + NOUN (PHRASE)
(+ **dâi: mái?**):

ขอน้ำเปล่าสองแก้ว(ได้ไหม)
kǒr náhm bplào sǒrng gâir-o (dâi: mái?)
Can I have two glasses of water, please?

If the noun is unquantified (e.g. 'water' rather than 'two glasses of water'),
then it is often followed by **nòy** ('a little') for politeness:

ขอน้ำหน่อย(ได้ไหม)
kǒr náhm nòy (dâi: mái?)
Can I have some water, please?

ขอข้าวหน่อย(ได้ไหม)
kǒr kâo: nòy (dâi: mái?)
Can I have some rice, please?

. . . **dâi: mái?** ('could I . . . ?') is an optional additional politeness expression.

<hr>

15.4.3 *Requests to do something oneself*

Requests to do something oneself can be expressed by the pattern, **kǒr** +
VERB (PHRASE) + **nòy** (+ **dâi: mái?**):

ขอดูหน่อย
kǒr doo nòy
Can I have a look, please?

ขอพูดกับคุณต๋อยหน่อยได้ไหม

kŏr pôot gùp kOOn dtŏy nòy dâi: mái?

Could I speak to Khun Toi, please?

Requesting someone to do something

Requesting someone to do something for you, or for someone else, is expressed by the pattern, **chôo-ay** + VERB (PHRASE); the request is made more polite by the addition of the mood particles **dôo-ay ná** or **nòy** (10.3), while . . . **dâi: mái?** ('could you . . . ?') can also be added at the end of the sentence for politeness:

ช่วยบอกเขาด้วยนะ

chôo-ay bòrk káo dôo-ay ná

Could you tell him, please?

ช่วยปิดประตูหน่อยได้ไหม

chôo-ay bpìt bpra-dtoo nòy dâi: mái?

Could you close the door, please?

To indicate the beneficiary of the action (i.e. who it is being done for), the pattern may be expanded to **chôo-ay** + VERB + **hâi** (+ BENEFICIARY) + **nòy/dôo-ay ná**:

ช่วยปิดทีวีให้หน่อย

chôo-ay bpìt tee wee hâi nòy

Please turn the TV off (for me).

ช่วยสั่งอาหารให้(ผม)ด้วยนะ

chôo-ay sùng ah-hăhn hâi (pŏm) dôo-ay ná

Please order food for me.

ช่วยแปลให้เขาหน่อยได้ไหม

chôo-ay bplair hâi káo nòy dâi: mái?

Please translate for him.

Two rather more formal words for requesting someone to do something are **ga-rOO-nah** and **bpròht**, both of which can be translated as 'please'; **ga-rOO-nah** often follows **chôo-ay** in very formal polite conversation, while **bpròht** can be heard at the beginning of public announcements:

ช่วยกรุณาบอกเขาด้วย

chôo-ay ga-rOO-nah bòrk káo dôo-ay

Please tell him.

โปรดทราบ

bpròht sâhp...

Please be informed that...

Both **ga-rOO-nah** and **bpròht** also occur commonly on public signs:

กรุณาถอดรองเท้า

ga-rOO-nah tòrt rorng táo:

Please remove your shoes.

กรุณากดกริ่ง

ga-rOO-nah gòt grìng

Please ring the bell.

โปรดเงียบ

bpròht ngêe-up

Please be quiet.

| 15.4.5 | *Requesting someone not to do something* |

The least confrontational way to ask someone not to do something is to use the expression **mâi dtôrng...** ('there's no need to...'). More direct requests employ the negative imperative **yàh...** ('Don't...') (11.8), which can be 'softened' by the addition of the mood particle **ná** (10.3) or made more tactful, polite and deferential by prefixing the polite request words **chôo-ay, ga-rOO-nah** or, more formally, **bpròht. hâhm...** ('to forbid') (11.8) is an unambiguous order rather than a request, commonly found on notices of prohibition; in speech it, too, can be 'softened' by the addition of the final particle **ná**:

ไม่ต้องปิดประตูนะ

mâi dtôrng bpìt bpra-dtoo ná

There's no need to shut the door.

ช่วยอย่าปิดประตูนะ

chôo-ay yàh bpìt bpra-dtoo ná

Please don't shut the door.

235

กรุณาอย่าปิดประตูนะ

ga-rOO-nah yàh bpìt bpra-dtoo ná

Please don't shut the door.

อย่าปิดประตูนะ

yàh bpìt bpra-dtoo ná

Don't shut the door, OK?

ห้ามปิดประตูนะ

hâhm bpìt bpra-dtoo ná

Don't shut the door, OK!

ห้ามเข้า

hâhm kâo

No Entry!

ห้ามสูบบุหรี่

hâhm sòop bÒO-rèe

No Smoking!

| 15.4.6 | *Inviting someone to do something* |

Inviting someone to do something, such as sit down, come in, start eating, is expressed by the pattern, **chern** ('to invite') + VERB (PHRASE); the mood article **sí** (10.3) is commonly added to **chern . . .** invitations:

เชิญนั่งซิครับ/คะ

chern nûng sí krúp/ká

Please sit down.

เชิญข้างในซิครับ/คะ

chern kâhng nai sí krúp/ká

Please come in.

เชิญซิครับ/คะ

chern sí krúp/ká

Carry on; go ahead; after you.

15.5 Misunderstandings

15.5.1 Expressing ignorance, uncertainty

Thai cannot use the same verb for knowing facts and knowing people or places; **róo** (informal) or **sâhp** (formal, deferential) mean 'to know facts' while **róo-jùk** means 'to know or be acquainted with people, places or things':

ฉันไม่รู้/ทราบ
chún mâi róo/sâhp
I don't know.

เขาไม่รู้จักผม
káo mâi róo-jùk pǒm
He doesn't know me.

ไม่รู้จักคำว่า...
mâi róo-jùk kum wâh...
I don't know the word...

ผมไม่แน่(ใจ)
pǒm mâi nâir (jai)
I'm not sure.

15.5.2 Expressing non-comprehension

There are two words for 'to understand': **kâo jai** and **róo rêu-ung**:

ผมไม่เข้าใจ
pǒm mâi kâo jai
I don't understand.

เขาไม่รู้เรื่อง
káo mâi róo rêu-ung
He doesn't understand.

เขาไม่เข้าใจว่าทำไมผมจึงไม่สนใจ
káo mâi kâo jai wâh tum-mai pǒm jeung mâi sǒn jai
He doesn't understand why I wasn't interested.

237

róo rêu-ung often occurs as a resultative verb with **fung** ('to listen') and **àhn** ('to read') in questions like **fung róo rêu-ung mái?** ('Do you understand (what you hear)?') and **àhn róo rêu-ung mái?** ('Do you understand (what you read)?'). In negative statements the word order is VERB (PHRASE) + **mâi** + RESULTATIVE VERB (11.2):

เขาฟังไม่รู้เรื่อง
káo fung mâi róo rêu-ung
He doesn't understand (what he hears).

ฉันอ่านไม่รู้เรื่อง
chún àhn mâi róo rêu-ung
I don't undertand (what I read).

tun ('to catch up with', 'in time') is also used as a resultative verb with **fung** to express the idea that non-comprehension is due to the speaker speaking too quickly:

ผมฟังครูไม่ทัน
pǒm fung kroo mâi tun
I don't understand the teacher (because he speaks too quickly).

15.5.3 | Asking someone to repeat, speak slowly, explain, translate, spell

อะไรนะครับ/คะ
a-rai ná krúp/ká?
Pardon?

พูดอีกทีได้ไหม
pôot èek tee dâi: mái?
Could you say that again?

พูดช้าๆหน่อยได้ไหม
pôot cháh cháh nòy dâi: mái?
Could you speak slowly, please?

There are two ways of asking what something means: **mǎi: kwahm wâh a-rai?** is a request for clarification or an explanation, while **bplair wâh a-rai?** seeks a translation.

... หมายความว่าอะไร
...măi: kwahm wâh a-rai?
What does ...mean?

... แปลว่าอะไร
...bplair wâh a-rai?
What does ...mean?

... ภาษาอังกฤษแปลว่าอะไร
...pah-săh ung-grìt bplair wâh a-rai?
What is ...in English?

ภาษาอังกฤษแปลว่าอะไร
pah-săh ung-grìt bplair wâh a-rai?
What is it in English?

ภาษาไทยเขียนอย่างไร
pah-săh tai kĕe-un yung-ngai?
How is it written in Thai?

สะกดอย่างไร
sa-gòt yung-ngai?
How do you spell it?

ช่วยเขียนให้หน่อย
chôo-ay kĕe-un hâi nòy.
Please write it down for me.

15.6   Socialising

Initial conversations between Thais and foreigners are likely to involve the exchange of personal information. Westerners tend to find some questions, like *Do you have any brothers and sisters?*, surprising and others, like *How much do you earn?* or *Why haven't you got any children yet?* – irritating, intrusive or downright impolite, as in fact most Thais would. But these are easily outweighed, for most Westerners, by the Thais' capacity for saying nice things, such as *You speak Thai well!*, *That's a nice dress you're wearing!* or *You're looking handsome today!* Westerners, perhaps unused to a culture of mutual personal compliments, often make the mistake of

239

taking compliments too literally and, even more often, do not even consider making a return compliment at the next opportune moment. Compliments can be accepted with a gracious kòrp-kOOn ('thank you') or modestly denied mâi ròrk krúp/kâ ('not at all'):

คุณพูดไทยเก่ง/ชัด
kOOn pôot tai gèng/chút
You speak Thai well/clearly.

– ไม่หรอกครับ/ค่ะ
– mâi ròrk krúp/kâ
– Not at all.

Other typical compliments include:

แต่งตัวสวย/แต่งตัวหล่อ
dtàirng dtoo-a sŏo-ay (to females)/**dtàirng dtoo-a lòr** (to males)
You look nice (i.e. are nicely dressed)!

ทำอาหารอร่อย
tum ah-hăhn a-ròy
Your cooking tastes good.

15.6.1 | *Greetings, introductions, farewells*

The basic greeting **sa-wùt dee**, often abbreviated to **'wùt dee** in speech, is used for both formal and informal greetings regardless of the time of day; it is often accompanied by a *wai*, a gesture in which the head is bowed slightly and the hands held in a prayer-like position, somewhere between neck and forehead height, depending on the status of the person being greeted. **sa-wùt dee** can also be used when taking leave.

More casual greetings are **bpai năi?** ('Where are you going?') and **bpai năi mah?** ('Where have you been?'), which do not normally require a precise answer; in the work place, **tahn kâo: réu yung?** ('Have you eaten yet?') is often more a midday greeting than the run-in to an invitation to lunch together.

สวัสดีครับ/ค่ะ
sa-wùt dee krúp/kâ
Hello, good morning/afternoon, etc.; goodbye

สบายดีไหม/เป็นอย่างไรบ้าง

sa-bai: dee mái?/bpen yung-ngai bâhng?

How are you?

– สบายดี/ก็…เรื่อย ๆ

– sa-bai: dee/gôr …rêu-ay rêu-ay

– Fine/Same as usual.

ไปไหน

bpai nǎi?

Hello (casual). (lit. Where are you going?)

– ไปเที่ยว/ไปธุระ/ไม่ไปไหน

– bpai têe-o/bpai tÓO-rá/mâi bpai nǎi

– I'm going out/going on business/not going anywhere.

ไปไหนมา

bpai nǎi mah?

Hello (casual). (lit. Where have you been?)

– ไปเที่ยวมา/ไปธุระมา/ไม่ได้ไปไหน

– bpai têe-o mah/bpai tÓO-rá mah/mâi dâi bpai nǎi

– I've been out/been on business/haven't been anywhere.

ทานข้าวหรือยัง

tahn kâo: réu yung?

Hello (informal, polite). (lit. Have you eaten yet?)

– ทานแล้ว/ยังครับ/ค่ะ

– tahn láir-o krúp/kâ/yung krúp/kâ

– Yes/No.

ขอแนะนำให้รู้จักกับ…

kǒr náir-num hâi róo-jùk gùp …

I'd like to introduce you to …

ยินดีที่รู้จัก

yin dee têe róo-jùk

Pleased to meet you.

ไปละนะ/ไปก่อน

bpai lá ná/bpai gòrn

Goodbye; I'm off now.

15.6.2 Finding out about other people

The basic personal questions below can be prefaced by **kǒr-tôht krúp/kâ** ('excuse me') as a sign of politeness.

คุณชื่ออะไร
kOOn chêu a-rai?
What's your (first) name?

คุณนามสกุลอะไร
kOOn nahm sa-gOOn a-rai?
What's your surname?

คุณเป็นคนชาติอะไร
kOOn bpen kon châht a-rai?
What nationality are you?

คุณมาจากไหน
kOOn mah jàhk nǎi?
Where do you come from?

ที่...ตรงไหน
têe...dtrong nǎi?
Whereabouts in...?

คุณเป็นคนจังหวัดอะไร
kOOn bpen kon jung-wùt a-rai?
Which province do you come from?

ทำงานอะไร
tum ngahn a-rai?
What (job) do you do?

ทำงานที่ไหน
tum ngahn têe nǎi?
Where do you work?

มีพี่น้องไหม
mee pêe nórng mái?
Have you got any brothers and sisters?

มีพี่น้องกี่คน
mee pêe nórng gèe kon?
How many brothers and sisters have you got?

อายุเท่าไหร่
ah-yÓO tâo-rài?
How old are you?

แต่งงาน(แล้ว)หรือยัง
dtàirng ngahn (láir-o) réu yung?
Are you married?

มีครอบครัว(แล้ว)หรือยัง
mee krôrp-kroo-a (láir-o) réu yung?
Are you married? (lit. Do you have a family?)

มีลูก(แล้ว)หรือยัง
mee lôok (láir-o) réu yung?
Do you have any children?

15.6.3 *Expressing congratulations, sympathy*

Congratulations and sympathy can be expressed formally using the expression **kŏr sa-dairng . . .** ('I would like to show . . .'), which may be followed by the final particles **dôo-ay ná** (10.3):

ขอแสดงความยินดี (ด้วยนะ)
kŏr sa-dairng kwahm yin dee (dôo-ay ná)
Congratulations!

ขอแสดงความเสียใจ (ด้วยนะ)
kŏr sa-dairng kwahm sĕe-a jai (dôo-ay ná)
I'd like to express my regret/sympathy.

15.6.4 *Telephone transactions*

The English word 'hello', with – depending on the speaker – a more or less Thai pronunciation (**hun-lŏh**), is used at the beginning of phone calls; the greeting/farewell **sa-wùt dee / 'wùt dee** or, more informally, **kâir née ná** ('That's all for now') can be used at the end of the call.

ขอพูดกับ . . . หน่อยได้ไหม
kǒr pôot gùp . . . nòy dâi mái?
Could I speak to . . ., please?

ใครพูดครับ/คะ
krai pôot krúp/ká?
Who's speaking, please?

คุณ . . . ใช่ไหมครับ/คะ
kOOn . . . châi mái krúp/ká?
Is that . . . ?

คุณ . . . อยู่ไหม
kOOn . . . yòo mái?
Is Khun . . . there?

ผม/ฉัน . . . พูดครับ/ค่ะ
pǒm/chún . . . pôot krúp/kâ
This is . . . speaking.

ช่วยพูดดังๆหน่อยได้ไหม
chôo-ay pôot dung dung nòy dâi: mái?
Could you speak up a little, please?

ไม่ค่อยได้ยิน
mâi kôy dâi yin
I can scarcely hear.

รอสักครู่ครับ/ค่ะ
ror sùk krôo krúp/kâ
Hold on a moment, please

สายไม่ดี
sǎi: mâi dee
The line's bad.

สายไม่ว่าง
sǎi: mâi wâhng
The line isn't free.

สายหลุด
săi: lòOt
I got cut off.

ขอต่อเบอร์ ...
kŏr dtòr ber ...
Could I have extension ..., please?

จะฝากข้อความไหม
ja fàhk kôr kwahm mái?
Do you want to leave a message?

ช่วยบอกคุณติ๋มว่า ...
chôo-ay bòrk kOOn dtĭm wâh ...
Please tell Khun Tim that ...

ช่วยบอกคุณติ๋มให้โทรมาถึงฉันด้วยนะ
chôo-ay bòrk kOOn dtĭm hâi toh tĕung chún dôo-ay ná
Please tell Khun Tim to ring me back.

แค่นี้นะ
kâir née ná
That's all for now.

แล้วจะโทรมาใหม่
láir-o ja toh mah mài
I'll ring back later.

เย็น ๆ จะโทรมาใหม่
yen yen ja toh mah mài
I'll ring back this evening.

ขอโทษ โทรผิดเบอร์
kŏr-tôht toh pìt ber
Sorry, I've got the wrong number.

Romanisation systems

There are many different ways of romanising Thai, each with its strengths and weaknesses. The system used in this book is a 'non-technical' system, similar to that used in *Teach Yourself Complete Thai*, *Robertson's Practical English-Thai Dictionary*, and *Fundamentals of the Thai Language*. It attempts to represent unfamiliar Thai sounds with combinations of letters, such as 'air-o', 'dt', 'bp' and 'eu-a', without resorting to using new symbols.

In the 1940s Mary Haas, an American linguist, devised a system for romanising Thai, which, with slight modifications (e.g. 'j' is often replaced by 'y'), is widely used by linguists describing Thai and in most of the Thai teaching materials produced in universities. It utilises phonetic symbols such as ŋ, ʔ, ɔ, ə, ɛ and ɯ, and **ph** and **th** to represent the consonant sounds in '*p*ay' and '*t*ea' respectively. Librarians and historians generally prefer the Library of Congress system, which unlike systems used in language-learning materials, does not attempt to represent tones.

This is how the title of the book *Political History of Thailand* would be romanised according to the three different systems:

ประวัติการเมืองไทย

Essential Grammar:	**bpra-wùt gahn meu-ung tai**
Haas-type system:	**prawàt kaan mɯaŋ thay**
Library of Congress:	**prawat kān mū'ang thai**

CONSONANTS

	initial	final	initial	final	initial	final
	Essential Grammar		Mary Haas		Library of Congress	
ก	g	k	k	k	k	k
ข	k	k	kh	k	kh	k
ค	k	k	kh	k	kh	k
ฆ	k	k	kh	k	kh	k
ง	ng	ng	ŋ	ŋ	ng	ng
จ	j	t	c	t	čh	t
ฉ	ch	t	ch	t	ch	t
ช	ch	t	ch	t	ch	t
ซ	s	t	s	t	s	t
ฌ	ch	t	ch	t	ch	t
ญ	y	n	j/y	n	y	n
ฎ	d	t	d	t	d	t
ฏ	dt	t	t	t	t	t
ฐ	t	t	th	t	th	t
ฑ	t	t	th	t	th	t
ฒ	t	t	th	t	th	t
ณ	n	n	n	n	n	n
ด	d	t	d	t	d	t
ต	dt	t	t	t	t	t
ถ	t	t	th	t	th	t
ท	t	t	th	t	th	t
ธ	t	t	th	t	th	t

	initial	final	initial	final	initial	final
	Essential Grammar		Mary Haas		Library of Congress	
น	n	n	n	n	n	n
บ	b	p	b	p	b	p
ป	bp	p	p	p	p	p
ผ	p	p	ph	p	ph	p
ฝ	f	p	f	p	f	p
พ	p	p	ph	p	ph	p
ฟ	f	p	f	p	f	p
ภ	p	p	ph	p	ph	p
ม	m	m	m	m	m	m
ย	y	–	j/y	j/y	y	y
ร	r	n	r	n	r	n
ล	l	n	l	n	l	n
ว	w	–	w	w	w	w
ศ	s	t	s	t	s	t
ษ	s	t	s	t	s	t
ส	s	t	s	t	s	t
ห	h	–	h	–	h	–
ฬ	l	n	l	n	l	n
อ	–	–	?	–	–	–
ฮ	h	–	h	–	h	–

	Essential Grammar	Mary Haas	Library of Congress
-ั๋	-orn	-ɔɔn	-ǭn
-ั๋ั๋	-un	-an	-an
-ั๋ั๋-	-um	-am	-am
-ัว-	-oo-u-	-ua	-ua
-อ	-or	-ɔɔ	-ǭ
-ัะ	-a	-a	-a
-ั	-u-	-a	-a
-ัว	-oo-a	-ua	-ua
-า	-ah	-aa	-ā
-าย	-ai:	-aay	-āi
-าว	-ao:	-aaw	-āo
-ำ	-um	-am	-am
-ิ	-i	-i	-i
-ิว	-ew	-iw	-iw
-ี	-ee	-ii	-ī
-ึ	-eu	-ɨ	-uʼ
-ื	-eu:	-ɨɨ	-ūʼ
-ุ	-oo	-u	-u
-ุย	-oo-ee	-uy	-ui
-ู	-oo	-uu	-ū
เ-	-ay	-ee	-ē
เ-	-e	-e	-e
เ-ย	-er-ee	-əəy	-ōei

	Essential Grammar	Mary Haas	Library of Congress
เ-อ	-er	-əə	-ōe
เ-อะ	-er	-ə	-oe
เ-ะ	-e	-eʔ	-e
เ-า	-ao	-aw	-ao
เ-าะ	-o'	-ɔʔ	-ǫ
เ-ิ	-er	-əə	-ōe
เ-ีย	-ee-a	-ia	-īa
เ-ือ	-eu-a	-ɰa	-ū'a
แ-ว	-air	-ɛɛ	-ǣ
แ-ั	-air	-ɛ	-æ
แ-ะ	-air	-ɛʔ	-æ
โ-	-oh	-oo	-ō
โ-ะ	-o	-o	-o
ใ-	-ai	-ay	-ai
ไ-	-ai	-ay	-ai

The verbs **hâi, dâi/dâi:** and **bpen:** a summary

The verbs **hâi, dâi/dâi:** and **bpen** often seem confusing to the learner because each has several quite different meanings. This section summarises and cross-references the main patterns in which they are likely to be encountered.

1   hâi

(a) SUBJECT + **hâi** + INDIRECT OBJECT + VERB (PHRASE) (5.11)

As a causative verb means 'to let someone do something' or 'to have someone do something':

เขาให้ฉันกลับบ้าน
káo hâi chún glùp bâhn
He let me/had me go home.

(b) SUBJECT + VERB + **hâi** + OBJECT + VERB (PHRASE) (5.11)

The manner of causation (e.g. telling, wanting, permitting someone to do something) can be specified by an appropriate verb preceding **hâi:**

ฉันอยากให้คุณช่วยหน่อย
chún yàhk hâi kOOn chôo-ay nòy
I'd like you to help me a bit.

(c) SUBJECT + **tum** + **hâi** + OBJECT + VERB (PHRASE) (5.11)

This pattern conveys a sense of intention or coercion on the part of the subject:

เรื่องแบบนี้ทำให้รู้สึกรำคาญเสมอ
rêu-ung bàirp née tum hâi róo-sèuk rum-kahn sa-měr
This kind of thing always makes me feel annoyed.

(d) SUBJECT + VERB (PHRASE) + **hâi** + INDIRECT OBJECT (8.3)

This pattern conveys the idea that the action is being carried out for the benefit of someone:

ผมซื้อให้คุณ
pǒm séu: hâi kOOn
I bought it for you.

(e) SUBJECT + **hâi** + DIRECT OBJECT + INDIRECT OBJECT (5.12)

hâi in this pattern, means 'to give':

เขาให้เงินฉัน
káo hâi ngern chún
He gave me money.

(f) VERB (PHRASE) + **hâi** + ADJECTIVE (7.1.5; 9.4)

hâi is also used as an adverb-marker in imperatives:

พูดให้ชัดหน่อย
pôot hâi chút nòy
Speak clearly, please!

2 **dâi/dâi:**

Note that **dâi** and **dâi:** are spelt identically in Thai script, but the vowel length varies according to the position of the word in the sentence.

(a) **dâi** + NOUN

When **dâi** occurs before a noun, it means 'to get':

คุณได้เงินเดือนเท่าไหร่
kOOn dâi ngern deu-un tâo-rài?
How much salary do you get?

(b) **dâi** + VERB (PHRASE)

When **dâi** occurs *before* a verb or verb phrase, it means 'to get to do something':

ฉันจะได้ไปเที่ยวลาว
chún ja dâi bpai têe-o lao:
I'll get to visit Laos.

(c) VERB (PHRASE) + **dâi:** (5.6.2)

When **dâi:** occurs *after* a verb or verb phrase, it means 'can, able to':

เราไปพรุ่งนี้ไม่ได้
rao bpai prÔOng née mâi dâi:
We can't go tomorrow.

(d) VERB (PHRASE) + **dâi:** + ADJECTIVE (7.1.4)

dâi: occurs as an adverb-marker *between* a verb or verb phrase and an adjective:

เขาพูดไทยได้ดี
káo pôot tai dâi: dee
He speaks Thai well.

(e) **mâi dâi** + VERB (PHRASE)

This pattern indicates either something did not happen in the past (5.7.7):

เราไม่ได้ไป
rao mâi dâi bpai
We didn't go.

or to contradict or correct a preceding statement or assumption (11.4):

เขาไม่ได้เป็นคนไทย
káo mâi dâi bpen kon tai
He's not Thai.

(f) INDEFINITE PRONOUN + **gôr dâi:** (4.8.7); VERB (PHRASE)/NOUN
    + **gôr dâi:**

gôr dâi: follows indefinite pronouns, verbs and nouns to show amenability, a lack of preference or indifference:

คุณไปเมื่อไรก็ได้
kOOn bpai mêu-rài gôr dâi:
You can go whenever you like.

วันนี้ก็ได้ พรุ่งนี้ก็ได้
wun née gôr dâi: prÔOng née gôr dâi:
Today is OK, tomorrow is OK, too.

ไปก็ได้ ไม่ไปก็ได้
bpai gôr dâi: mâi bpai gôr dâi:
Going is fine by me, not going is fine, too

(g) VERB (PHRASE) + **dâi:** + TIME EXPRESSION (14.7.5)

When followed by an expression of time, **dâi:** expresses the idea of duration of time ('for . . .'):

ผมเรียนได้ไม่กี่ปี
pŏm ree-un dâi: mâi gèe bpee
I didn't study for many years. (i.e. I didn't have many years' schooling).

3   bpen

(a) **bpen** + NOUN (5.1.1)

As the verb 'to be', **bpen** cannot normally be followed by an adjective
(5.2); the negative is either **mâi châi** + NOUN, or + **mâi dâi bpen** + NOUN:

ลูกสาวเป็นคนน่ารัก
lôok săo: bpen kon nâh rúk
The daughter is cute.

เขาไม่ได้เป็นเพื่อน
káo mâi dâi bpen pêu-un
He's not a friend.

(b) VERB (PHRASE) + **bpen** (5.6.2)

After a verb or verb phrase, **bpen** means 'can' in the sense of 'knowing
how to do something':

เขาว่ายน้ำไม่เป็น
káo wâi: náhm mâi bpen
He can't swim.

(c) VERB (PHRASE) + **bpen** + NOUN (PHRASE) (7.1.3)

When **bpen** occurs between a verb phrase and a noun phrase it functions as an adverb marker:

จะแปลเป็นภาษาไทยอย่างไร
ja bplair bpen pah-săh tai yung-ngai?
How would you translate it into Thai?

(d) VERB (PHRASE) + **bpen** + EXPRESSION OF TIME (14.7.5)

bpen occurs with expressions of time to express the idea of duration of time:

เขาอยู่ที่เมืองไทยเป็นเวลานาน
káo yòo me-ung tai bpen way-lah nahn
They've been in Thailand a long time.

(e) **bpen** + DISEASE

bpen followed by the name of a disease is used to translate 'to have/get' an illness or disease.

คุณเป็นหวัดใช่ไหม
kOOn bpen wùt châi mái?
You've got a cold, haven't you?

Glossary

Adjectives in Thai occur after the nouns they describe; they do not occur with the verb 'to be'. Adjectives also function as **stative verbs**; thus, **dee** is both the adjective 'good' and the stative verb 'to be good'. Adjectives and adverbs often take the same form in Thai; thus **dee** is both the adjective 'good' and the adverb 'well'.

Adverbs often occur after verbs. They can describe a single action, where they often take the same form as adjectives, or they can describe the whole sentence.

Aspect is concerned with whether the action of a verb is complete, ongoing or habitual; it is marked in Thai by **auxiliary verbs**.

Auxiliary verbs only occur with other verbs; Thai auxiliary verbs include **modal verbs** and time and **aspect** markers.

Causative verbs in Thai convey a range of meanings, including allowing something to happen, causing something to happen, either intentionally or unintentionally, and compelling someone to do something.

Classifiers are attributed to every noun and are used primarily, but not exclusively, in noun phrases involving numbers, such as 'three daughters', 'four glasses of orange juice', and so on.

Compounds are combinations of two words to make a new word. Compounding is an important device in Thai for creating new nouns, adjectives and verbs.

Concessive clauses concede a point, which is then often countered in the following clause. In English they usually begin with 'although'; in Thai the following clause is usually introduced by 'but'.

Conditional clauses commonly begin with 'if' and state a condition under which the following clause holds true. In Thai, the 'if' word is often omitted.

Consonant class Thai consonants are divided into three classes – low, mid and high; the class of the initial consonant in a syllable is one of the factors that determines the tone of the syllable.

Consonant clusters are combinations of two consonant sounds, such as **bpl-**, **kw-**, **gr-**; in Thai they occur only at the beginning of a syllable. The class of the first consonant in the cluster is one of the factors that determines the tone of the syllable.

Dead syllables are one of two types of syllable in Thai (see also **live syllables**); dead syllables are those which end in either a **-p**, **-t**, **-k** sound or a short vowel.

Demonstratives are words like 'this' and 'that'. Thai demonstrative pronouns and demonstrative adjectives are distinguished by tone, pronouns having a falling tone and adjectives a high tone.

Directional verbs occur after a verb or **verb phrase** to indicate the direction of the action in relation to the speaker.

Intensifiers modify adjectives and adverbs, expressing the degree to which that quality is present (e.g. 'very', 'fairly', 'hardly'); many adjectives in Thai take their own specific intensifier (cf. '*pitch* black').

Live syllables are one of two types of syllable in Thai (see also **dead syllables**); live syllables are those which end in an **-m**, **-n**, **-ng** consonant sound, a long vowel sound, or the Thai letters -ย, -ว, เ-า, ไ- , ใ-.

Modal verbs express possibility, probability, ability, necessity, volition and obligation. Most, but not all, Thai modals occur before a verb or verb phrase; not all modals are negated in the same way.

Noun phrases consist of a noun modified by one or modifying words, such as numbers, **demonstratives** or **adjectives**. **Classifiers** play an important role in noun phrases in Thai.

Personal pronouns Thai has a much more complex system of personal pronouns than English; choice of the appropriate pronoun is determined not only by gender and number, but also by age, social status, context and personality; kin terms, status/occupation terms, personal names and nicknames are commonly used as pronouns. Pronouns are commonly omitted when it is clear from the context who is being addressed or referred to.

Quantifiers are words like 'all', 'some', 'many' and 'every'. In Thai **noun phrases** some quantifiers behave like numbers and others like **adjectives**.

Reduplication most commonly involves the repetition of an adjective or an adverb. It can serve a number of distinct functions, including making the meaning less precise, intensifying the meaning and signalling a command. A small number of nouns can be pluralised by reduplication.

Resultative verbs occur after another verb to describe the state that results from the action of the first verb (cf. 'I shot him *dead*.').

Sentence particles occur at the end of an utterance. They include question particles, which serve a grammatical function, and polite particles, mood particles and exclamatory particles, which have a communicative function.

Stative verbs describe a state rather than an action. Adjectives in Thai also function as stative verbs.

Subordinate clauses are dependent on the main clause in the sentences. They include concessive, conditional, purpose, reason and relative clauses.

Tone the pitch assigned to each syllable. Standard Thai has five tones – mid, high, low, rising and falling.

Topicalisation involves placing a word or phrase other than the subject at the beginning of a sentence in order to highlight it and make it the 'topic' of the sentence.

Unreleased consonants occur when the airstream is closed to make the sound, but not re-opened; the final 'p' in English 'yep!' is often pronounced as an unreleased consonant. In Thai, the final consonants -p, -t, -k are unreleased.

Verb phrases consist of a verb and optionally, its objects (direct and indirect) and any modifying **adverb**. In this book the convention VERB (PHRASE) is used to mean 'verb or verb phrase'.

Verb serialisation is an extremely common feature of Thai in which a number of verbs sharing the same subject follow one another with no intervening conjunctions (e.g. 'and') or prepositions (e.g. 'to'). The verbs can refer to a series of either consecutive or simultaneous actions.

Wh- questions are questions which begin with 'wh-' in English (i.e. 'who?', 'whose?', 'what?', 'which?', 'where?', 'when?', 'why?'); 'how?' is also normally included in this category.

Bibliography and further reading

Abramson, Arthur S. (ed.) (1997) *Southeast Asian Linguistic Studies in Honour of Vichin Panupong*. Bangkok: Chulalongkorn University Press.

Angkab Palakornkul (1972) *A Socio-linguistic Study of Pronominal Strategy in Spoken Bangkok Thai*. Unpublished PhD. diss. University of Texas, Austin.

Brown, J. Marvin (1967–69) *AUA Language Center Thai Course* (3 vols). Bangkok: American University Alumni Language Center.

—— (1979) *AUA Language Center Thai Course: Reading and Writing* (2 vols). Bangkok: American University Alumni Language Center.

Campbell, Russell N. (1969) *Noun Substitutes in Modern Thai: a study in Pronominality*. Mouton: The Hague, The Netherlands.

Campbell, Stuart and Chuan Shaweewongse (1957) *Fundamentals of the Thai Language*. Bangkok: S. Bunyasiribhandu.

Chamberlain, James R. (ed.) (1991) *The Ram Khamhaeng Controversy: Collected Papers*, Bangkok: Siam Society.

Cooke, Joseph R. (1968) *Pronominal Reference in Thai, Burmese and Vietnamese*. Berkeley and Los Angeles: University of California Press.

—— (1989) *Thai Sentence Particles and Other Topics*. Canberra: The Australian National University.

Delouche, Gilles (1991) *Méthode de Thaï* (2 vols) (Langues de l'Asie – INALCO). Paris: L'Asiathèque.

Diller, Anthony (1985) 'High and low Thai: views from within', in D. Bradley (ed.) *Language Policy, Language Planning and Sociolinguistics in South-East Asia*. Canberra: Papers in South-East Asian Linguistics no. 9, Pacific Linguistics A-67.

—— (1991) 'What makes Central Thai a National Language?', in C. J. Reynolds (ed.) *National Identity and Its Defenders: Thailand, 1939–1989*. Victoria, Australia: Monash University, Centre of Southeast Asian Studies (Monash Papers on Southeast Asia no. 25).

Domnern Garden and Sathienpong Wannapok (1994) *Thai-English Dictionary*. Bangkok: Amarin Printing and Publishing pcl.

Gething, Thomas W., Harris, J. G. and Pranee Kullavanijaya (eds) (1976) *Tai Linguistics in Honor of Fang-Kuei Li*. Bangkok: Chulalongkorn University Press.

Haas, Mary and Heng Subhanka. (1945–48) *Spoken Thai* (Holt Spoken Language Series). New York: Henry Holt. (Repr. n.d. Ithaca, New York: Spoken Language Series.)

—— (1964) *Thai English Student's Dictionary.* Stanford: Stanford University Press.

Harris, Jimmy G. and Chamberlain, J. R. (eds) (1975) *Studies in Tai Linguistics in Honor of William J. Gedney.* Bangkok: Central Institute of English Language, Office of State Universities.

Higbie, James and Snea Thinsan (2001). *Thai Reference Grammar: the structure of spoken Thai.* Bangkok: White Lotus.

Huffman, Franklin E. (1986) *Bibliography and Index of Mainland Southeast Asian Languages and Linguistics.* New Haven and London: Yale University Press.

Iwasaki, Shoichi and Preeya Ingkaphirom (2005) *A Reference Grammar of Thai.* Cambridge: Cambridge University Press.

M. R. Kalaya Tingsabadh and Arthur S. Abramson (eds) (2001) *Essays in Tai Linguistics*, Bangkok: Chulalongkorn Press.

Kuo, William (1982) *Teaching Grammar of Thai.* Berkeley, California: Centre for South and Southeast Asia Studies.

Manas Chitakasem and Smyth, David (1984) *Linguaphone Thai Course.* London: Linguaphone Institute.

McFarland, George B. (1944) *Thai-English Dictionary.* Stanford: Stanford University Press.

Moore, Christopher G. (1992) *Heart Talk.* Bangkok: White Lotus.

Moore, John and Saowalak Rodchue (2005) *Colloquial Thai.* London: Routledge.

Mori, Mikio (1984) *Thai* (Asian and African Grammatical Manual, no. 14c). Tokyo: Gaikokugo Daigaku (Institute for the Study of Languages and Cultures of Asia and Africa).

Noss, Richard (1964) *Thai Reference Grammar.* Washington D.C.: Foreign Service Institute.

Palmer, Adrian (1974) *Small Talk.* (AUA Language Center Thai Course, Dialog Book A), Bangkok: American University Alumni Language Center.

—— (1977) *Getting Help with your Thai* (AUA Language Center Thai Course, Dialog Book B). Bangkok: American University Alumni Language Center.

Robertson, Richard (1969) *Robertson's Practical English-Thai Dictionary.* Rutland, Vermont and Tokyo: Charles E. Tuttle.

Smalley, William A. (1994) *Linguistic Diversity and National Unity: Language Ecology in Thailand.* Chicago and London: University of Chicago Press.

Smyth, David (2001) 'Farangs and Siamese: a brief history of learning Thai', in M. R. Kalaya Tingsabadh and Arthur S. Abramson (eds) (2001) *Essays in Tai Linguistics*, Bangkok: Chulalongkorn Press, pp. 277–85.

—— (2010) *Complete Thai.* London: Hodder Education.

Thianchai Iamwaramet (1993) *A New Thai Dictionary with Bilingual Explanation.* Bangkok: Ruam San.

Vichin Panupong (1970) *Inter-sentence Relations in Modern Conversational Thai.* Bangkok: The Siam Society, 1970.

Voravudhi Chirasombutti and Diller, Anthony (1999) 'Who am "I" in Thai?
– The Thai first person: self-reference or gendered self?', in Jackson, P. A.
and Cook, N. M. (eds) *Genders and Sexualities in Modern Thailand*. Chiang
Mai, Thailand: Silkworm Books, pp.114–33.

Yates, Warren and Absorn Tryon (1970) *Thai Basic Course* (2 vols.). Washington
D.C.: Foreign Service Institute.

Yuphaphann Hoonchamlong (2007) *Thai Language and Culture for Beginners*
(2 vols.). Manoa: University of Hawaii.

Thai language sources

นววรรณ พันธุเมธา (๒๕๔๘) *ไวยากรณ์ไทย* กรุงเทพฯ: โครงการเผยแพร่ผลงาน
วิชาการคณะอักษรศาสตร์ จุฬาลงกรณ์มหาวิทยาลัย, ๒๕๔๘

— (๒๕๕๕) *คลังคำ* กรุงเทพฯ: อมรินทร์

เรืองเดช ปันเขื่อนขัติย์ (๒๕๔๑) *ภาษาศาสตร์ภาษาไทย* ศาลายา นครปฐม: สถาบันวิจัย
ภาษาและวัฒนธรรมเพื่อพัฒนาชนบท มหาวิทยาลัยมหิดล

วง วรรธนพิเชฐ (๒๕๕๓) *พจนานุกรมไทย-อังกฤษ* ฉบับ *New Age* กรุงเทพฯ: บริษัท
ไทยเวยส์ พับลิเคชั่น จำกัด

Index

ability and permission: **dâi:, bpen**
    and **wǎi** 70–1
abstract nouns 32
address, terms of 42–9
adjectives (stative verbs)
    94–108
  comparison 103–8
  compounds 95–6
  intensifiers 98–101
  modification 96–8
  reduplication 101–2
  superlatives 107–8
adverbial phrases 111–4
  bpen + noun phrase 113
  dâi: + adjective 113
  dôo-ay + noun phrase 112
  doy-ee + verb phrase 112
  doy-ee + noun phrase 112
  hâi + adjective 114
  yàhng + verb phrase 111–2
adverbs 109–22
  comparison 115–7
  degree 120–22
  frequency 119–20
  manner 109–14
  modification 114–5
  time 117–9
apologies 231–2

bahng 121, 208–9
bâhng 120–2, 190–1
because 138, 186
bpen 254–5
by 129–31

classifiers 34
  with adjectives 39, 40
  with cardinal numbers 36, 39
  with demonstratives 38
  with quantifiers 37
  with ordinal numbers 38, 40
comparison
  adjectives 103–8
  adverbs 115–7
  degrees of comparison 103
  equal comparisons 104–5, 115–6
  excessives: 'too . . .' 106–7, 116
  interrogative comparisons 105–6
  negative comparisons 106
  quantities: 'more/less than . . .'
      212–5
  superlatives 107–8, 116–7
compounds
  adjectival 95–6
  nouns 29–34
  verbs 65–6
consonants
  classes 14
  clusters 6–7, 19
  double functioning 22
  final 6, 14
  initial 5, 12–13, 19
  names 12–13
  pronunciation 5–7
  silenced 22
  written form 12–13

dates 219
dâi/dâi: 252–4

days of the week 216
  parts of the day 217
dead syllables 17
direct and indirect objects 91–2
direct and indirect speech 85–6,
    143, 193
distances 207
distribution: 'per' 207–8

exemplification 142

for 127–9
from 132

gahn + noun, gahn + verb 31–2
gahn têe 138–9
give 91–2
gôr 135
. . . gôr dâi 58–9
gum-lung + verb (phrase) . . . 76
gum-lung ja + verb (phrase) 76

hâi 251–2
however (whatever way) 58

imperatives 110, 114, 143,
    155–7
inviting someone to do something
    236

ja + verb phrase 74
ja . . . réu yung? 179–80

ker-ee + verb (phrase) 77–8
kin terms 46–7
kûng + preposition 124–5
kwahm + verb 32

. . . láir-o 74–5, 78, 177–80
. . . láir-o gôr . . . 190
live syllables 17–18
location: têe and yòo 123–4

measurements 206–7
misunderstandings 237–9
  ignorance, uncertainty 237
  non-comprehension 237–9
months 217

names
  personal 25
  place 25–6
necessity: 'must' and 'need' 72–3
negation 158–73
  auxiliary verbs 160–2
  mâi + verb (phrase)
  mâi châi 164
  mâi cherng 164, 172
  mâi dâi + verb (phrase) 62, 78,
      162–3
  mâi mee 164–5
  main verbs 158
  mí and hăh . . . mâi 173
  modifying negatives 165–6
  negative causatives 167–70
  negative comparisons
  negative conditional clauses
      171–2
  negative expressions 173
  negative imperatives: yàh and
      hâhm 166–7
  negative past tense
  negative questions 170
  'neither . . . nor . . .' 164
  resultative verbs 159–60
  saying 'no' 172
noun phrases 34–41
nouns 25–41
  abstract 31–2
  borrowings 27–8
  compounds 29–34
  common 26–7
  proper 25–6
numbers 194–215
  averages 204
  cardinal numbers 195–8
  sùk and dtûng + cardinal number
      198–9
  collective numbers 204
  decimals 203
  fractions 202
  idiomatic expressions 205–6
  multiples 203
  once, twice 201
  ordinal numbers 199–200
  percentages 203
  Sanskrit numbers 200–1

obligation 73
otherwise 171

pai: + preposition 125
particles 145–57
  exclamatory particles 144
  mood particles 149–57
    dôo-ay 149
    lá/la 150
    lâ 151
    . . . ná 151–2
    . . . nâ/nâh 152–3
    nòy 153
    ngai 153–4
    . . . ròrk/lòrk 154–5
    sí/sì/see/sêe 155–6
    tee 157
    tèr/hèr 157
  polite particles 145–9
    há 147
    hâ 147
    já 147
    jâ/jăh 148
    ká 147
    kâ/kâh/kà 147
    kăh 147
    krúp 146
    krúp pŏm 146
    wá/wâ/woy-ee 148
    yá/yâ 148
  question particles 174–80
    . . . châi mái? 176
    . . . lĕr/rĕu:? 175–6
    . . . mái? 174–5
    . . . ná? 176
    . . . réu bplào:? 177–8
    . . . réu mâi? 178
    ja . . . réu yung? 179–80
    . . . (láir-o) réu yung? 178–9
pêrng + verb (phrase) 77
politeness 230
possession 41, 54
possibility and probability 69–70
prepositions 123–32
pronouns 42–60
  demonstrative 54–5
  emphatic 52–3
  indefinite 55–9

interrogative 55
kin terms 46–7
occupation terms 48–9
omission of 43–4
personal 42–6
possessive 54
reciprocal 54
reflexive 50–2
relative 59–60
sacred 49–50
pronunciation 5–10

quantification 194–215
  approximation: about 210–11
  as many as . . . 215
  less than . . . 214
  more than . . . 212–4
  quantifiers 208–9
  negative quantification 210
  restriction: only 211–2
questions 174–93
  alternative questions 192
  asking the time 228–9
  how? (manner) 186–7
  how? (degree) 187–8
  how/what about . . .? 191–2
  how many? 189–90
  how much? 188–9
  indirect questions 193
  negative questions 170–1; 185–6
  yes/no questions 174–80
  WH- questions + bâhng 190–1
  WH- questions + dee 190
  what? 182–3
  when? 185
  where? 184
  which? 183
  who? 181
  whose? 181
  why? 185–6

reduplication
  adjectives 101
  adverbs 110–11
  nouns 27
requesting
  information 232–3
  something 233

someone to do something 234
someone not to do something
    235–6
to do something oneself 233–4
romanisation 2, 246–50

seasons 220
socialising 239–45
    greetings, introductions, farewells
        240–1
    finding out about other people
        242–3
    expressing congratulations,
        sympathy 243
    telephone transactions 243–5
somebody, anybody, nobody 56
something, anything, nothing 56–7
somewhere, anywhere 57–8
spelling irregularities 21–4
stress 10
subordinate clauses 136–42
    additive clauses: 'apart from' 141
    conditional clauses: 'if' 137–8;
        171–2
    concessive clauses: 'although' 140
    purpose clauses: 'in order to'
        140–1
    reason clauses: 'the fact that/
        because . . .' 138–9
    'the more . . . the more . . .' 141
    time clauses 142

tahng + right/left 126
thanks 230–31
têe 32–3, 59, 86–7, 123–4
time 216–29
    adverbs of time 117–9
    telling the time 225–229
    time clauses 142
    useful expressions 220–5
tones 8–9
    tone change 9
    tone marks 18
    tone rules 17–20
topicalization 133–6

verbs 61–93
    causatives 87–90
    compounds 65–6
    directional verbs 67–9
    modal verbs 69–74
    passives 83–5
    resultative verbs 66–7
    serialization 92–3
    stative verbs 64–5
    time and aspect 74–82
        actions about to happen 76
        actions that have just happened
            77
        attained states 74–5
        changed states 79
        completed actions 74–5
        continuous actions 76
        future actions 74
        negative past tense 78
        past continuous tense 78–9
        single and habitual actions in
            the past 77
        verb (phrase) + ao 80
        verb (phrase) + sĕe-a/sá 81–2
        verb (phrase) + wái 79–80
    to be: bpen, keu:, mee, yòo 61–4
    verbs of emotion + têe . . . 86–7
    verbs of utterance . . . +
        wâh . . . 85–6
vowels
    pronunciation 7–8
    silent final vowels 22
    unwritten vowels 20
    written form 15–16

want to . . . 73
whenever 57
whichever 58
whoever 56
with 131
word order 36–41, 133–6
writing system 11–24

years 218–9
yòo 64, 76, 123